Plant Hunting in Nepal

ROY LANCASTER

Plant Hunting in Nepal

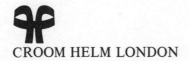

CROOM HELM LONDON

© 1981 Roy Lancaster
Croom Helm Ltd, 2-10 St John's Road, London SW11

British Library Cataloguing in Publication Data

Lancaster, Roy
    Plant hunting in Nepal.
    1. Plants – Collection and preservation
    I. Title
    579'.6'095496   QK359.5

    ISBN 0-7099-1606-X

Printed in Great Britain by
Redwood Burn Ltd., Trowbridge,

CONTENTS

LIST OF ILLUSTRATIONS

Erratum: In plate section; Valley Above Topke Gola Down which the Expedition Travelled to their First Base Camp, should read, Ridge Above the Lower Arun Valley with Chamlang (left) and Makalu (right) in the Background.

LIST OF GENERIC NAMES AND THEIR
ENGLISH EQUIVALENTS

Throughout this book botanical names have been used when referring to plants except in those few instances where an established English name exists, in which case both names are given. For readers who find botanical names a nuisance, or worse a barrier to their enjoyment of this book, the following list, it is hoped, will help familiarise them with at least some of the most well-known examples used.

Botanical Name	English Name	Botanical Name	English Name
Abies	fir	Lonicera	honeysuckle
Acer	maple	Mandragora	mandrake
Aconitum	monkshood	Meconopsis	poppy
Adiantum	maidenhair fern	Musa	banana
Alnus	alder	Pedicularis	lousewort
Allium	onion	Pinus	pine
Anaphalis	pearly everlasting	Populus	poplar
		Prunus	cherry
Arundinaria	bamboo	Pyracantha	firethorn
Betula	birch	Pyrus	pear
Carpinus	hornbeam	Quercus	oak
Corylus	hazel	Rheum	rhubarb
Cupressus	cypress	Rhus	sumach
Euonymus	spindleberry	Ribes	currant
Euphorbia	spurge	Rubus	raspberry or bramble
Fagopyrum	buckwheat		
Ficus	fig	Salix	willow
Hedera	ivy	Sambucus	elderberry
Ilex	holly	Sorbus	rowan or whitebeam
Impatiens	touch-me-not		
Larix	larch	Taxus	yew
Leontopodium	edelweiss	Tsuga	hemlock fir

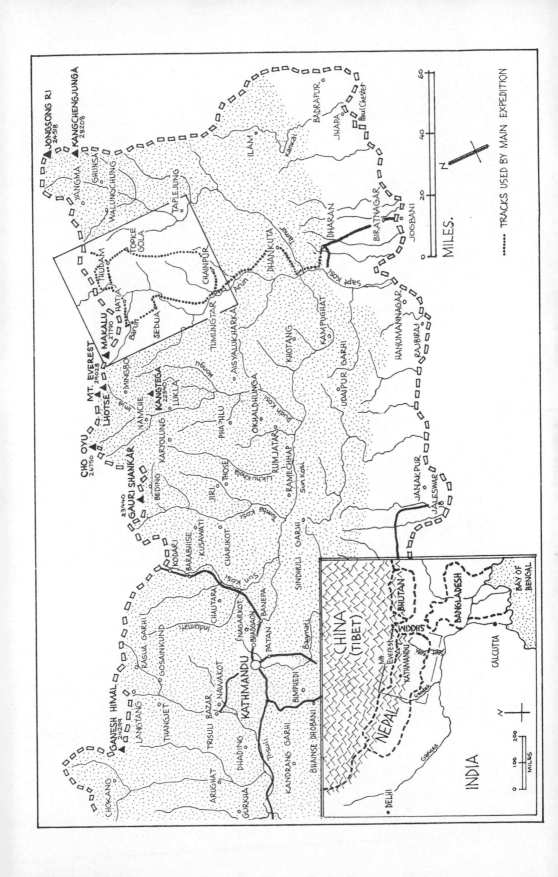

TRACKS USED BY MAIN EXPEDITION

MILES.

JONGSONG RI 24·518
KANGCHENGJUNGA 28·208
YANGMA
GHUNSA
WALUNGCHUNG
TOPKE GOLA
THUDAM
HATIA
MAKALU 27·790
SEDUA
Barun
MT. EVEREST 29·028
LHOTSE
Mingbo
CHO OYU 26·750
NAMCHE
KANGTEGA 22·340
LUKLA
GAURI SHANKAR
BEDING
KARYOLUNG
23·440
TAPLEJUNG
CHAINPUR
TUMLINGTAR
AISYALUKHARKA
Hongu
PHAPLU
OKHALDHUNGA
Dudh Kosi
RUMJATAR
RAMECHHAP
THOSE
Likhu Khola
JIRI
Tumba Kosi
CHARIKOT
KUSAWATI
Sun Kosi
SINDHULI GARHI
KODAKI
BARABHISE
Indrawati
CHAUTARA
NAGAKKOT
BHADGAO
BANEPA
Sun Kosi
PATAN
KATHMANDU
Baomati
BIMPHEDI
BHAINSE DHOBANI
KANDRANG GARHI
NAWAKOT
TRISULI BAZAR
Trisuli
DHADING
GURKHA
ARUGHAT
THANGJET
LANGTANG
GOSAINKUND
RASUA GARHI
GANESH HIMAL 24·299
CHOKANG

ILAM
Kankai
TAPLEJUNG
Arun
DHANKUTA
Jhinne
DHARAN
BADRAPUR
JHAPA
Bad Chester
BIRATNAGAR
JOGBANI
Sapt Kosi
HANUMANNAGAR
RAJBIRAJ
KAMPUGHAT
KIOTANG
UDAPUR GARHI
JANAKPUR
JALESWAR

CHINA (TIBET)
NEPAL
Mt. Everest
KATHMANDU
SIKKIM
BHUTAN
Gandak
Sapt Kosi
BANGLADESH
BAY OF BENGAL
CALCUTTA
Ganges
DELHI
INDIA

MILES
0   100   200

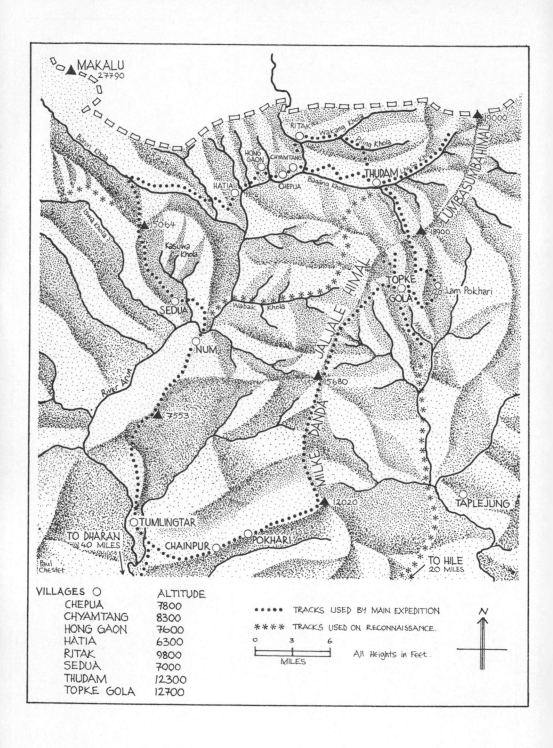

MAKALU
27790

Barn Khola

RITAK
Wakang Khola
Pling Khola

HONG
GAON   CHYAMTANG
HATIA   CHEPUA   Bagang Khola   THUDAM   Hass khola

15064
Kasuwa
Khola

SEDUA   Wabak   Khola

NUM

River Arun

7553   15680

JALJALE HIMAL

TOPKE
GOLA   20 Lam Pokhari

Mewa Khola

TUMLINGTAR

TO DHARAN
40 MILES   CHAINPUR   POKHARI

12020   TAPLEJUNG

TO HILE
20 MILES

Paul Chester

UMBASUMBA HIMAL

19000

18900

MILKE DANDA

VILLAGES ○	ALTITUDE
CHEPUA	7800
CHYAMTANG	8300
HONG GAON	7600
HATIA	6300
RITAK	9800
SEDUA	7000
THUDAM	12300
TOPKE GOLA	12700

••••• TRACKS USED BY MAIN EXPEDITION

**** TRACKS USED ON RECONNAISSANCE.

0   3   6
MILES

All Heights in Feet.

N

ACKNOWLEDGEMENTS

The writing of this book has been a story of help and encouragement and sometimes gentle bullying. Margaret Body gave me constant advice and support and Joan Parsons had the unenviable task of deciphering my notes for typing. Subsequent work on the manuscript was bravely undertaken by Hilary Bachmann and my wife Sue. Sue also kept my nose to the grindstone when deadlines loomed. Hatton Gardner generously gave of his time and expertise in proof-reading and in the compilation of the indices whilst Paul Chester executed in record time the excellent sketches which grace these pages.

As for the botanical aspects of this book I have to thank the staff of the Botany Department of the British Museum (NH) for their help and guidance and in particular Sue Sutton who bore with characteristic patience and phlegmatism my queries and demands. Such errors and imperfections as there may be are my own responsibility.

To my friends and to all those who, at various times urged me to record in writing the fun and enthusiasm of my talks I extend my warmest thanks and gratitude.

Dedicated to the memory of my friend Len Beer who died in 1976.
Without his loyalty and companionship
this book could never have been written.

Swayambhu
Bhuddist
Temple,
Kathmandu

Paul Chesker

1 PREPARATIONS

It was a chill March day with an overcast sky; an unkempt rose scraped the panes of my office window. I stared at the list of names on the sheets before me on the desk, and for the umpteenth time read carefully through the 159 entries under the genus *Salix*, beginning with *S. acutifolia* from Europe and ending with *S. yezoalpina* from Japan.

I was checking the page proofs of *Hilliers' Manual of Trees and Shrubs*, and a task which over the last five years had seemed unending was now nearing completion. The phone rang and, my eyes not leaving the list of names, I answered automatically, 'The Hillier Gardens and Arboretum, Roy Lancaster here'. The voice on the other end asked a simple question. 'I am leading a plant collecting expedition to East Nepal, can you come?' My gaze shifted from the proofs to the blank sky outside. 'Could you repeat that,' I asked incredulously. The voice obliged and it was then I recognised my informant as Len Beer, with whom I had spent a happy year at Hillier's back in 1962. Beer was now horticulturalist at the University College of North Wales, Bangor and this was his second attempt to organise an expedition to the Himalaya.

Beer explained how a member of his five-man team had suddenly withdrawn to join another expedition and that I had next option on the vacancy. 'We intend leaving in September and will probably be away for three months, can you get time off?' Beer asked.

'Time off?' My mind was in a whirl — 'Time off? — of course I can get the time off. If it means losing my job I shall get the time off.'

15

Beer seemed satisfied and outlined the plans and objectives of the expedition. He then mentioned a problem. 'Before I can say for sure that you can join us you will have to meet the others, John, Dave and Martin. Can you come up for an interview one weekend?' I replied that I could, and a date was fixed.

Ever since my schooldays at the Castle Hill County Secondary in Bolton I had dreamed of plant hunting abroad. In those happy far-off days my plant hunting revolved round the moors, spinneys and road-sides of South Lancashire. Even slag heaps and flooded subsidence (known locally as flashes) yielded their treasures. My initiation into the plant world had begun with my discovery of a Mexican tobacco plant (*Nicotiana rustica*) growing on an allotment close to my school, and my subsequent interest in foreign plants led me to all manner of sites from a hen-pen at Knob End to the fabulous Crown Wallpaper tip at Darwen. In the latter place rejected scum from the vats of the nearby factory gave birth to the most exotic plants, of which the ice plant *Cryophytum crystalinum* and the date palm *Phoenix dactylifera* ruled supreme.

An unforgettable 18 months as a national serviceman in Malaya introduced me to a completely new world of plants and gave me the desire for travel in foreign lands. Meanwhile I was earning my living as a gardener and slowly becoming familiar with plants of the temperate zones.

I forget when I first read about the famous plant hunters, but I had long known some of the plants they had introduced. I do remember reading accounts by Ernest Wilson of his travels in China, and there was the memorable epic of the long chase, a gripping life-or-death true story related by George Forrest.

However in March 1971 I had reached the stage where it was no longer enough for me to read of others' adventures. Not enough to read how Forrest or Kingdon Ward had felt on first surveying the vast colourful rhododendron tapestries covering the Tibetan plateaux, or standing beneath tall fir and spruce in some staggering river gorge. I wanted to know how *I* would feel in those shadowed forests, listening to the rain on a high canopy, or wading through Himalayan scrub full of plants familiar from English gardens. Maybe now that dream was about to come true.

Next morning, I walked through the arboretum with a new sense of purpose, my eyes searching for those plants with a claim to Himalayan ancestry. I noted *Euonymus hamiltonianus*, a big deciduous spindle-berry, and nearby the drooping funereal foliage of the coffin juniper *Juniperus recurva* var. *coxii*, *Spiraea bella*, *Ephedra gerardiana* and *Cotoneaster microphyllus*. I was heading for Jermyns House, home of Harold Hillier, head of the firm and family, to find out whether I would be leaving for Nepal with or without official blessing. He had agreed to meet me in his study, a small room with four exits, one leading through French windows onto a paved area. This exit was flanked by a tall cinnamon barked tree from Santa Catalina called *Lyonothamnus floribundus* var. *asplenifolius*, and by a large bushy specimen of *Magnolia delavayi*, a magnificent Chinese evergreen with leathery paddle-like leaves.

Mr Hillier sat at his bureau sifting through a sheaf of papers. The interview was brief and to the point. All he would say after hearing my inarticulate reasons for wanting to go was, 'I shall consult my partners and let you know our decision'.

It was a few days before I was asked again to Mr Hillier's study. The meeting was shorter than before but the answer had been 'Yes'! Later that day I made a phone call to Beer to tell him the news and we discussed my trip to Bangor in order to meet the other expedition members. On the appointed weekend I drove to Bangor and thence to Beaumaris on the Isle of Anglesey where Beer had a flat above a hair-dresser's shop. Later the same day we drove into Bangor and made our way to a Chinese restaurant. John Witcombe, bare browed, bearded and slight in build was a lecturer in plant genetics and a vice-president of the university mountaineering club. He was in charge of the Agricultural Project and was hoping to make seed collections of culti-vated plants and those of potential economic importance. Martin Mortimer, an agricultural botanist, was to assist Witcombe. He had long dark hair and sported a drooping moustache. The fourth member of the group, Dave Morris, was the tallest and looked down at me from a height of six feet. A research botanist, he was the expedition's organiser and would assist Beer in the work of the Horticultural Project.

I attempted to justify my inclusion in the team, Beer supporting my case with vigour and conviction. Questions were fired at me. Why did I want to go to Nepal? What did I know of the plants we might find? What was my knowledge of Himalayan plants in cultivation? I then found myself relating my life history, emphasising my early interest in plants and subsequent experience with plants in cultivation. The questioning continued until, our meal finished, we left the restaurant and retired to the nearest pub where the grilling was continued over pints of beer. We then made our way to a hall of residence on the University Campus where Morris had a room and here the debate continued. I was asked if I had any medical knowledge. I replied that I had not. Did I think it wise or essential to have a medical man as a member of the expedition? I said I would feel happier if there were, to which they replied that a medical man had applied to join the expedi-tion and it was either him or me. Twice I was asked to leave the room whilst they debated in private and I drank cups of coffee in the kitchen. On the second occasion I was called back to find the members silent and serious — they had come to a decision. I forget now who told me but it was probably Beer. 'We would like you to join the expedition,' he said rather formally. The others looked expectant and then their faces creased and all hell let loose as congratulations were shouted, my hand was pumped and back slapped. I believe that tears actually came to my eyes but we all seemed to be laughing after the tension of the evening and a drink was called for to toast the occasion.

This was to be the first of several weekends in Bangor, and at an early stage it was agreed that I should be responsible for organising the food for the expedition. This entailed writing letters to manufacturers in the hope of donations or discounts. During the next few months, as a result of my efforts, a large assortment of dehydrated soups, meats and vegetables found their way to our Bangor headquarters, demonstrating the generosity of manufacturers in supporting worthwhile and well-organised projects. We had high hopes of supplementing this basic fare with fresh locally grown products. Meanwhile Morris was busy with the thousand and one things which are an expedition organiser's lot, principal among which was the business of raising money. We were offering shares in the seed we hoped to collect, Ordinary shares at £25 and Special shares at £50. Several correspondents with special interests in *Primula*, *Rhododendron* and other specific genera bought the more expensive shares to secure first choice or larger quantities in their chosen groups. Of course we all rose to the challenge of selling shares and eventually something in the region of £1,500 was raised this way. Initially the expedition budget was set at £6,000 but later was increased to £7,000. Many trusts, scientific institutions and private concerns made generous donations and each expedition member made a personal contribution of £100.

Witcombe, in the meantime, was selecting equipment, including tents, sleeping bags, boots, warm clothing, compasses, seed bags and envelopes. A certain amount of climbing gear was purchased which reminded me that Witcombe, Morris and Mortimer were experienced climbers. I compared their manoeuvres in the mountains of North Wales with my strolls up and down the 300 ft of St Catherine's Hill near Winchester, and I had unhappy dreams of being left behind on the first day of our march into the hills of Nepal.

Organisation of the expedition had begun the previous August and much of the groundwork had been completed by the time I joined the team. We had secured the blessing of Sir George Taylor, FRS, Director, Royal Botanic Gardens, Kew and Sir Charles Evans, Principal, University College of North Wales, as patrons, and Professor P. Greig-Smith, also of the University College of North Wales, had agreed to be our home agent.

Beer's contact with the Botany Department of the British Museum (Natural History) had resulted in the loan of plant-collecting material such as presses, drying paper and several packing cases. John Williams of that department was particularly helpful. He had visited Nepal on four occasions as a member of plant-collecting expeditions and knew some of the problems we might be facing. Another person whose help proved invaluable was Frank Ludlow. As the remaining member of that famous partnership Ludlow and Sherriff, his advice was supremely sound. Both Beer and I met him on visits to the British Museum, and before leaving England he spoke to me of the things to be careful about in the Himalaya. 'The most important thing is to look after your stomach,' he said. 'Treat it gently and sensibly and you won't go far wrong.' After all the discussion about the plants we would see this was a wise after-thought. Without a qualified doctor in the team our physical well-being would be in the hands of Morris. Taking professional advice, he assembled pills, ointments, tinctures and drugs, together with bandages, plasters, splints and enough bits and pieces to satisfy an army of hypochondriacs.

During this time I was briefing myself on the Himalayan flora, especially that relating to Nepal. Beer knew the alpine plants to search out and Witcombe was similarly well informed on the broad range of cereal crops he would find. Although I had already promised myself to look at everything that grew, walked, crawled or flew, I was looked upon by the others as the woody-plant expert, and it was this diverse group which claimed much of my attention. I was acquainting myself with those trees and shrubs in gardens which had originated in Nepal or thereabouts. Much as I am familiar with a plant in cultivation, when I see that plant in its native state I am deeply moved. It is like meeting an old friend in a strange place far from home.

Visits to the gardens at Kew, Wisley and Exbury brought me into contact with Nepalese plants, but one of my most significant experiences happened at Wakehurst Place in Sussex. I was being taken round by the man in charge, Tony Schilling, who had lived and worked in Nepal for two years and was well attuned to the country and its people. He took me to a place in the garden which was the closest thing in Sussex to a Himalayan glade. We made our way along a path which led into a steep-sided valley filled with rhododendrons and large trees. After a few minutes we stopped beneath a giant beech. 'Close your eyes and don't open them until I tell you,' Schilling said. As I hung onto Schilling's jacket we continued along the path and plunged to our right, down a sharp incline. Hard leaves cracked underfoot. We stopped and Schilling told me to open my eyes. I found myself supported by a tall stem, one of several forming a colony on the slope above the stream. My eyes followed the nearest stem upwards to a dense canopy some 20 ft above. We were standing in a plantation of the noble tree rhodo-dendron, *R. arboreum*, which I had been told covered the lower regions of the Nepalese peaks. Schilling also pointed out a Himalayan bamboo, and across the valley a giant *Magnolia campbellii*, another native of Nepal. Many other Himalayan plants were shown to me and months later when in the Himalaya, I remembered that Wakehurst Place had been a convincing, albeit in miniature version, of the real thing.

It had been agreed that Beer should leave alone for Nepal in June on a three-month reconnaissance, during which time he would locate and mark worthwhile plants in flower for seed collection later. He would also check on suitable routes and promising collecting locations and camp sites. Beer's departure caused a great flurry of activity as stores and equipment were assembled and packed to accompany him.

Expeditions rely on many things, not least good fortune — so too this one. Arrangements had been made with the Royal Air Force to fly expedition members and baggage from England to Singapore on one of their regular weekly flights, space permitting. We should have to use civil airlines only in order to get us from there to Kathmandu.

Beer reached Kathmandu on 9 June. Our main contact there was Mike Cheney of Mountain Travel, a well-known and experienced trekking firm. He was to arrange for Sherpas as interpreters and camp staff, and cooking equipment and would help us obtain trekking permits for the area to be visited. An approximate route had been decided earlier but had been modified as time went by and new information became available. We intended our operational area to be in the north-east corner of the country, mainly between the Tamur and Arun rivers (87 °10'E and 87 °40'E). On 3 August, a little over two months after Beer's departure, Witcombe flew out to begin a similar but shorter reconnaissance investigating crops grown at lower altitudes. With him went the main bulk of food and equipment which, together with Beer's allowance and that of the remaining members of the team, amounted to more than one ton overall.

During this period we received several letters from Beer, deep in the hills and by all accounts having a hard time of it. Summer in the Himalaya brings the monsoon, and this year's rains were the worst for more than a decade. He wrote of swollen rivers, dangerous bridges, landslips and leeches, and suggested an altogether unwelcome environment.

On the evening of 14 September I was driven to Oxford and met Morris and Mortimer at a small hotel. We worked into the night writing last-minute letters, compiling lists, packing, unpacking, then packing again, in a room which resembled a quartermaster's store after an earthquake. In the early hours of the morning we staggered to bed and thanks to Ken Burras, Superintendent of the University Botanic Garden, who lent us a small truck and driver we arrived at RAF Brize Norton in time to take off at 2.30 p.m. on 15 September.

We made two stops on our flight to Singapore. First, briefly, Bahrain in the early hours and then the tiny island of Gan in the Maldives, south-west of Sri Lanka. The runway began and ended by the sea and there were coconut palms, flame-flowered poincianas — *Delonix regia* —

and the equally brilliant flowers of the African tulip tree – *Spathodea campanulata*.

By mid-afternoon we were 35,000 ft above Sumatra, a vast green forested land intersected by winding ochre-coloured rivers. An hour later we touched down at Changi Airport, Singapore, to be met by the fragile figure of Yong Fan Chin. I had known Yong some years previously when he was a student first at Hillier's Nursery and then at Kew and I had written to tell him of our expedition and our passage via Singapore. We had the rest of the day and all the next to enjoy the island and Yong insisted on being our guide and provider; it was a brief respite from the organisation and headaches that we had left in England and which most assuredly awaited us in Nepal. We spent the rest of that day and the next relaxing in Singapore, enjoying its food and its rich variety of plants.

Frangipani (*Plumeria* sp.) was particularly plentiful with flowers of white, pink, yellow and red. So too the ubiquitous bougainvilleas clambering over walls and houses and into the branches of trees, their flowers varying from orange, crimson and purple to a rather dirty white; cassias with yellow flowers and long truncheon-like pods; scarlet-trumpeted *Hibiscus rosa-sinensis*; flame poincianas and yellow-flowered *Thevetia peruviana*. I was particularly struck by a line of clove trees (*Syzygium aromaticum*) whose flower buds are the cloves of commerce; even the crushed leaves were clove scented.

After further stops at Bangkok and Calcutta we were on our way to Kathmandu. We approached the Nepalese border through dense cloud which gradually thinned as we flew high above a vast white mantle whose horizons seemed boundless and whose surface was incredibly even, save for a series of eruptions to the north. It was some minutes before we realised that these 'eruptions' were of a solid nature – it was our first view of the Himalaya. The plane banked suddenly and descended at an alarming rate into the cloud layer. We were flying over the Mahabharat Lekh, the range of mountains stretching in an east-west direction through southern Nepal, for many centuries the main barrier between this once remote kingdom and the outside world to the south. Green terraced hillsides gave way to equally green fields as the plane sank lower into the widening valley of Kathmandu. We could see strange buildings and trees, many of unfamiliar hues, and the brown band of the Bagmati River. A crowd was gathered around the terminal building. From the seething throng a figure emerged dressed in an orange T-shirt and baggy khaki shorts; it was Beer.

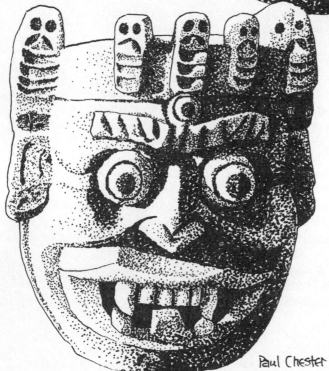

Paul Chester

Hibiscus
rosa-sinensis

2 CITY OF THE GODS

'And about time, too,' was Beer's first greeting, accompanied by a grin and followed by much back-slapping. He was obviously pleased and relieved to see us, the last contingent, and whilst he and Morris sorted out the baggage for Customs' inspection, Mortimer and I drove into the city in a car that was long past retiring age. The road was pot-holed and strewn with reclining cattle which our driver negotiated at speed as though taking part in some giant obstacle race. Other cars raced ahead, their lurching shapes obscured by great clouds of dust which entered our vehicle to leave a grey deposit on its occupants.

In a short while we were moving through narrow streets between wooden canopied buildings and all around us a sea of people and a din of car hooters and clanging gongs and bells as a religious parade passed by. Then we turned through a narrow opening and pulled up at the entrance to the Panorama Hotel. It was a tall building with white-washed walls, a dark entrance and a constant coming and going of tricycles and taxis. Perhaps the best amenity was the view from the hotel roof which attracted most guests at some time or another but most of all in the early morning and evening when the sun rinsed the landscape in gold.

Eventually Beer and Mortimer arrived with the baggage and for the next hour we listened to Beer recounting his adventures in the hills, occasionally throwing in questions which he answered with authority and obvious enjoyment. There had been many problems, most of which he had overcome and it seemed the greatest disappointment to him had been the non-arrival of many of our letters and news of the expedition's organisation in the UK. Difficulties of travel and certain unexplained delays had been the main culprits and the next hour therefore was spent in bringing Beer up to date with the situation.

When we finally ventured into Kathmandu it was mid-afternoon and hot. The next few hours brought a bewildering series of pictures and impressions as we walked through narrow streets, dust underfoot, flanked by shops whose open fronts exhibited an incredible array of goods. Strange sights and smells assailed us on all sides and there was a constant babble of unfamiliar tongues. Fruit-sellers abounded, their pumpkins, papayas, durians, mangoes and bananas tumbling into the street in piles. The bazaar areas were seething with people of many distinct races — Newars, Thamangs, Rais and several others. The temples rose like islands from a sea of wooden and whitewashed hovels. This contrast between the exotic and the ordinary amazed us. One minute we would be walking down a thoroughfare of temples and carved exteriors, the next we would turn into an alleyway of filth and stench where mangy dogs scrabbled and scavenged like rats, eating whatever man had discarded or deposited. The splendour, magic, mystery and the squalor of the city roused alternating feelings of wonder and disgust, and our heads swam with the whole colourful experience as we wound our way back to the hotel.

We found Ed Hammond sitting in the hotel lobby, who was leader of a small climbing expedition, the other members of which were travelling from Britain in a jeep. We had met during the previous spring and he had given us a great deal of useful information and advice based upon his previous visits to Nepal. It was growing dark when Hammond suggested a place to eat, whereupon we hailed a taxi and piled in. The small candlelit restaurant was apparently full when we arrived but a table and chairs were extracted from a particularly dense concentration in the darkest corner and we were soon seated. The room was full of foreigners like ourselves, many of them members of climbing teams, whilst others were on long overland hikes. Others had come to Nepal to make special studies, and then there were those here as volunteers helping in various social or agricultural projects. American, Australian, New Zealand, Japanese, German, French, Danish and British accents combined in a multiple conversation with loud exclamations, table banging and hand waving, indicating the various national temperaments. It was exciting to be part of such a gathering and the sense of adventure and the unknown lay thick in the air.

The heat and excitement made sleep impossible for me that night. We had returned to our hotel during the early hours after a marathon session of story-telling and jokes accompanied by glasses of rakshi which, like most initially nasty brews, improved as the night wore on.

During the previous day we had made brief telephone contact with Major Tom Spring-Smyth and his wife Jenny who had arranged to take us to see the Kathmandu Botanical Garden at nearby Godavari. After breakfast next morning the Spring-Smyth's arrived at the hotel in a jeep complete with picnic basket. I had met Spring-Smyth on two occasions in England, both in the Hillier Arboretum. Joining us for the trip to Godavari was Dawa, a Sherpa guide, who had been sirdar (chief Sherpa) with Beer's party and who had been engaged in the same rôle for the main expedition. The route to Godavari led us through Patan, a place of temples and wooden structures both domestic and religious. The dusty road looked as if a squadron of planes had bombed it and Morris's head beat a regular tattoo on the roof of the jeep as we lurched first this way then that. All round lay paddy fields splashed white with cattle egrets, and when we passed through small villages we saw scenes of domesticity.

Eventually we arrived at the Botanical Gardens, situated at the foot of a densely forested 9,050 ft hill known as Phulchoki. The garden had been cut from the forest and contained a number of native plants which occurred in far greater numbers in the thickets outside. A particularly large specimen, some 60 ft high, of *Stranvaesia nussia* caught our attention, so much that we decided to have our picnic beneath it. This is a handsome evergreen, with rather leathery leaves varying from lanceolate to obovate, and with flattened heads of white flowers during summer. It is occasionally met with in gardens and collections in the milder regions of southern and western Britain, but is generally too tender for our climate. Scattered throughout this area was a wild pear — *Pyrus pashia* — a small thorny tree with ovate, sometimes taper-pointed leaves, which on strong or sucker shoots were often deeply three lobed. A few flower clusters still showed, quite attractive with their white petals and red anthers, but the branches were mainly hung with small fruit up to 1 in. across, rounded, hard and acid to the taste. Later we came across a man going through the fruits searching for and eating those which had ripened, turning brown and soft (bletted).

A small stream ran through the garden and the banks were peppered with the rich blue single pea flowers of *Parochetus communis* which grew here as freely as the white clover — *Trifolium repens* — in Britain. I had often seen this little gem cultivated in cool houses in England, and in particular I remember it being sown annually on the sandstone rock garden at the University Botanic Garden, Cambridge. It was a thrill to see it in the wild.

In the scrub around the garden's boundary, three shrubs caught our attention — *Berberis asiatica* reached 10 ft in height and its evergreen leaves, 1.5-3 in. long, were elliptic to rounded and few spined. They were hard and leathery in texture and made conspicuous by the striking whiteness of their undersurface. This handsome shrub has been tried in the Hillier Arboretum but without success because it is liable to frost damage. *Sarcococca hookerana* was an evergreen with strong growths up to 7 ft tall. The leathery leaves were 4-6 in. long and rather narrow, ending in a slender point. The wood of this shrub is hard, like boxwood, and further east is used for walking sticks. In cultivation it is only suited to the warmer regions of the British Isles and has been long superseded by its more ornamental Chinese variety *digyna*. *Pyracantha crenulata*, the Himalayan firethorn, grew here in some quantity. Its narrow, minutely-toothed leaves and small orange-red fruits are no competition for the popular firethorns in cultivation, and its tender nature also prevents it from becoming better known in British gardens.

We left the garden and drove along a track which wound its way through the forest and up the side of Phulchoki. Many plants caught our attention and I was pleased to see *Coriaria napalensis* throwing its long arching stems 6 ft in the air. Unfortunately this handsome shrub is only suitable for the warmer areas of the British Isles although is has succeeded for several years in the Hillier Arboretum.

On the lower slopes *Alnus nepalensis* formed colonies with dark green stems 60-70 ft high and handsome slender-pointed leaves 4-6 in. long, the petioles with conspicuous stipules. It is a pity that this alder is so tender because in the British Isles its attractive foliage, bark and autumnal catkins would be in great demand among tree planters and landscape architects.

Although long past flowering, the Himalayan musk rose – *Rosa brunonii* – impressed by its powerful scrambling growths reaching into trees and swamping lesser fry. Hips were swelling but still retained the green of youth. *Stachyurus himalaicus* put in an appearance between the 5,000 and 6,000 ft contours. Its flower spikes were already formed, lining the undersides of the branches ready for the long winter ahead. Unlike the Japanese *S. praecox* of our gardens, this species has dusky red flowers and is quite startling as a result. It is vigorous in growth, reaching 8-10 ft, but unfortunately is too tender for all but the mildest areas of the British Isles. I remember a large specimen growing in a border on the north side of Jermyns House in the Hillier Arboretum during the mid-1960s. It flowered but timidly two years running before succumbing to a persistent frost.

We left the jeep parked by the track and scrambled up the steep slope beneath trees of a handsome evergreen oak – *Quercus semecarpifolia*. Many were gnarled specimens 30-40 ft high or more and the fallen leaves of summer lay in thick carpets crackling under our feet. The current leaves were obovate to oblong in shape, 3-4.5 in. long, dark glossy-green above and covered with a dense pale buff to rust-coloured felt beneath, even the young growths were similarly covered. The leaves varied in amount of toothing, those on old trees entire or few toothed, whilst on vigorous, especially sucker growths, they were spine toothed and larger. Occasionally we came across stumps where trees had been felled and these had produced dense growths bearing prickly leaves as hostile almost as those of an English holly. This diversification of armature is not unusual with evergreen oaks and is commonly seen in the holm oak − *Q. ilex* − in Europe. *Q. semecarpifolia* has an immense range in the wild from Afghanistan to W. China, reaching an altitude of 12,000 ft in the western Himalaya. It is strange, therefore, that it should be so rare in cultivation, the only tree I had previously seen being one from the NW Himalaya introduced by acorns sent to R. S. Gamble of East Liss, Hampshire in 1900.

Sharing the same zone as the oak were two other handsome evergreen trees, one of which, *Rhododendron arboreum*, formed characteristic dense, gently tapered columns up to 40 ft or more. The other tree was another species of oak − *Q. lamellosa* − an attractive tree 50-60 ft high with striking sweet chestnut-like leaves 6-10 in. long. These were boldly toothed and parallel veined, and the glossy dark-green of the upper surface contrasted effectively with the glaucous undersurface. It is little wonder that Sir Joseph Hooker, who saw this tree in Sikkim, regarded it as the noblest of all oaks.

As the tree cover thinned out a little towards the summit of the hill, several small perennial plants became more frequent, including two species of pearly everlasting *Anaphalis triplinervis* and *A. busua*. Both had grey woolly stems and foliage, those of the latter narrow and lacking the distinctive triple-venation of the other. In full flower was *Roscoea purpurea*, a member of the ginger family, with erect leafy stems to 1.5 ft and lovely orchid-like pale purple flowers.

Two white-flowered perennials appeared in the shape of *Thalictrum javanicum* and *Anemone vitifolia*. The former preferred shady places, throwing up erect stems 1-2 ft high, whilst the *Anemone* sought the sun. A curious saprophytic plant was the diminutive *Monotropastrum humile* which poked its creamy-white flower spikes above the leaf mould of the rhododendron and oak forest floor.

On our return to the jeep we encountered several well-known shrubs, of which *Hypericum uralum* was the most frequent. Its graceful habit with arching frond-like stems, small leaves and yellow flowers like nodding buttercups was a constant pleasure.

Hydrangea aspera is a variable species which is not surprising considering its distribution, which stretches from Nepal eastwards through China to Formosa, and then leaps a couple of thousand miles south to appear in Java and Sumatra. Many of these forms are too tender for British gardens and the plants we found growing on Phulchoki would doubtless fall into this category. There were several specimens from 6-10 ft high with large velvety hairy leaves, pale beneath, and flattened heads of blue-tinted fertile flowers surrounded by conspicuous white-ray florets. Interestingly, this species was first described from Nepal in 1825, though the hardy forms in cultivation today are of

Chinese origin, several having been collected by the great plant hunters E. H. Wilson and George Forrest. Both *Viburnum cylindricum* and *V. erubescens* were present in some quantity, the former with its unusual leaves which are covered above with a thin coating of wax. When scratched or folded the wax ruptures and turns grey, and Beer chose a large leaf on which to draw a face with a sharp-ended twig. Both species are of borderline hardiness in Britain, but I had seen several specimens of *V. cylindricum* in large collections such as Exbury Gardens and three large specimens grew in the Hillier Arboretum.

A Himalayan privet — *Ligustrum indicum* (*nepaulensis*) — occurred frequently in open scrubby areas and an evergreen form of *Daphne bholua* appeared as scattered individuals over a wide area of forest and clearing. Climbing in the main stems of several trees was an ivy — *Hedera nepalensis* — with ovate entire or three-lobed leaves. It looked very similar to our native species *H. helix*, but the fruits, when they ripen in spring, are amber-yellow rather than black, otherwise it is just as effective, and hardy. As if called to complete the partnership, we found a Himalayan holly — *Ilex dipyrena* — forming a small tree up to 20 ft. The oblong, slender pointed, dull-green leaves measured 4-5 in. in length with entire or spine-toothed margins, borne on short purple-tinged petioles. The fruits were green and immature. Several trees had been cut down recently and the resultant sucker growths carried leaves which were fiercely armed with large spine-tipped teeth. Phulchoki opened our eyes to the rich variety of the Nepalese flora and yet it was merely the beginning, the first glimpse, the initial taste of things to come.

The next morning we awoke early. This was to be a day of visiting and organisation, beginning with Mike Cheney, a friendly, capable man of immense activity. He introduced us to our Sherpas — Da Norbu, Namgyal, Pema our cook, Namcha, Perma and Jangbu and of course, Dawa our sirdar whom we had already met. The latter accompanied us on a shopping spree for last-minute stores and equipment which included five black umbrellas made in the Republic of China. These would serve the dual purpose of protecting us from the hot sun and the worst of the rain — a comforting thought even to adventurers.

Another foray took us to the palatial Singha Durbar, the city's administrative centre, whose lawns were parched and fountains choked with debris. Inside the gull-white walls lay a quiet dark world, a rabbit-warren of corridors and offices, each with its attendant cluster of people outside the doors. Here we applied for our visa extensions and our trekking permits for the north-east.

Whilst still in England I had received a request from Spring-Smyth to bring two small plants of the dawn redwood — *Metasequoia glyptostroboides*. He had a hunch that this tree, as yet unknown in Nepal, might prove suitable as a rapid source of timber. The two specimens we carried, however, were destined as gifts to the British and American Embassies in Kathmandu, and on our last day before heading east, we joined the Spring-Smyths for a luncheon engagement at the British Embassy. The Ambassador and his wife were charming to us and showed great interest in the aims of the expedition as explained by Beer and Morris. We then selected a place in the garden where the dawn redwood might flourish and related to our hosts the story of this remarkable tree, of how it was known only as a fossil until 1941 when living trees were discovered in a remote corner of Central China and later introduced to the world by the Arnold Arboretum, Massachusetts.

The afternoon we spent on a final tour of the city beginning with the Annapurna Hotel. However it was not the hotel so much as the surroundings that interested us. In a garden opposite the hotel entrance stood a group of tall conifers from Australia — *Araucaria bidwillii*. One of these was dead and from a distance its naked branches appeared strung with fruits like withered plums. Closer inspection revealed these 'fruits' to be Indian fruit bats or flying foxes (*Pteropus giganteus*). They hung by the claws of their feet with their wings folded around them like a cloak. The only movement came from an occasional outstretched wing, but they kept up a continuous chatter reminding me of a British rookery. Their main activity takes place at dusk when they fly to the fruiting trees where they eat and then rest and digest their meal for several hours before flying back to their roosting trees before dawn.

The trees of Kathmandu are a mixed bag including several intro-duced from Australia during the nineteenth century. Pride of place must go to the occasional giant gums — *Eucalyptus* species — which dominate the squares and grounds in which they are planted. *E. globulus*, the Tasmanian blue gum, seems the most common. Another magnificent tree is the Australian silk oak — *Grevillea robusta* — which is not an oak at all but is related to the waratah. This is a popular pot plant in Europe where its finely divided fern-like leaves and reddish-purple young growths are much appreciated for decorating conservatories and halls. It is too tender for growing permanently out of doors however, which is why the sight of such large trees as those in Kathmandu interested me. In spring their dense clusters of golden-yellow flowers bring an added pleasure.

Those of us familiar with the bottle-brushes — *Callistemon* species — were amazed to see large tree specimens of *C. citrinus*, their drooping wand-like branches moving in the slightest breeze. *Jacaranda mimosifolia* from Brazil was commonly planted along main roads and in recreation areas, but its panicles of incredible lilac-blue flowers would not be appearing until the spring.

Many colourful shrubs crowded gardens and parks alike and included the ubiquitous *Hibiscus rosa-sinensis*; *Lagerstroemia indica*; Chinese persimmon — *Diospyros kaki* — and the loquat — *Eriobotrya japonica*.

29

Bougainvilleas scrambled everywhere over walls, fences, roofs and into lofty trees, bringing a dazzle of colour which, intensified by the sun, was almost blinding.

The following morning our plane was due to leave Kathmandu at 11 a.m. and we were up and about in plenty of time to have our baggage transported, to and checked in, at the airport. We were flying south-east to Biratnagar, just north of the Indian frontier, where we would meet up with Witcombe, the fifth member of our party who had come out in August to do the crop reconnaissance. An aircraft was trundling along the runway to the airport terminal as we fought our way through the crowded arrival and departure hall. But it appeared that something was wrong with the engine and mechanics swarmed over and under the fuselage, while the waiting passengers walked over to watch the action. The efforts of the mechanics were mystifying to me so I left the others and watched the circling griffon vultures high above.

At last the trouble was located and dealt with and soon we were all aboard and the plane was racing down the runway. Minutes later, at a height of 15,000 ft, we peered below us to the north where peculiar rib-like hills rose from the valleys, whose water courses appeared dry and filled with silt. Further north the hills grew progressively larger until on the horizon, stretching east-west like some gigantic white wall, we saw the Himalayan massive, regularly punctuated by peaks in excess of 20,000 ft. The plants we had come to collect would be found mainly below the snow-line, between the 10,000 ft and 15,000 ft contours. In order to reach this area we would need to follow the ridges, travelling north, maintaining as far as possible an even speed and height in order to keep within our schedule.

There was neither steward nor stewardess on our flight, no boiled sweets, nor friendly reassuring noises from the captain, and our descent to Biratnagar airport was signalled by a sudden loss of height accompanied by a rapid movement of the adrenalin. My first glimpse of the airfield, while still aloft, revealed a short runway in a parched field with what appeared to be cattle wandering about. On landing I was able to confirm that cattle had indeed been occupying the runway and had been pushed away by a cowherd just prior to our landing. Now safely down, the plane was immediately surrounded by interested villagers and their assorted dogs, whilst the cattle returned to bask on the hot surface of the runway. Beer, who had flown in the previous day, was waiting to meet us.

For the next few days we were to be guests of the Officers' Mess at the British Gurkha Headquarters at Dharan, and their hospitality had extended even to the provision of a jeep to carry us and our luggage to the camp some miles north of Biratnagar. We found Witcombe discussing the money situation with a rather benign bank manager who immediately offered us cigarettes and cups of tea and threw in what he explained was a Muslim Christmas Card for luck. Witcombe looked tired and thinner than when we last saw him and later we heard that he had been ill whilst in the hills and had returned in a weak and unhappy state by horseback. Our arrival, however, seemed to cheer him and during the subsequent journey to Dharan we rarely stopped talking. The only interruptions came when we saw things of interest in the surrounding villages and fields. In some areas by the road jute (*Abutilon avicennae*) was being grown. The fibre comes from the stem of this tall herbaceous plant, a member of the mallow or hollyhock family (*Malvaceae*), so fields are thickly planted to encourage long slender stems. In a group of dead trees in the middle of a cultivated area we saw some strange-looking birds with scrawny necks and hunched shoulders. One or two rose on heavy wings at our approach and we recognised them as adjutant storks, ugly birds with grotesque ruddy pouches hanging from their chests. The roadside telegraph wires were a favourite perch for a host of interesting smaller birds including the black drongo with its characteristic deeply forked tail and the small green bee-eater, a delightful species with slenderly pointed bill and tail. Once we saw a blue jay or roller, a brilliant flash of blue, like a giant kingfisher.

Two common inhabitants of the rice fields were the white cattle egret and a biscuit-coloured relative of the bittern, appropriately known as the paddy bird. In the forest the all black jungle crow contrasted with the slightly smaller black-and-grey house crow — a bird similar in appearance to the European hooded crow — which frequented villages and towns.

We spent the next few days sorting and repacking our food and equipment and Dawa, our sirdar, arrived with 24 porters, Sherpas from the village of Sedua, who had just returned from a Japanese climbing expedition to Makalu. We agreed to employ them at ten rupees per day and sent them off to Tumlingtar to establish our first camp while we waited for the weather to clear in the hills. Because of the crop research being tackled by Witcombe and Mortimer, the Food and Agriculture Organisation of the United Nations had offered to fly us and our baggage into Tumlingtar, thus saving us an initial four or five days of hard slogging on foot. Eventually the Pilatus Porter arrived and the first two of us, Beer and myself, were being shuttled north towards a seemingly impenetrable barrier of hills and ravines.

Satyrium nepalense

Paul Chester.

3

UP THE MILKE DANDA

It was a curious sensation flying above foothills, any one of which would have ranked as a mountain in Britain. The slopes were steeply terraced and intensely cultivated with what appeared from our height to be pocket-handkerchief-size rice fields. We saw the River Tamur where it joined the Sun Kosi and then we headed up the valley of the Arun. Suddenly the valley widened on all sides and before us on a raised plateau stood the village of Tumlingtar some 1,500 ft above sea level. We could see no runway, just a level area of rough grass onto which our pilot lowered his plane with the expertise born of long experience.

A plane landing in the valley was not such a common event that it passed unnoticed and it was not long before a good-sized crowd had assembled to watch us unload our gear. One man, clad only in a pair of shorts, was covered from head to foot in a white powdery substance and looked as if he had fallen into a vat of flour. We were told that he came from a village on the hillside above and that he had been engaged in white-washing the walls of his house when the sound of the approaching plane had caused him to drop everything and come running to see what it was all about. Another man with bow legs and an engaging smile wore a pair of spectacles in which one lens was missing and the bridge stuck together with plaster. He was introduced as panchayat leader, the head man of the village, and when we made to shake hands he placed his own together and greeted us with a 'Namaste'.

32

We smiled and repeated the greeting which then spread through the crowd. The pilot meanwhile had turned his plane round and taken off, and two trips later the expedition's five members and Sherpas were standing on the plateau surrounded by an assortment of bags, boxes and baskets.

Pema, the cook, got busy with preparing a meal as we began the task of re-sorting the baggage into 60 lb porter loads. After lunch we made our way through fields planted with maize, a bean of some kind and, surprisingly, cotton. Forty years ago cotton was commonly grown in the hills of Nepal. It was a shifting cultivation with a rapid turnover and resulted in the destruction of huge areas of virgin forest. The industry declined, however, mainly due to the importation of cheap yarns from India. We found ourselves at the edge of a deep ravine through which the Sabhaya Khola flowed to join the River Arun at the foot of the plateau. We reached the river after a long dusty climb and plunged naked into the cold water. The surrounding soil was a red laterite which baked in the sun and dazzled the eyes. It was therefore pleasant lying in the fast-running water wedged between large rocks staring at the hillsides above. Two hours later we climbed out of the ravine and returned to camp. During our absence the tents had been erected and fuel brought from the village.

Tumlingtar was something of a modern miracle. Ten years earlier it did not exist because of the malarial mosquitoes which swarmed from its waters. Then DDT had been introduced and the mosquito was said to be no more. The plateau was certainly fertile and it was claimed that the best chillies in Nepal were grown here. We assumed that by best they meant the hottest as we learned when we were served a curry at dinner that night.

At breakfast next morning we discussed the non-appearance of our porters hired in Dharan; but half an hour later 19 men, women and children padded into camp carrying home-made bamboo baskets and an assortment of bamboo sheets and ropes. We needed more porters so Dawa, Namgyal and Da Norbu were sent to recruit some in the village. In the early evening Dawa returned with extra porters, a strange looking bare-footed bunch of various ages. One of them gave me a cigar which he had made by rolling together the dried leaves of *Lyonia ovalifolia*, a large shrub or small tree of the *Ericaceae*. It had a strong flavour, and though crude compared with western versions, was nevertheless an acceptable substitute and cost nothing.

That night we were besieged by all manner of biting insects, most of which homed in on the light cast by a Tilley lamp which we sat around writing our letters and diaries. The shrill sounds of crickets and other creatures of the dark filled the air but failed to prevent us from sleeping through until a call from Pema announced the day of departure. It was 5.30 a.m. and it was just beginning to get light. Through the steam of our porridge we could see the porters arriving in dribs and drabs to stand in small groups awaiting instructions. Then Dawa and his assistants began issuing orders and the groups broke up and milled around the piles of baggage, sorting and weighing each item, discarding it if it proved too bulky or heavy. With the pale light of dawn bathing the valley our camp looked like a scene from an ancient history book of the east. The porters scurried about testing each other's load, talking, shouting and arguing like a pack of hounds in a mêlée. They were a mixed group, Sherpas from Sedua, Chetris from the valley, Thamangs and Limbus. Some of the women wore rings in their ears and ornamental nose pins. They would be carrying loads as heavy as those of the men and were being paid the same rate, ten rupees per day, approximately 40 pence. The bamboo baskets were home-made and cone-shaped so that the bulk of the load occurred at the top end. A band passes around the basket and round the carrier's forehead so that the weight is borne mainly by the head. The porters, as a result, develop strong neck and shoulder muscles, contrasting with their often thin legs. All possess broad, flattened feet with wide gaps between the first and second toes from long use as an anchor in the making of bamboo ropes and straps.

Half an hour after leaving camp we left the plateau and followed a steep track down into the valley to the edge of the Sabhaya Khola. At this point the water was waist deep and running fast, too fast for the porters to chance fording. A discussion took place and a man was sent down river to summon the ferryman and his boat. Meanwhile we settled ourselves in the rocks and had a lunch of chapattis and eggs, the porters doing likewise, some of them using as bowls the leaves of the sal tree — *Shorea robusta* — pinned together with slivers of bamboo. My hat had just fallen into the river and been carried away, when the ferryman appeared paddling towards us in a dugout canoe. It was with some difficulty that he steered to where we waited, the current continuously threatening to push his craft back in the direction he had come. At last he moored and we were better able to examine the boat, which was simply a tree trunk hollowed out with hatchet and fire. He told us it had taken him four days to make at a cost of 800 rupees. Stepping into the craft I could not help but notice the handsome outcrop of bracket fungus which had established itself for 2-3 ft along the water level down one side.

There was no let up in the steepness nor the direction of the track which climbed straight up and out of the valley heading for the distant ridge above. We were moving in an easterly direction towards the village of Chainpur, which we hoped we would reach in time for tea. It certainly had not looked too great a distance on our map, but then the map was an unknown quantity as we were to discover many times in the days to come. Any excuse to stop for a rest on that long haul was quickly taken and we began to take photographs on all sides and at regular intervals. Once, it was a colourful pair of grasshoppers (*Aularches miliaris*) copulating in the grass, another time it was a group of three hoopoes in nearby scrub, their black-and-white barred wings attracting our attention and that of one of our young porters who shouted to us and laughed pointing a finger in their direction.

Pines were frequent on these hills sporting large handsome bunches of 9-15 in.-long grey-green, drooping needles. These were the chir pine — *Pinus roxburghii* (*P. longifolia*) — a three-needled species occurring from Afghanistan in the west to Bhutan in the east. Here above the Arun it grew at 3,000 ft and individual trees reached 50-60 ft in height, though there was evidence that many larger specimens had long since been felled. The chir pine is too tender for general cultivation in the British Isles, although I understand it has been grown with reasonable success in Cornwall and elsewhere.

After what seemed like a month we found the track gradually levelling out and looking ahead we saw that a number of porters had stopped to rest in the shade of two huge trees with vast spreading boughs. Crawling the last few feet we sank thankfully to the ground to lie on our backs staring up at the high mosaic of green leaves and needled sunlight. The trees were the banyan — *Ficus benghalensis* — and the bo-tree *F. religiosa* — both popular as village trees and both commonly planted above steep tracks in the foot-hills to give welcome shade to weary travellers. Here in Nepal they were referred to as 'people's trees' or as 'marriage trees' because their branches interlocked. The leaves of the banyan were elliptic and short pointed, rather like those of the evergreen magnolia (*Magnolia grandiflora*), with a rounded- or heart-shaped base strongly contrasting with those of the bo-tree which were remarkably like those of a black poplar (*Populus nigra*) but with a characteristic and conspicuous 'drip-tip'. It was dark before the dancing lights on the ridge ahead announced our arrival at Chainpur and the rough and rivened course of the track gave way to a paved main street. We tramped along the street to where a brick and wooden building stood before an open grassy space. This was the British Medical Centre, one of several operating in Nepal for the treatment of various ailments, but especially tuberculosis. At the time of our visit there were four British nurses in residence. They welcomed us and made a large kettle of tea which soon helped us forget the long march.

It was with difficulty that we hauled ourselves up the ladder into the Centre's attic, where our torches revealed piles of boxes, bottles and stores of one kind or another. We needed no rocking that night and apart from the occasional involuntary kick when rats ran over our legs, we slept soundly until morning when Pema awoke us with mugs of hot tea. The porters were already assembled outside, having spent the night in various hostelries around the village. Now we could see Chainpur

35

sitting astride a 4,500 ft ridge, its houses strung out along a single paved street eventually climbing the hill in a series of broad steps. It was a holiday — Dashira — and many of the shop fronts had been freshly painted for the occasion. Chainpur was an isolated Newar stronghold as evidenced by the comparative cleanliness and intricate carvings on stone and wood exteriors. Around the wall of the Medical Centre was a narrow stone band in which numerous faces of animals and humans had been delicately carved, and it might well have been taken from an old English cathedral or church. There were many merchants and craftsmen living here, especially those dealing in metalwork, and their tapping and banging could be heard all through the day and into the night. Outside on the village square a huge swing had been erected on bamboo uprights. Small children were being pushed to what seemed a terrifying height without their showing any sign of fear — on the contrary they were queuing up for the experience and once in the seat screamed to be pushed higher and yet higher. As we stood watching this entertainment we saw gliding high above us on the warm thermals a group of six Himalayan griffon vultures, as magnificent on the wing as they are repulsive on the ground.

The sun had so burned my legs in Tumlingtar that I could not bear to wear trousers and yet I needed somehow to protect them, so I decided to make a cotton skirt similar to those being worn so gracefully by the women and purchased two yards of a suitable material, which I proceeded to wrap around my lower half, tucking the end piece securely into my waist band. The merchant and his cronies, not realising the material was meant for me, were startled by my antics and broke into loud guffaws when I tried my first steps in the new creation, but I had wrapped it round too tight and could walk only with difficulty. In view of the gathering audience, and to save further embarrassment, I decided to keep moving until safely out of the village before attempting a readjustment. I managed a further two or three yards before tripping up at the feet of the local policeman. Beer and Morris were no help and actually asked me for an encore. That was it, and without further ado I abandoned the skirt, revealing my bright pink legs protruding from corduroy shorts. Once we had left the village well behind I again donned my skirt, this time taking care to wrap it loosely. It survived only until the next day when the rains came.

We entered a scrub area where we were surprised to encounter a familiar fern from home — the bracken — *Pteridium aquilinum*, which is said to be one of the most cosmopolitan of all plants. It was certainly common in these parts, whilst two evergreen trees — *Lithocarpus elegans*, with large leathery leaves, and *Schima wallichii* — occurred as isolated specimens. Both trees were heavily pruned, whilst the latter with a fairly hard close-grained, reddish wood was used for plough-shares and in house building. Neither would be hardy in the British

Isles. In the branches of one of these trees two small, brilliantly coloured birds were active. Their fiery-red and glossy black plumage identified them immediately as male scarlet minivets.

Our path ran freely along the ridge now and afforded views of hillsides devoted to rice, creating pale green bands snaking round the contours. The village of Side Pokhara appeared ahead of us and we noticed its pond on the outskirts choked full of water hyacinth, those on the marginal mud much larger and greener than those in the water. They were in full flower and quite beautiful and I should not have been at all surprised to see them decorating houses and shops in the village, but their value was far more prosaic — they were used as pig fodder. The water hyacinth seemed a very long way from its native Amazon, and nearby in a garden grew another alien, *Datura suaveolens* from Tropical America, its large white trumpet flowers hanging from the axils of the upper leaves. The smaller species of *Datura* such as *D. metal* have been cultivated in Nepal and in India certainly for a very long time. J. D. Hooker, in his Himalayan Journals published in 1854, described the use of this plant's seeds as a drug by thieves who frequented travellers' resting places.

By nightfall the porters had collected bundles of faggots, and fires were crackling and sparkling in many directions attracting people from a wide area who came to watch us eat. They were dressed in their best clothes because of the holiday and some of the men had their foreheads dyed deep pink or studded with pink or orange rice; more people, returning from a religious ceremony, arrived and they all milled about among the many camp fires, talking and shouting, whilst a boy blew continuous blasts on a horn, the light from the fires flickering on their faces, and the smoke curling in a dozen trails through the street. It was a warm night, with the stars out in full, and we slept out on the wooden porch of a house.

The next morning we climbed the steep hillside through terraced fields of rice and small vegetable patches where buckwheat — *Fagopyrum esculentum* — presented masses of white flowers to lighten the green around. There were houses scattered over a wide area and the track we followed snaked its way past many of these, which were usually stone based with wooden and bamboo superstructures. Sometimes we were invited to stop and examine some inmate with a troublesome sore or sprain or maybe worse. It was in such a house that we were invited to have our lunch, and as soon as Pema and the kitchen porters arrived they got busy preparing our meal on the family fire. Meanwhile our hosts busied themselves making us feel comfortable, mats were placed on the floor for us to sit on and we were offered roasted corn to eat. The house was a typical one of two storeys, each of a single room. A notched log led from the living area in which we sat through a gap in the ceiling to the sleeping quarters above. The fire lay in a depression in

37

the floor and the smoke made its exit via the open windows and door. The living area was becoming quite crowded, and as the porters arrived they too squeezed inside to escape the rain. Small fires were lit and pots of water and rice were set to boil. The room became so warm and full of smoke that Morris decided to sit on the porch outside, where he soon busied himself flicking leeches off his legs. Although we were at the end of the monsoon period which lasts from June to September, the hillsides were quite wet. The leeches favoured the bushes and low vegetation bordering tracks, dropping onto any passing animal, be it pig, cow or man.

I remembered being advised by someone before leaving, to sprinkle a pinch of salt on their tails. Considering the number of leeches we did encounter we would have needed a large barrel to have dealt with them all. An old ex-Indian Army officer had even described to me in gory detail the effects of a leech attack, 'A tiger leech will drain your arm of blood in an hour, your leg in two hours and your whole body in a day.' As if that were not bad enough he then proceeded to tell me about the dreaded bull leech which was on record as growing up to four inches or three times the size of the tiger leech, although he had once shot a giant specimen fully six inches long. The next time we met a few weeks before my departure the colonel unwittingly repeated the story but this time his bull leech had gained three inches whilst the appetite of his tiger leech had increased to the point where it had drained the body of his gun bearer as he slept in the night. I had not the heart to tell him that I had been on very friendly terms with leeches in Malaya many years previously when serving in Her Majesty's Forces. I knew well their capacities, and knew also that the simplest method of persuading them to disengage was to touch them with the lighted end of a cigarette. Unlike the weevil, the bug, the spider and other maligned creatures of this world, the leech has to my knowledge never been celebrated in poetry or song and is likely ever to remain one of nature's contemptibles.

Cherry trees grew in some quantity around this and other houses in the neighbourhood. When we enquired of their origin, we were told that they were wild and that they had pink flowers in December. They were heavily lopped for firewood and as a consequence had the appearance of giant hat stands. We were later to identify them as *Prunus cerasoides*.

Many familiar shrubs had appeared during the last thousand feet of the climb, chief amongst which were *Pyracantha crenulata* and *Viburnum cylindricum*. *Lyonia ovalifolia* formed a large shrub or occasionally a small tree up to 30 ft in height. This is a most attractive, almost spectacular sight, in late May and June when the racemes of white pitcher-shaped flowers crowd the branches creating a singular effect, especially when seen from afar. Its leaves are used in the manufacture of native cigars or cigarettes and it was common for our porters to stop and stuff their pockets with the leaves for later use. It is a pity that this species is rarely seen in cultivation. In the Hillier Arboretum it is merely represented by the Japanese var. *elliptica*, which has inferior flowers.

An evergreen — *Symplocos theifolia* (*lucida*) — occurred as a dense shrub with clusters of blue fruits, and the retaining walls around each house were clothed with moss and *Selaginella* spp. in which were embedded pink polygonums of several kinds, ferns, begonias and other small flowering plants. By mid-afternoon we had left cultivation behind and now walked through pastures with scattered islands of trees and scrub. We had reached the Milke Danda, a euphonious name for the ridge which would be our companion for the next few days. We were, at this point, approximately 7,000 ft above sea level and life was becoming exciting as more and more plants appeared to indicate the approach of the cool temperate zone. The scrub included *Sarcococca hookerana* and *Mahonia napaulensis*, the latter not very spectacular out of flower and rarely seen in cultivation where most plants so named usually prove to be another Himalayan species — *M. acanthifolia*. In some areas the hard bright-yellow wood of the *Mahonia* is used to make handles for the kukris carried by most village men. The wood of *Rhododendron arboreum* is also used for this purpose.

The pastures were studded with the slender pink flower spikes of *Spiranthus sinensis*, a pretty little orchid which, according to the latest authority, belongs to the variety *amoena*. This species has an incredible distribution, being found from Afghanistan in the west right through the Himalaya to China, Siberia, Japan, Malaysia and Australia.

Our track then left the open spaces and entered an evergreen forest in which the two main trees *Rhododendron arboreum* and *Castanopsis tribuloides* formed a dense dark canopy. The former was variable in leaf indumentum, ranging in colour from silver through buff to brown. Those with thin silver-backed leaves generally have crimson flowers and are more tender in cultivation, coming as they do from lower altitudes. The *Castanopsis* surpassed in size the 30-40 ft columns of the *Rhododendron* and several specimens must have been in excess of 60-70 ft. The dark green, toothed, chestnut-like leaves were pale or subglaucous beneath. The prickly-fruit clusters were borne in dense spikes, each capsule, when opened, containing two to three nuts. Both trees were full of epiphytic plants, especially lichens, ferns and orchids, and included *Agapetes serpens*, an unusual member of the *Ericaceae*, with slender trailing stems each lined with a double rank of narrow box-like evergreen leaves from the axils of which hung a profusion of tubular, inch-long, red-veined flowers. At its point of attachment with the tree the stem of the *Agapetes* becomes conspicuously swollen into a hard turnip-like structure. One specimen we found still attached to a fallen branch had a swelling the size of a football. I have always wanted to see this plant tried in some of the moist, mild, woodland gardens of the west, such as Caerhayes in Cornwall, but frost in any guise would probably dispatch it and it will, I suppose, remain forever a cool house or conservatory subject in Britain.

The forest floor supported a wide variety of shrubs and herbs especially *Impatiens* spp. with yellow, pink or purple flowers. Two were later identified as *I. puberula* and *I. hobsonii. Eupatorium adenophorum*, a bushy sub-shrub up to 3 ft crowded the paths and formed drifts in glades and open spaces. It occurred over a wide altitudinal range and had accompanied us from the plateau at Tumlingtar. In the darkest places there were giant clumps of *Sarcococca saligna* (*pruniformis*) with stems several feet high. This species is very occasionally seen in cultivation, being suitable only for mild areas. Growing in moss on the forest floor we found a small creeping shrublet with small shiny leaves and prickly stems. It looked very similar to a plant Spring-Smyth had once brought to the Hillier Arboretum which has since been identified as *Zizyphus nummularia*.

Mahonia napaulensis was now frequent and included many old gnarled specimens covered with epiphytes. We also collected seed of two large thorny *Zanthoxylum* spp. One had pinnate leaves with a winged rachis and axillary clusters of small, wrinkled, orange-red, peppercorn-sized fruits. Both male and female plants occurred, and it reminded me of the American sp. *Z. americanum*, the toothache tree whose sharp-tasting shoots and fruits were once chewed by the Indians to relieve toothache. It proved to be *Z. acanthopodium*, whilst its companion, whose red fruits occurred in terminal clusters, was *Z. oxyphyllum. Symplocos theifolia* here formed a handsome evergreen tree up to 50 ft with clusters of immature greenish fruits.

Eventually we chose a glade in which to make camp for the night and helped our Sherpas to erect the tents. The glade was full of *Sambucus adnata*, forming extensive patches in the manner of *S. ebulus*, the Dane's elder. It differed from that species however in the large flattened corymbs of orange, ripening to red, fruits. These fruits are sometimes taken as a laxative, a power which is lost however on their being cooked.

Many climbers thrust their way into the canopy and we quickly recognised the grey downy leaves of the Himalayan musk rose — *Rosa brunonii* — even without the masses of fragrant white flowers. Equally powerful were the stems of a giant bramble — *Rubus paniculatus* — which scrambled and clawed its way into several neighbouring trees to send its branches tumbling down from heights of 40-50 ft, terminating in crowded inflorescences of white flowers followed by small blackberries. Its ovate-lanceolate leaves were cream or grey felted beneath. A single plant grown from this seed was planted out in the Hillier Arboretum. We were pleased to find a climbing honeysuckle — *Lonicera glabrata* — despite its name a softly hairy twiner carrying axillary pairs of black shiny fruits. One of the most exciting finds however was *Clematis buchananiana*, a strong-growing climber with trifoliolate leaves and drooping panicles of tubular-bell-shaped, greenish-yellow flowers an inch long. The entire plant (including flowers) was clothed with a dense pale tomentum.

On a much smaller scale were two very choice plants with slender twining stems. The first of these — *Dicentra scandens* — had the typical locket-shaped flowers of the tribe, 0.75 in. long, white with a greenish puckered mouth. They hung in loose clusters to be replaced by 1 in. long, bullet-shaped, pale purple fruits. The leaves were much divided and fern-like. *Tripterospermum volubile* belongs to the gentian family and was at one time assigned to *Gentiana*. It twined its way into large bushes or small slender-stemmed trees, bearing its long pointed ovate to ovate-lanceolate leaves in pairs. The nodding tubular deep-blue flowers, up to 1.5 in. long, were borne singly from the leaf axils and gave way to fruits which reminded me of small purple radishes 1-1.25 in. long. An occasional plant with white flowers was seen.

The above four climbers grew on the edge of the clearing, although the last two favoured shadier places. None as far as I am aware is in general cultivation, being somewhat tender in nature, although all but the honeysuckle would be well worth their place in a conservatory with just enough heat to keep away the worst of the winter cold. Seed of the *Dicentra* and *Tripterospermum* germinated and plants were grown at Hillier's Nursery but they perished before flowering.

Our campsite was at approximately 7,800 ft and for up to an hour after our arrival the porters were turning up thoroughly soaked and anxious to get a fire started. Dawa told us he had paid two porters off because they had changed their minds about going any further, whilst he had sacked another two after finding them lying in a house drunk on rakshi. He had, however, managed to hire an extra five porters.

It was dark by 6 p.m. and we busied ourselves by the Tilley lamp writing plant notes and pressing material. In the house where we had taken our lunch we had been given soya beans (*Glycine max*) but we then did not connect these hairy pods with the soya-bean milk which Morris, Mortimer and I had sampled in Singapore. Soya beans were being grown by the villagers along the edges of their fields. The main crop in this area appeared to be maize (*Zea mays*) which was later underplanted with finger millet (*Eleusine coracana*) to ripen after the maize was harvested.

Witcombe and Mortimer were sharing a tent as were Morris and I, whilst Beer had his own. At some obscure hour in the night we heard a commotion from Witcombe's and Mortimer's tent and at breakfast next day we were told that John had suddenly awoken to find his hair wet and sticky, which when Mortimer shone his torch on it proved to be blood from a leech bite. Pema too had been bitten on the ankle but did nothing about it until much later when it had turned septic.

The rain had not stopped and we climbed into a change of clothes and donned our boots before doing a quick exploration of the campsite and its environs. Two polygonums I recognised at once like old friends — *Polygonum campanulatum* was very common on the edge of the clearing and alongside the several streams nearby. Its leaves were beautifully parallel veined beneath and clothed with a silky fawn tomentum, whilst the clusters of flowers were typically white with a pink tinge. The other species was almost certainly *P. alpinum*, forming handsome bushy clumps to 3 ft covered with panicles of snow-white flowers. It grew in similar places to the other but lacked the far creeping habit. Scattered across the grass of the glades and clearings were at least three species of *Anaphalis* including the narrow leaved *A. busua* previously seen on Phulchoki. Another species which somewhat resembled *A. triplinervis* was later identified as *A. contorta*, which as far as I am aware is not in cultivation.

The main party moved off leaving Beer, Morris and me to collect seed. Pema had stayed behind to cook us a light lunch, after which we all set off up the track. After a short while we entered *Rhododendron arboreum* forest and everything darkened. It was eerie as we picked our way through the tall crooked stems dripping with mosses and lichens, now and then obscured by drifting patches of mist. It put me in mind of J. R. Tolkien's description of Mirkwood in 'The Hobbit'. We passed through several small clearings containing rock outcrops on which grew large colonies of *Cautleya cathcartii*, evidently quite at home in the thick pelt of leaf mould in which it spread its roots. It grew equally happily on mossy tree trunks. This species is closely related to *C. spicata* and is similar to it in flower. It was named after J. F. Cathcart (1802-51), a .Calcutta judge and amateur botanist. The fruits we collected have subsequently produced established plants in the Hillier Arboretum, Wakehurst Place and several other gardens in England.

Climbing all the while the track led us through the evergreen forest onto an open ridge. Here *Piptanthus nepalensis* (*laburnifolius*) formed great thickets together with an equally robust *Elsholtzia fruticosa* (*polystachya*) whose 5-6 ft shoots produced, from their tips, branched spike-like racemes of small creamy-white flowers. *Edgeworthia gardneri* and *Daphne bholua* became frequent, suckering to form clumps up to 6 ft tall, whilst I was surprised to see *Hydrangea heteromalla* growing as an epiphyte. There were several specimens of the *Hydrangea* 8-10 ft tall perched in the crotches of trees an equal distance from the ground, and then we found one growing normally, a large tree-like specimen of 25 ft with a single trunk. The flowers occurred in broad flattened corymbs, both fertile and ray florets white, the latter 1-2 in. across. This species is variable, more so than *H. aspera*, and many forms from China especially at some time have been treated as separate species.

Mixed with the *Piptanthus* in the more sheltered sites we recognised *Leycesteria formosa*, the so-called Himalayan honeysuckle, with its characteristic jade-green hollow stems and white flowers protruding from clusters of purple-tinted bracts. The dark purple juicy berries are a favourite food of several birds, especially the many pheasants which skulked about in the undergrowth.

Beer pointed out to me *Pieris formosa* growing just below the ridge path on the SE slope. It formed large bushes up to 15 ft, but much higher amongst the trees. Most of the upper reaches of this slope were covered with scrub and one of the commonest components was *Spiraea micrantha*, its erect 5-6 ft stems terminating in broad flattened corymbs of white flowers. Where it pushed its way through the branches of the *Pieris* it reached 10 ft. On the edge of the forest we found 15 ft specimens of an evergreen with dark green, narrow serrated leaves arranged in pairs along the twigs. We decided that it was probably *Osmanthus suavis* which one sees occasionally in cultivation in the warmer regions of the British Isles and elsewhere. It produces in spring the sweetly scented white flowers which are a trade mark of the genus.

By now we had attained somewhere in the region of 8,800 ft and the track ran a comparatively level course, snaking in and out of the forest heading north-east. At this altitude other trees made an appearance and Beer and I were overjoyed to see our first wild *Magnolia* – *M. campbellii* – even though we had missed its white flowers by several months. A large-leaved sycamore-like maple proved to be *Acer sterculiaceum* (*villosum*) and accompanying it in some quantity was *A. campbellii* commemorating Dr A. Campbell (1805-74), Superintendent of Darjeeling and Political Agent to Sikkim. He was a friend of J. D. Hooker, accompanying him on his famous journey through Sikkim in 1849, during which time they were seized and made prisoners by Sikkim Bhotiyas (Tibetans).

I was surprised to see a yew tree growing in the forest and then others appeared exactly resembling our native *Taxus baccata* in appearance but referred to by some authorities as a separate species *T. wallichiana*. According to J. D. Hooker, the red bark of this tree was used to make a dye for staining the foreheads of Brahmins in Nepal, and maybe this is the source of the dye we saw being used for this purpose in Side Pokhara. Beneath the forest canopy a bamboo ran riot pushing between stems and rocks, out into the open and into the scrub. Its slender bluish-green canes reached 10-15 ft with characteristic scabrous internodes. The narrow leaves, 4-7 in. long, we were later told are commonly given to cattle and ponies as fodder. It proved to be *Arundinaria maling* (*racemosa*) which is rare in cultivation, although I remember once examining a whole drift of it growing in Hillier's Chandler's Ford Nursery in the 1960s.

The flora here was tremendous and neither Beer nor I could contain our excitement as each new plant appeared. Morris, whose horticultural experience was understandably limited, was infected by our enthusiasm and searched as diligently as we for seed and specimens of each new find. A single shrub of what appeared to be a *Corylopsis* sp., possibly *C. himalayana*, grew by the track, and whilst I was examining this Morris emerged from the thicket triumphantly holding a section of creeper from which hung a large sausage-shaped purple pod. The leaves were compound, composed of five pointed leaflets 3-6 in. long and there was no doubt that it was *Holboellia latifolia*, a forest climber with twining stems up to 15 ft or more. *Vaccinium retusum* grew as an epiphyte on several trees, its wiry stems 1-3 ft long, densely clothed with obovate, notched, evergreen leaves 0.75 in. long and carrying terminal racemes of small blue-black berries.

Hypericum uralum appeared again and with it the handsome *Berberis insignis* with smooth thornless stems 4-5 ft high, sporting clusters of large dark evergreen leaves up to 5-7 in. long boldly edged with spine-tipped teeth. This striking shrub is sometimes found in *Berberis* collections in Britain but is not the hardiest of species.

We found the track narrowing beneath a tall bush of *Enkianthus deflexus*, and then skirting a rock face exposed to the south-east. The rain was blowing into our faces all the while but this was suddenly forgotten when we saw several 1-2 ft stems of a lily above our heads. Each was clothed with linear leaves and supported a single terminal nodding capsule and all around were small seedlings, especially plentiful at the base of shrubs. It was *Lilium nepalense* whose strange green flowers in June are stained deep crimson at the base within. It was quite at home in the mossy chinks and pockets and some seedlings were growing on the moss-carpeted rock itself. Sharing the same situation but preferring the fully exposed rock was a *Pleione* sp., unfortunately not in flower. The small flattened pseudobulbs clung to the rock surface like limpets and were loosely covered by a 0.5 in. layer of moss. The whole rock face was running with water, a situation which must dramatically change after the monsoon when the sunny weather of autumn would shrivel the moss and dry out the face until the snow of winter arrived. We were so pleased about the lilies and fussed about the pleiones looking for a sign of seed capsules but with no success. Instead we found the delicate golden-backed fronds of a pretty fern — *Cheilanthes farinosa* — which thrived here despite the seemingly unhelpful conditions. This is a most variable fern in which maybe several species are involved and I cannot understand why it is rarely seen in cultivation. It would surely enjoy the damp shady walls beloved of our native spleenworts. On reflection, however, it may be of border-line hardiness, though collections from the highest altitudes might prove more successful. It is a pity that hardy ferns figure so infrequently in the introductions of plant collectors unless, of course, the collector is a pteridologist. We saw many excellent ornamental ferns in Nepal and made numerous spore collections. As the light faded we hurried along the track past many tempting pieces of forest and hillside. Another *Clematis* sp. — *C. tongluensis* — scrambled over neighbouring vegetation and its general aspect suggested a relationship with the well known *C. montana*. A single flower with four narrowly elliptic, creamy-white tepals confirmed our diagnosis.

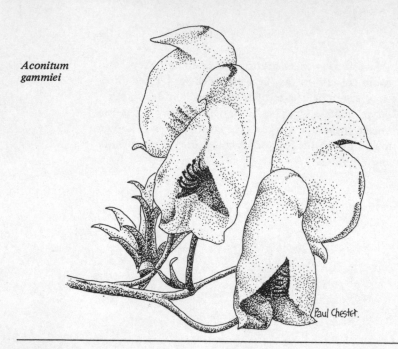

Aconitum gammiei

4 LOST IN THE MIST

The gales of the night had played havoc with the camp and the large jouster tent had been blown down and its metal frame broken. The gales had spent themselves but the rain remained to remind us of the heavy cloud which hid the sky. Dawa and several porters left soon after breakfast and headed up the hill on their way to the village of Topke Gola several days' journey away, whilst the rest of us spent the day collecting in what seemed a botanically rich area.

Our presence on the Milke Danda was based solely on a story Beer had heard on his reconnaissance. He had travelled to Topke Gola on foot from Dharan via Dhankuta, Hile and Taplejung, following first the Tamur Valley and then the Mewa Khola to establish his base camp. On his return journey he had stayed one night in a hill village and huddled round a fire with the Sherpas and porters. The porters chatted with a group of villagers talking of the journey and the strange foreigner who collected flowers and seeds, not to eat but to press between paper and to store in bags. One of the villagers spoke of a sacred lake high on the mountains of the Jaljale Himal above the Milke Danda. According to the storyteller, on a special occasion each year, shepherds and others would go on a pilgrimage to the lake which was set in a place where many wonderful flowers grew. Dawa had translated the story to Beer and on repeating the story to us on our arrival at Dharan we had agreed, after some discussion, that the lake might be worth a visit even if it did mean a new and high route unknown to our Sherpas and

Paris polyphylla

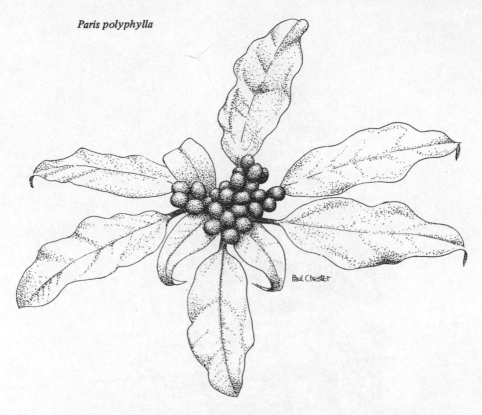

Paul Chester

porters who preferred lower, well-known routes in the valleys. This route up the Milke Danda through the Jaljale Himal to Topke Gola was full of promise and a sense of the unknown — anything might happen; we had instructed Dawa to leave indications of any change of route so that we might follow in his footsteps.

Beer, Morris and I meanwhile returned along the ridge to the rock face where we made a detailed search for more seed of the lily. We found a large individual carrying three plump capsules and again many seedlings growing mostly at the base of *Spiraea micrantha* clumps. It was whilst we were so engaged that the rain ceased and on turning round we could see a long streak of blue on the south-east horizon. From then on the weather improved and with it our attitude, which until then had been one of resistance against the rain and leeches. *Rosa sericea* was plentiful with its small nodding, pear-shaped, red and yellow hips, but out of flower this is a poor relation compared with its blood-winged Chinese variety *pteracantha*.

We returned to camp for lunch and then plunged into the forest on the north-west slope to spend a happy afternoon in what was to us a paradise. There were *Magnolia campbellii* 60-70 ft high, their branches green with algae and moss. We grubbed in the litter beneath these trees

47

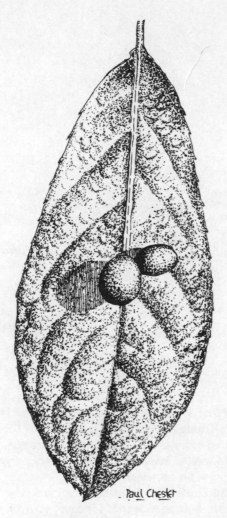

*Helwingia
himalaica*

Paul Chester

but most of the fruits were worm-ridden. A large poplar — *Populus
jacquemontiana* var. *glauca* — had sticky buds and ovate-cordate, grey-
green leaves, glaucous beneath, borne on angular shoots. As far as I
could remember I had neither seen nor heard of it in cultivation. Both
maples of the previous day — *A. sterculiaceum* and *A. campbellii* —
were plentiful with individuals 50-60 ft in height. A third maple —
A. pectinatum — was present here growing to a similar size and with
three-lobed leaves on red petioles, the veins beneath clothed with
fulvous hairs. Even the fruits, in pendulous clusters, had attractive
red wings. A small tangled currant occurred as an epiphyte on several
trees and proved to be *Ribes laciniatum*, but of no ornamental merit.
We were struck by the various members of the *Araliaceae* present, in
particular *Pentapanax leschenaultii* which reminded me of a large leaved

Firmiana. The ground where this small tree flourished was swampy and crowded with ferns of the *Dryopteris* clan. The sinister mottled stems of *Arisaema nepenthoides* thrust their way through the low vegetation bearing dense orange-red fruiting spikes. Red fruits also appeared on *Paris polyphylla*, where they formed a dense terminal cluster above a ruff of seven to nine slender leaves, the whole carried on a stem 8-9 in. from the forest floor. Creeping about nearby was a miniature bramble — *Rubus calycinus* — which formed carpets of kidney-shaped leaves 1-2 in. across. From the axils of many leaves small raspberry-like fruits were borne on 1-1.5 in. stalks. It was a most attractive creeper and is now established in cultivation from this seed.

I was excited to encounter a shrub whose red berries were produced in pairs, apparently from the upper surfaces of the long-pointed leaves. It was *Helwingia himalaica*, a member of the dogwood family — *Cornaceae*. I remembered having seen the black-berried Japanese species — *H. japonica* — at the University Botanic Garden, Cambridge, when a student and remember also the then Director, John Gilmour, demonstrating that the apparent abnormality is due to the fusion of the peduncle with the petiole and midrib. We found more *Holboellia latifolia* and collected its purple pods and there was more of the climbing gentian — *Tripterospermum volubile*. Growing in the shadiest parts of the forest was a peculiar brown fruiting spike belonging to a parasite *Hymenopogon parasiticus* and another *Cautleya* sp. — *C. spicata* — colonised the moss-capped boulders.

Just before returning to camp we discovered several scattered trees of a whitebeam which I thought was *Sorbus cuspidata*, but which was later identified as *S. hedlundii* by the Armenian authority Eleonora Gabriellian. They were trees of 60-70 ft with large leaves varying in shape from elliptic to rotund elliptic. The leaves were white tomentose beneath with rust-coloured midrib and veins, resembling in this character a tree grown under this name in the Hillier Arboretum. We collected a number of fallen fruits the size of small crab apples coloured green or russet with brown speckles. Several young trees from this seed are now established in the Hillier Arboretum and elsewhere.

By now the sky was clear and the sun shone on the hills around highlighting the snow-capped peaks to the north which included Makalu. The turf around the campsite was full of *Satyrium nepalense*, a small orchid, the majority of whose relatives are found thousands of miles to the south in South Africa. This species was a charmer showing its pretty pink flower spikes a few inches above the short grass and colouring the open ridge as far as the eye could see. Growing as a companion, though less spectacular, was a miniature *Elsholtzia* — *E. strobilifera* — with elongated pale pinky-purple flower cones in branched heads.

That evening, after de-leeching, we spent several hours pressing specimens and cleaning seed whilst the Sherpas played a game of

49

hand-ball outside in the moonlight. One of the Sherpa porters from Sedua poked his head into our tent, and after watching us for a while retreated, but not before he had picked up some cast-away *Arisaema* fruits which he popped into his mouth.

The following morning was one of the most enjoyable awakenings I have ever had. It began as usual with a loud rasp as the tent was unzipped. As I freed myself from my sleeping bag I saw Pema's smiling face, returned his greeting and watched hot tea being poured from a tin kettle into an enamel mug. The rays of the rising sun pierced the steam illuminating the interior with a warm orange glow. By the time Morris was awake the porridge had arrived and this we ate after first stirring in a large helping of syrup. By the time we had washed and dressed the sun was up and on the northern horizon Makalu and its attendant peaks glistened from a fresh fall of snow. We left Pema and the others to pack up the camp and followed the track up a grassy slope until it entered once again the *Rhododendron arboreum* forest. Conditions were so gloomy here that we had difficulty in keeping to the track which resembled one of several nearby gullies worn by floodwater from the recent heavy rains. Occasionally the canopy high above parted to allow in a long shaft of sunlight which showed several stems swaddled in moss and lichens. In this soft, moist, vertical strata many epiphytes had found a comfortable home; these are plants which, tired of the eternal rat-race on the forest floor, have taken the 'elevator' to the upper floors (branches) of the tree and now earn for themselves, with a few adaptions, a relatively easy living.

After a long steep climb we emerged into the light and saw the track moving up through open scrub with scattered deciduous trees and rhododendrons. Amongst the latter *R. cinnabarinum* and *R. barbatum* were now prominent with the plum-coloured flaking bark of the latter species particularly pleasing. *Stachyurus himalaicus* and *Enkianthus deflexus* appeared, both with individual specimens up to 18 ft high. There were several large trees of *Populus jacquemontiana* var. *glauca*, their leaves on long petioles fluttering constantly in the breeze. The evergreen clumps of *Pieris formosa* now became dominant reaching 18-20 ft high pierced only by the stout trunks of many whitebeams — *Sorbus hedlundii* — up to 70 ft tall. Then one of my favourite trees, a birch, turned up. This was the Himalayan birch — *Betula utilis* — an extremely variable species in leaf, shoot and colour of bark, which is not surprising considering its distribution along the Himalaya from Afghanistan to China. Its status is hotly contested by the rival factions of the 'splitters and lumpers' club, the latter seeing it as one variable species, whilst the splitters divide it into at least three species — *B. jacquemontii* in the west, *B. utilis* in the Himalaya and *B. albo-sinensis* in China. There are several creamy-barked forms of *B. utilis* in cultivation whilst those we found on the Milke Danda and elsewhere possessed orange-brown or coppery bark, peeling in tassels and curls, especially below the main branches.

More *Lyonia ovalifolia* and *Piptanthus nepalensis* appeared as scattered shrubs, and then we discovered two 25 ft trees of *Sorbus insignis*. I was familiar with this species from a tree in the Hillier Arboretum grown from seed collected by Kingdon Ward in the Naga Hills, Assam in 1928. I was unaware, however, that it occurred in Nepal. The handsome, large, pinnate leaves were composed of 15 broad leaflets whose polished dark-green upper surfaces shone in the morning sun. I climbed into the branches in order to grasp the small, deep red, unripened fruits produced in dense corymbs. Sitting in this tree looking out over the surrounding rhododendrons I felt a tremendous satisfaction. Surrounded by plants which previously I had known only in cultivation, I found it hard to believe my good fortune and took a few deep breaths of Himalayan air to reassure myself that it was real. I now realised that at last the dreams of my youth were coming true and I began to sing at the top of my voice. My singing, however, was heard only by a pair of white-cheeked bulbuls who flew from a nearby rowan to disappear further down the ridge. I then looked around but Beer and Morris were nowhere to be seen and my gaze was met by a heavily laden porter who had stopped in his tracks and now stared incredulously in my direction. Laughing I climbed out of the tree and set off up the track in pursuit of my colleagues. It was not long before I caught them up, as they had stopped to collect the fruits of a small rowan – *Sorbus kurzii*. The fruits were white, flushed pink, whilst the glossy-green pinnate leaves, borne in tight rosettes, were already turning crimson and orange. It was quite new to me and as far as I knew unknown in cultivation. W. S. Kurz (*c*.1833-78) was a German botanist who collected plants in the East and was at one time Curator of the Calcutta Herbarium. Beneath this tree we found *Skimmia laureola*, the male form of which is such an outstandingly good evergreen shrub in cultivation with its dense conical or rounded clusters of greenish-yellow flowers. As with most, if not all the skimmias, the flowers are sweetly scented which is more than can be said for the leaves which emit a pungent aroma when bruised. It became quite common by the track, stunted in the open, reaching 4 ft in shade.

We found red fruits in abundance on *Cotoneaster microphyllus* var. *thymifolius* which formed low mounds and mats of densely packed stems on grassy banks and hillocks. The tiny evergreen leaves were a dark polished green, and so tightly did these mounds knit together that one could stand on them without damaging their symmetry. This variety is regarded as a species – *C. integrifolius* – by the German authority G. Klotz.

At 9,800 ft we found another *Sorbus* with bold pinnate leaves and conspicuous stipules on the young shoots. It was a tree 18 ft high but unfortunately with no fruits. I picked specimens for a photograph because this tree reminded me of one growing in the Hillier Arboretum which we had originally received as seed labelled *S. insignis* from the Darjeeling nursery firm of Ghose.

The ridge narrowed and boulders crowded the track as we picked our way through low scrub which consisted of dwarf rhododendrons, *R. anthopogon* being the most common with its greyish-green leaves, followed by *R. lepidotum* with sage-green linear leaves. Amongst these we found two isolated specimens of *R. ciliatum* and *R. glaucophyllum*. Flowering herbs peppered the turf and I was pleased to see the trailing slender growths of the annual *Cyananthus inflatus* whose bright blue flowers protruded from hairy inflated calyces. In places it contrasted with the yellow flowers of *Corydalis juncea*, another annual. At one point where the ground sloped steeply into a gully, a company of *Aconitum spicatum* appeared from the undergrowth. This handsome monkshood bore 2.5-3 ft stems crowded with blue-purple helmeted flowers and would be a worthwhile addition to any herbaceous border or island bed in the garden, though I have not heard that seed we then collected has resulted in this plant becoming generally grown in cultivation.

We were now above 10,000 ft and still the track continued upwards, now into a mist which had stealthily crept along the ridge. Beer and I became separated from the others and we decided to move a little more quickly, ignoring the plants — we could not see them anyway. At a height of 11,000 ft I felt dizzy suddenly so I told Beer to go on whilst I sat down to catch my breath. I am glad that I did because growing in the turf at my feet was *Gaultheria trichophylla*, a choice little suckering shrublet 3-4 in. high with tiny ciliate, thyme-like leaves and sporting oblong to ovoid fruits 0.5 in. long, coloured a deep blue. It was quite plentiful on these open slopes and must have presented a pretty sight with the sun on the fruits. After a while I felt better and proceeded up the hill in Beer's wake to find myself almost immediately at the camp which had been pitched on a level area. The voices of Witcombe and Morris guided me to the kitchen where I found the group chatting over mugs of hot tea. It was a good campsite with water nearby and plenty of fuel. It always caused me grief, each time we established camp, to hear the sound of chopping in the forest and to see the Sherpas and porters emerging dragging branches and logs for the several fires. At this camp we were surrounded by Rhododendron thicket in which grew *R. barbatum*, *R. hodgsonii*, *R. campanulatum*, *R. campylocarpum* and *R. cinnabarinum*. To see these being cut, though in a limited way, set me to wondering what would have been the reactions of those Edwardian owners of the great Rhododendron collections in Cornwall where a visiting enthusiast needed a passport to *see* the treasures let alone touch them! *Rhododendron hodgsonii* was certainly a handsome species with attractively flaking, pinky-brown stems up to 18 ft. The leaves of young specimens measured 10-15 in. and their shining deep-green upper surfaces had a sprinkling of hoar-like indumentum. On older specimens the leaves were reduced in size. The undersurface of the leaf was clothed with a pale buff indumentum which became silvery on exposure to the light. On a springtime visit two years later I saw this species bearing tight rounded heads of magenta-purple flowers, while in the sheltered forest lower down on the Milke Banjgang I found forms with larger looser trusses of pink flowers. *R. hodgsonii* was certainly valued by the hill people for its hard wood which was used for cups, bowls and other implements and made the best fires. The leaves too were used for lining baskets and for carrying food within the village or camp. We also later found them useful as fans on warm days. This notable *Rhododendron* was named by J. D. Hooker after his friend B. H. Hodgson (1800-94), a British resident in Nepal and an amateur naturalist of some repute, his main interest being mammals and birds (Hodgson's pied wagtail). Accompanied by Dr Thomson he greeted Hooker and Campbell on their release from captivity in 1849.

R. arboreum had been left behind down the ridge but the other species which replaced it proved equally dominant, forming almost impenetrable thickets up to 15 ft high. Through these thickets grew two trees, *Betula utilis* and the East Himalayan silver fir — *Abies densa*. This species is the cause of much discussion, even argument, in botanical circles. It has been called *A. spectabilis*, and before that *A. webbiana*, but in *An Enumeration of the Flowering Plants of Nepal*, vol. 1, published in 1978, the Spanish botanist J. do Amaral Franco distinguishes three species of *Abies* in Nepal. *A. pindrow* in the west, *A. spectabilis* in west and central Nepal and *A. densa* in the east. According to Franco, *A. densa* differs from *A. spectabilis* mainly in its bark soon becoming scaly, its brownish (not yellowish) twigs and its broader leaves. Our trees certainly had brown shoots and scaly bark, but their most striking feature was the dark glossy-green leaf with two broad bands of chalk-white stomata beneath. These were densely crowded in two ranks along the branches. Young trees raced up to the ridge from sheltered gullies, of conical shape and strong and virile. Meanwhile, stout-stemmed older trees occurred as isolated individuals on the ridge itself, blasted by a hundred years or more of winds and storms, their once fine raiment now tattered and torn, hanging in long streamers. Their boughs sagged from the vegetable encrustations of countless decades of epiphytes. Some trees were in fruit, the sloe-black, barrel-shaped cones lining the upper sides of the top branches like midnight candles.

These thickets, where tracks if any belonged to small creatures, were the haunt of beautiful birds like the Blood Pheasant which went mostly unseen. However, one of these birds, a male, was somehow caught by a porter who brought it triumphantly into camp. It was grey and green above with blood-red throat, tail, legs and eye patch. Several times we heard the Impeyan Pheasant but only once did we see it. I was leading a small contingent of porters one day through bamboo and rhododendron thicket when a large bird flew onto a branch some 15 ft to my left. We froze and watched fascinated as it turned slowly round as if on a pivot. A shaft of sun acting as spotlight highlighted the multitude of colours in the bird's plumage, blue, green, purple and chestnut. It reminded me of one of those magical birds from a children's storybook, because as suddenly as it had appeared it was gone, its silent glide carrying it from our view back into the shadows.

The next morning the sun was shining and our eyes saw a wonderful sight. It was as though a piece of sky had fallen into our camp overnight because our hands and knees sank into a turf full of blue gentians belonging to two small annual species *Gentiana prolata* and *G. sikkimensis*. Both grew no more than 3 in. high and bore tubular flowers, the former in groups of three, the latter in heads of five to nine. We decided against taking photographs of blue flowers so early in thé day, due to the quality of the light, and agreed to do it later. Breakfast finished, Morris and I walked back along the ridge to where the previous afternoon the mist had intervened in our plant collecting. A breeze blew our hair and the views were magnificent. To the north-west Makalu and Everest dominated the skyline, whilst Kanchengjunga appeared in the north-east. Large carpets of trailing reddish stems on banks and boulders proved to be *Polygonum vacciniifolium*. The multitude of short erect flower spikes were a deeper pink than those normally encountered in cultivation and coloured the sides of the track for some distance. Trailing down a wet rock face was another species — *P. emodi* — with long woody stems and long narrow leaves with revolute margins. The flower spikes were even more slender than those of *P. vacciniifolium*, and the individual flowers were crimson. Of the two, *P. vacciniifolium* is the better garden plant because of its hardiness, freer flowering and tidier habit. It is also more adaptable to different situations and will take sun or shade. To complete a trio of polygonums we then found *P. milletii* growing on boulders and rock ledges. The leaves were heart shaped, much larger than those of the others, and the dense spikes of deep rose-red flowers were carried aloft on 9-12 in. stems. The name commemorates Charles Millett, an official of the East India Company during the early nineteenth century and an amateur botanist. In the same rocks grew *Codonopsis dicentrifolia* forming 9-12 in. clumps of slender-stalked prettily divided leaves. The blue flowers 1-1.5 in. long were borne in long terminal panicles creating delightful fountains from a distance. Most plants grew on the SW or SE faces of the rocks, their roots deeply entrenched in vertical crevices. At the foot of these and other rocks, in the moist shady spots, occurred numerous rosettes of *Meconopsis napaulensis* with pale green, densely hairy, pinnatisect leaves. One plant supported a 3 ft central stem carrying a few late, nodding, lilac-blue flowers.

Clumps of *Anemone polyanthes* were scattered over the hillside, but in fruit they gave little indication of their merit when in flower. This robust perennial throws up one to several erect downy stems to 2 ft, bearing several large white or pink-tinted flowers in June and July. It is highly desirable and should be in every garden in England but regretfully I have never seen it in cultivation.

I was keen to reach a *Sorbus* sp. which hung its clusters of pink, turning to white, fruits in the denser parts of the Rhododendron thicket. Its small neat leaves with numerous tiny leaflets identified it as *S. microphylla*, a charming small tree as yet rare and little known in general cultivation. We later saw this species in many places and it appeared to be the most commonly occurring member of its genus above 10,000 ft. We discovered that many plants preferred the company of rocks and cliffs and we examined every outcrop within easy reach. On one of those a handsome purple-flowered onion – *Allium wallichii* – occupied a grassy ledge and its acquisition caused us considerable trouble. According to a recent report by J. F. Dobremez, this species is an important medicinal plant containing steroids, flavonoids and polysaccharoides. It is used for altitude sickness and as a stimulant.

It was whilst we were clawing our way along a particularly tricky rock ledge that we noticed that the sun no longer warmed our backs, and when we looked around it was to find that the mist spewing up from the valleys had joined with cloud from above. For the next hour we ignored the rain which rushed in from the south-west, but gradually conditions became worse and we returned to camp where the disappearance of the sun had caused the gentians to close and become invisible in the grass.

Towards the end of the afternoon, the weather cleared and the sunshine persuaded Beer and me to explore the hillside above camp where a dwarf *Berberis* sp. formed colonies no more than a foot high. It was a densely branched shrub with suckering reddish shoots and obovate spine-toothed leaves 0.5 in. long which were a polished dark-green above and a contrasting glaucous beneath. The single yellow flowers changed to oblong to obovoid deep red fruits 0.5-0.66 in. long. It reminded me of *B. concinna* and in the event proved to be the closely related *B. erythroclada*, a species named by the Rev. W. Ahrendt. Ahrendt had based his name on a herbarium specimen collected by F. Kingdon Ward in SE Tibet and the abundant seed which we collected constituted its first introduction into cultivation. Plants are now growing quite happily in the Hillier Arboretum and elsewhere. We called on two Sherpa boys to continue picking seed whilst we did a reconnaissance along the ridge. Returning as dusk settled on the ridge, we stopped and turned to the north before descending to our camp. To the north-west Mount Everest and her attendant peaks riding on a sea of cloud were painted a rich gold from a setting sun and appeared like ships in a Turner painting. To the north-east lay the pale massive of Kanchengjunga bathed in moonlight. The contrast was at once startling and humbling and for some time after returning to camp the experience occupied our thoughts. The night remained calm and we sat around the camp-fire talking and working. A last look at the outside world before going to bed revealed a moon-washed landscape in which the only movement was clouds rising like goosedown from the valleys below.

Another day began with the sun and a blue sky to cheer us. Meanwhile six porters had decided to return to their farms and this necessitated several of their colleagues having to carry loads of 90 lb for which they were paid extra. Even so, two loads had to be left behind with Namgyal until we could send porters back from the next camp. All day we walked along a gently rising ridge track, our view into the valleys obscured by rising mist. By mid-afternoon it was drizzling and we became steadily soaked, our toes squelching in waterfilled boots.

Anaphalis spp. shared the hillsides with *Cremanthodium* spp., whose nodding, yellow, daisy heads were as charming as they were characteristic. *C. reniforme* was the most commonly seen. Occupying sizeable areas of bank was *Gaultheria pyroloides* forming close mats and carpets of prostrate stems and evergreen, obovate to elliptic-obovate leaves 1.5-2 in. long bearing an attractive reticulate venation. In other areas the tufted growths of *Cassiope fastigiata* were found, though unfortunately long past flowering. Rosettes of *Primula petiolaris* shared the banks with the peculiar moss-like *Saxifraga brachypoda*. We crossed a wide stretch of pasture where clumps of *Euphorbia himalayensis* were turning fiery-red and orange. We then realised what it was we had seen several times already that day. Occasionally, through breaks in the mist and cloud, we had caught glimpses of distant hillsides apparently alight, and had puzzled over this each time. The autumn display of the *Euphorbia* was certainly a sight to be remembered and provided us with the only hint of warmth on an otherwise cold wet trek.

Passing through a region of rocks and boulders I spotted a small deciduous *Cotoneaster* which reminded me of the Chinese *C. adpressus*. Its leaves were possibly smaller but they had the same shape (broad-ovate to obovate) and shine.* Specimens of a similar species collected on a later occasion have been identified as *C. cavei* and this shrub is now in cultivation from an introduction by my Dutch friend Harry van de Laar.

Rhododendrons continued to be the dominant shrub cover. A colony of *Bergenia ciliata* appeared beneath trees on a wet slope, the leaves orbicular and hairy. It was near this point that we found a 5 ft specimen

*Bertil Hylmo, the Swedish authority on the genus, has pronounced this a new species — *C. milkedandai*.

of *Daphne bholua* with leaves striped creamy-white. It was quite acceptable as variegations go but there was no way that we could have brought it successfully home.

The continuing rain and mist were such that we were forced to spend the next two days in camp, each day hoping for a change in the weather. Witcombe and Mortimer had decided that they would be going no further along the ridge and scouted around for a track leading west. Some of the time we spent drying paper for the presses. This had to be done over the fire in the kitchen shelter and here the conditions were very difficult. The wet fuel caused clouds of acrid smoke to fill the shelter, necessitating a hasty retreat every few minutes. The Sherpas and porters on the other hand seemed untroubled, merely averting their faces when the smoke came their way, or at worst, screwing their eyes tight until it changed direction.

An occasional search in the vegetation below the camp brought further trophies to the press or seed bag. In the valley, where the porters had taken up residence, a group of 50-60 ft bird cherries — *Prunus cornuta* — bore long racemes of red, turning to black, fruits. The elliptic leaves were glaucescent beneath and up to 6 in. long. A small tree from this collection is now growing strongly in the Hillier Arboretum. Two bushes of *Potentilla fruticosa* were found and on the same slope a rather nibbled hummock of *Juniperus communis* var. *saxatilis*. The rhododendrons had been joined by another species — *R. thomsonii*. In fact, this one species excluded all others in the area immediately below the camp and their flaky reddish-brown bark and dark blue-green orbicular leaves were made even more attractive when wetted by the rain. The seed capsules still retained their characteristic cup-like, fleshy, green calyx, though the deep red bell-shaped flowers were now but a memory. This beautiful species was first introduced to cultivation from Sikkim by J. D. Hooker in 1850 and is a parent of many lovely hybrids. It is named after Thomas Thomson (1817-78), a Scots doctor, one time Superintendent of the Calcutta Botanic Garden, and the other member, with Hodgson, of the welcoming party who greeted Hooker and Campbell on their release from captivity in 1849. It is interesting to note that these three people, Campbell, Hodgson and Thomson, all had rhododendrons named after them by Hooker. Other friends were likewise honoured, including Dr H. Falconer (1808-65), M. P. Edgeworth (1812-81), Major Madden (1805-56), R. Wight (1796-1872) and Lady Dalhousie (1786-1839). Hooker himself was likewise honoured by Thomas Nuttall with the naming of *R. hookeri* discovered in 1849 in Assam by T. J. Booth.

On 9 October we parted company with Witcombe and Mortimer. The members of the Horticultural Project then set off up the ridge, anxious to leave the camp and its memories of rain and mud, of smoke and leeches, swollen legs and coughs. The mist was now so thick that one could barely see the man in front and every so often the porters would call to each other to maintain contact. I stopped at one point to re-adjust my rucksack and when I continued I could not see the porter ahead of me. I hurried to catch him up and followed the track which had suddenly narrowed along the hillside to a point where it disappeared into a bamboo thicket. I could hear my heart thumping rapidly as I realised I had missed my way. I just stood and listened and thought I heard shouts coming from below, so downhill I went, crashing through the bamboo, tripping and tumbling several times in my hurry to reach the others. I eventually cleared the bamboo and my heart dropped when I found the ground falling in a series of steep cliffs into what looked like a vast smoke-filled cauldron. It was a deep ravine from which mist spewed and I knew then that the calls I had heard were tricks of the mist, echoes maybe, and I was now lost. I sat down and thought it out carefully. The first thing I must do was to retrace my steps through the bamboo thicket. This I did slowly and painfully because the slope was steep and the broken bamboos sharp and lethal. At last I was back where I started and I then slowly followed the track back to the ridge. In an area of low scrub I noticed another track veering away to run steeply into a narrow ravine. I noted also the large imprints of Morris's boots in the mud and I followed the track all the way down to where my colleagues waited at the base of a huge cliff. I was not the only one to go astray and it took the rest of that day for the porters to arrive, tramping down the ravine in dribs and drabs until all were accounted for. There was no sense in our continuing that day so we simply made our camp by the cliff, erecting a screen to keep out the worst of the rain.

Whilst waiting for Pema to cook the supper we watched one of our porters preparing his. In one dish he made a tacky substance, deldo or tsampa, by mixing millet flour with water. In another dish, chillies were boiled in water to make a soup. All mixing was done with a spatula made on the spot from the wood of *Rhododendron hodgsonii*. He then took a pinch of the deldo and dipped it in the chilli before popping it into his mouth. During the day the porters chewed on cobs of corn and it was common to find discarded cobs on tracks even in remote areas. Porters provide their own food which they carry in a sack, or when available in a plastic bag. Their main meal would be tsampa or rice, curried or otherwise with chillies. When passing through villages they can and usually do supplement their diet with whatever they can buy — fruit, vegetables, eggs or a chicken being the usual fare.

That night a thunderstorm broke and attacked our position with full force. As we lay wedged at the base of the cliff in a deep ravine, thunder cracked in loud peals and lightning came in jagged fingers. All night long we heard branches and trees crashing around us in the forest. Eventually we dropped off and when we awoke at breakfast it was difficult to decide whether or not we had all suffered the same night-mare. Beer was lying in a pool of water which had accumulated from the cliff face whilst Morris was soaked from the rain driving in from the ravine. As for me, I had lost the previous night's draw for sleeping positions and had ended up sandwiched between the other two, as a result of which I had been warm and dry. A bowl of hot porridge and a mug of scalding sweet tea put new life into us and we needed it to face the now inevitable mist and drizzle. We picked a bagful of dark blue fruits from a carpet of *Gaultheria pyroloides* and more fruits of *Sorbus kurzii*. A small, loose-limbed *Ribes laciniatum* provided us with a number of red currants and accompanying this shrub as an epiphyte on several trees was *Vaccinium nummularia*, a small evergreen with slender, densely rusty-hairy stems crowded with small obovate leaves and bearing terminal clusters of black berries.

The track moved off uphill and we followed puffing and sweating and cursing until new plants caused us to linger. One such was a rather pretty blue sowthistle — *Cicerbita macrantha* — with stems 12-18 in. high clothed with pinnatisect leaves and bearing nodding blue flower-heads. Unfortunately in cultivation this plant proved to be coarse in growth and unsuitable for the rock garden. We came upon a rhubarb with large cordate leaves and 3 ft dense panicles of red flowers. It was later named as *Rheum acuminatum*. *Juniperus squamata* appeared in increasing numbers, forming scrubby patches 4-5 ft high, with spreading branches and shoots nodding at the tips. The awl-shaped leaves were greyish-green and the fruits black. A superb red form of *Polygonum vacciniifolium* turned up but regrettably no seed was available.

We moved through a zone of low scrub in which dwarf rhododen-drons, *Potentilla fruticosa*, *Berberis* spp. and a *Spiraea* sp. dominated. Many herbs now put in an appearance and we were particularly taken with a dwarf *Delphinium* — *D. viscosum* (*trilobatum*) — with three-lobed leaves and 6-9 in. downy stems bearing several large, pale-yellow downy flowers. Attractive as it was on these alpine slopes, this was another plant which proved ineffectual in cultivation. A plant grown from this seed in the Hillier Arboretum was rather weedy with small greenish flowers on taller stems. A yellow saxifrage — *S. hookeri* — vied with the comparatively large deep-blue bell-shaped flowers of *Cyananthus lobatus*, whose slender trailing stems were clothed with small deeply lobed or fingered leaves. Trailing too, were the long growths of a climbing monkshood — *Aconitum gammiei* — which scrambled over junipers, producing its slate-blue helmeted flowers in profusion. The Scot, George Gammie (1864-1935) was botanist and Superintendent in turn of the Saharanpur and the Lloyd Botanic Gardens before being made Curator of the Calcutta Botanic Garden.

Several louseworts — *Pedicularis* spp. — were common here and an *Androsace* sp. whose tight green mounds had long since flowered. The plant that pleased us the most however was the fabulous *Corydalis cashmeriana* with its sky-blue flowers sprinkled in the grass. It seemed to grow best in the competition provided by grass and other low herbage and extended over a large area of hillside.

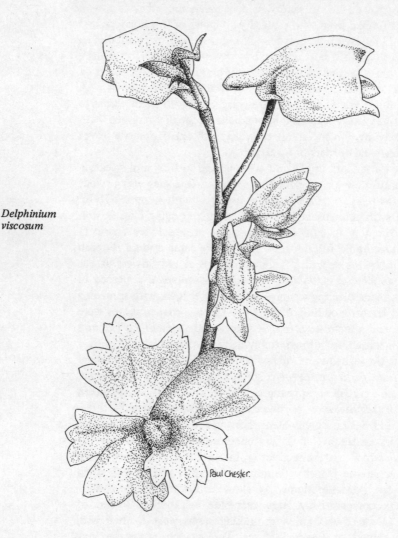

Delphinium viscosum

Paul Chester.

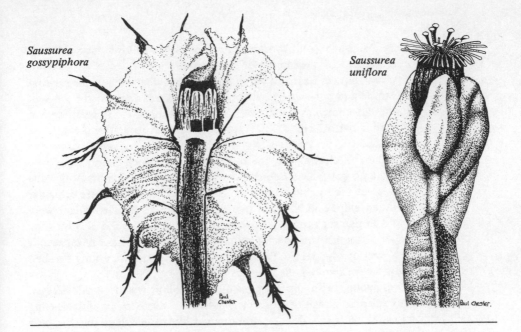

Saussurea gossypiphora

Saussurea uniflora

5   RHUBARB HILL

All that night I tossed and turned and could not get warm. Cold damp-
ness seeped up through the groundsheet and the tent seemed damp
inside. When dawn came at last, we found that we were camped in the
middle of a bog. Pema, anxious to establish a camp and hampered by
mist, had assumed the wet ground to be rain soaked as elsewhere. Little
wonder that the night had been so frustrating. The conditions now
however were bright, and blue sky was evident in patches. The bog, a
soggy area of grasses and sedges, was spattered with the rosettes of at
least three different *Primula* spp., two of which we were able to have
named. The most obvious was *P. obliqua*, a striking plant forming
stout clumps of finely toothed, strap-shaped leaves, covered beneath
with a yellowish farina. The fruiting capsules were borne in umbels
terminating stout 1-1.5 ft scapes. Although past flowering these plants
were made attractive by the rich butter colour or golden-yellow suffu-
sion of the leaves as they left their summer green behind them. It was a
common species which occurred throughout these mountains between
the 13,000 and 14,000 ft contours, often colouring the hillsides from
afar. The second species — *P. dickieana* — was much smaller with
oblanceolate leaves 1-2.5 in. long, distantly toothed in the upper half.
The umbels of fruit capsules were carried on a 6 in. slender scape. Seed
of both species was plentiful and we filled several paper packets. Beer
had seen both species in flower elsewhere during his reconnaissance and
described those of *P. obliqua* as cream in colour and an inch or more

61

across, whilst those of *P. dickieana* varied from white to lavender with a yellow eye and measured over 1 in. across.

Our campsite was situated a few hundred feet below the ridge at 13,500 ft and our route now lay north-eastwards through the range of mountains known as the Jaljale Himal. We scanned the ridge above and noticed a narrow col whence poured a small stream. The sun seemed imminent and we decided to climb the hillside to see what lay on the other side. Following the line of the stream we soon found many new plants amongst which *Bergenia purpurascens* was the most noticeable because of the bright crimson of its fleshy leaves. These were orbicular to broad elliptic in shape. Large patches of this excellent plant were found in damp places, especially by the water's edge but also on rock ledges. Although this species colours in cultivation I have never seen it as it was on the Jaljale Himal. The purple flowers were long finished and we were able to collect lots of seed.

Competing with the *Bergenia* for late colour was *Aster himalaicus*. This splendid alpine daisy formed patches of ovate leaves with clasping bases. It occupied drier, better-drained situations than the *Bergenia* and enjoyed full sun and wind. The flowerheads 1.5-2 in. across comprised a yellow disc surrounded by purple ray florets. They were carried singly on erect hairy stems, in some instances their numbers hiding the leaves beneath. After a while we could spot this plant from a distance as purple patches on the hillside. Plants raised in the Hillier Arboretum from this seed have proved vigorous and hardy though taller in the stem and with slightly smaller flowers.

A prostrate willow with small, narrow, rosemary-like leaves formed large mats, its leaves turning yellow creating golden splashes in the grass. *Cassiope fastigiata* was plentiful on hillocks and banks but as we approached the col *Rhododendron anthopogon* and *R. setosum* took over, their dense low clumps occupying large areas and swamping lesser plants. One bush of the former species still sported a late cluster of reddish flowers, darker even than those of the Award of Merit clone 'Betty Graham' raised from Ludlow & Sherriff seed by the Coxes of Glendoick.

The sun broke loose from a bank of cloud just as we breasted the col at a height of 14,000 ft. The spine of the ridge was relatively narrow and the ground fell away steeply to the north. Stretching across the horizon to the north-west we saw a series of snow-clad peaks and ridges. Six superb mountains dominated our vision from west to east — Chamlang 24,183 ft — Baruntse 22,150 ft — Lhotse 27,885 ft — Everest 29,029 ft — Makalu 27,790 ft and Chomolonzo 22,150 ft.

Suddenly a thick mist descended and obliterated the view along with Beer and Morris. An hour later it began to clear, draining from the steep slopes like some ghostly double tide, leaving the ridge isolated like a whale in the foam. I rose to my feet and walked to the edge of the northern escarpment peering down a gully which revealed a single silvery vein of water. Something then caught my eye which caused my heart to race. Less than a hundred yards away there appeared a dozen snowballs lying in the grass. I moved quickly in their direction and as I approached the objects looked less like snowballs and more like balls of cottonwool. It was only on close examination however that I discovered these strange objects were living plants. It was one of those curious members of the *Compositae* known as *Saussurea gossypiphora*, a bizarre member of a large and variable genus of plants related to the thistles. I was able to photograph and examine the plants in some detail. The short stem was provided with long, narrow, sharply toothed leaves and carried at its summit a single, or sometimes several, thistle-like flowerheads. The entire plant was densely clothed with long, silky, white hairs which took the form of a cottonwool-like mass, completely enveloping all but the tips of the leaves.

The cottonwool is a protective measure, like a fur coat, insulating the flowers from the extremes of heat and cold common at such altitudes. But the *Saussurea* has a secret to reveal. In the top of the cottonwool ball is an aperture just large enough to allow a bumble-bee access to the flowers. Even when the plant is covered by snow, which it is sometimes at flowering time, the bee can still carry out its task because the process of respiration within the cottonwool creates just enough warmth to melt a passage through to the outside world which the bee finds its way down. This observation was first made by A. F. R. Wollaston (1875-1930) during the 1921 British Everest Expedition. Wollaston watched the bees entering and leaving the snow-holes then scraped away the snow to reveal the *Saussurea*. We collected seed from several specimens but none of our shareholders reported successful germination, and so this strange and remarkable plant retains its reputation as being impossible to cultivate, a fact not altogether surprising considering the combination of growing conditions in its native environment.

I had been so enthralled with the saussureas that I had not noticed Morris's arrival. When the mist blanketed the ridge he had gone back to camp where he had lunch before returning to look for me. Beer was also in camp so I accompanied Morris down the slope still talking about the latest find. We picked our way through alpines whose late flowers gave lie to the opinion of those pundits in England who had doubted that we would see much in flower. *Cremanthodium ellisii* (*plantagineum*) with narrow-toothed, plantain-like leaves and a single nodding yellow daisy on a 6-9 in. stem; *Saussurea uniflora* with solitary erect stems 6-8 in. high clothed with conspicuous purple-flushed bracts and bearing a single terminal, blue, thistle-like flowerhead; a *Gentiana* sp., possible *G. depressa*, with pale-blue trumpets, white and green speckled within, dark striped without. *Polygonum vacciniïfolium*, clothing rocks with leafy trailers and a myriad pink or red miniature spears; *Tanacetum atkinsonii* (*Chrysanthemum atkinsonii*), with finely divided leaves and yellow daisy flowers; blue *Swertia* spp. and *Cyananthus lobatus*. These and several others, including *Aster himalaicus* and *Delphinium viscosum*, created colourful tapestries of a kind one normally associates with the European Alps in June.

The next two days were long and frustrating. We followed the ridge keeping to the 14,000 ft contour, heading first in an easterly then in a northerly direction. In one place the track diverged and neither porters nor Sherpas knew which one we should take. Then someone spotted a cone of rocks nearby and on taking this apart we discovered a message left by Dawa with instructions to follow the left-hand track. The mist stayed with us for most of the time usually accompanied by rain or drizzle. Once the mist parted and we gazed into a deep valley where *Abies densa* forest gave way to alpine rhododendrons, their dark carpets enlivened by the gold splashes of *Primula obliqua* foliage.

Seed collecting was restricted to the few bright periods when the mist cleared or thinned out. Interesting plants continued to appear but the weather conditions made certain that we missed many more. On one hillside grew a *Rhododendron* which strongly reminded me of *R. campanulatum* ssp. *aeruginosum*. It formed a dense low colony several acres in extent, the leaves were oblong-elliptic, 4-5 in. long, of a striking sea-green above and covered on the underside with a pale, almost white, indumentum, becoming buff tinged with age and finally, on old leaves, a rich rust colour. The remarkable uniformity of height, habit and leaf colour contrasted markedly with the specimens of typical *R. campanulatum* all around.

The two most fascinating flowering plants we encountered during this period were *Corydalis meifolia* and an *Aconitum* sp. close to *A. staintonii*. The first was a strikingly glaucous plant with deeply divided leaves and racemes of black and yellow flowers. It always grew in running water and beneath waterfalls. The *Aconitum* reached no more than 3 in. high, bearing one or two large blue-helmeted flowers. It occurred on grassy slopes in some profusion and grew from a small tuber. A *Salix* sp. formed carpets and mats and may have been *S. lindleyana*, but the abundant seed we collected, being of short viability, failed to germinate.

At the end of one day we climbed up a scree where boulders, loosened by the porters' feet, hurled downwards so that we were forced to seek refuge beneath a rock outcrop. It was not a pleasant experience to hear but not to see rocks tumbling towards us and we were thankful therefore when we had attained the ridge above. All that day it had poured with rain and our route had taken us across screes, through streams and bogs, up cliffs and narrow gullies, and all this in dense mist. Our maps were of little help and only our compass and the experience of our porters had kept us on the right track. It was frustrating knowing that we were passing through superb terrain with mountain peaks and valleys and yet unable to see and appreciate it.

Now the rain had turned to sleet as we continued along the ridge. A party of birds flew from a large slab-like rock and their rufous tail feathers and the white patch on their backs told us they were Impeyan pheasants. They called both on the wing and when stationary with something like a curlew's cry, but shorter. On the same ridge we saw a covey of Himalayan snowcocks, the males with grey-spotted plumage. About the size of guineafowl, they appeared on the track ahead of us and rather than fly simply ran away into the mist.

We decided to camp amongst a jumble of large boulders at 14,000 ft. It was several hours before the last porter staggered in and as each one arrived I gave him a generous pinch of tobacco and a sheet of British Rail lavatory paper to make cigarettes. This had become a daily ritual, and considering the appalling conditions in which the porters carried it was small reward. Still barefoot they tramped through ice-cold rivers and torrents, across sharp-edged screes dressed in little more than loin-cloths, with just a blanket to sleep in. The last porter to arrive, a small and sickly looking man, was so tired he crawled under a nearby rock and, wrapping himself in his blanket, fell fast asleep. The wood carried from lower altitudes was wet and took a long time to burn, by which time Beer, Morris and I had climbed into our sleeping-bags, but even they were wet. Somehow we got to sleep but we were awoken at 5.30 the next morning to the sound of something banging hard on our tent. We unzipped our bags and flap to investigate the cause of the disturbance. The scene which met our gaze as we looked through the tent entrance was like something from a Christmas card. Snow had fallen heavily during the night and one of our Sherpa boys, Dorje, had gone round beating it from the tents. There was no question about continuing our journey that day so we set about looking for firewood. This we found after tramping some distance downhill. It was another new *Rhododendron*, forming thickets at the base of a cliff and below the snow-line. The leaves were elliptic to elliptic-obovate, 5-8 in. long including the stout grey petiole, acute, broad cuneate to almost rounded at base, covered beneath with a thin, smooth, shining, buff indumentum. The flower buds were stout and coloured the same grey as the petioles and last year's shoots. It proved to be *R. wightii*, named after Robert Wight (1796-1872), an assistant surgeon in the East India Company and Superintendent of the Madras Botanical Garden.

Growing on the edge of the snow we found a delightful little *Cremanthodium* with the usual nodding yellow daisy head on a 3-4 in. stalk and a rosette of small deeply divided dandelion-like leaves. We saw it on many subsequent occasions and it proved to be *C. pinnatifidum*. A flash of colour then caught our eyes and we saw a wall creeper quartering the rock-face above our heads. The red wing feathers and white spots in an otherwise greyish attire were quite outstanding.

We watched for a time the mist alternately forming and dispersing in the valley below before retracing our steps up the hillside. The sun in the meantime appeared and warmed our backs, throwing our shadows across the snow. On returning to camp we found Pema carrying a large and curious plant. It was cone-shaped, 3 ft long and composed of pale-green bracts. Beer recognised it as *Rheum nobile*, the noble rhubarb, which he had seen during his reconnaissance. The rhubarb is eaten raw or cooked by the Tibetans but gives the westerner stomach ache and in no way can it be confused with that familiar companion of custard. Beer and I climbed the rocks above the camp to a place pointed out by Pema and there found many more. They towered through the snow like green rockets ready for blast-off. We collected several specimens, breaking the stems away from the basal rosette of large orbicular-cordate leaves. The typical triangular dock-like fruits were carried in crowded fingers at intervals along the stout 3-3.5 ft stem, each cluster arising in the axil of a large, conspicuous, scallop-like, apple-green bract which concealed and protected the fruits, collectively forming a dense column. Beer told us that at flowering time in June/July, these columns are squatter and are a startling milk-white. The plant appeared to be monocarpic, as those which had flowered seemed spent. We found many non-flowering rosettes however, and it appeared fairly common on the grassy slopes of the hill.

Like most of the slopes we had crossed this one had water moving freely through the surface layers but never lingering long enough to cause waterlogging. Only in a normal autumn would it in any way become dry, and then only comparatively so. It struck me that the rich flora of these alpine slopes were blessed with that mythical condition oft quoted in nurserymen's catalogues as 'a moist well-drained soil'.

Back in camp we found Morris trying to persuade the porters to go and collect wood. They grumbled about the snow but eventually moved off leaving behind the small sickly porter and another who was lame. We sat around the fire bagging seed of the rhubarb, stopping only once to observe a large raptor gliding across the hillside above camp. From its size, comparatively long tail, heavy wings and rufous-coloured neck we guessed it to be a Himalayan golden eagle.

When we awoke the next morning the snow was still lying around but the sun was out and the views were breathtaking. During breakfast we looked eastward across a series of ridges and valleys to the massive of Kangchengjunga (28,208 ft), whose several peaks seemingly supported the sky. Only once had this holy mountain been climbed, by a British team in 1955, and even then they had stopped short of the main summit in deference to the wishes of the Indian, Nepalese and Sikkim

Members of the Expedition Above Thudam. Standing (Left to Right): Dave Morris, the Author and Len Beer (Leader). Seated (Left to Right): Pema (Cook), Dorje, Namgyal, Dawa (Sirdar) and Tende

Looking from East to West along the Spine of the Himalaya. Makalu (27,790 ft) is the Peak in the Centre Background

Bergenia purpurascens at 13,500 ft (Jaljale Himal)

Dichroa febrifuga at 7,400 ft (Lower Arun)

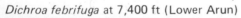

Lentopodium monocephalum at 16,500 ft (Lumbasumba Himal)

Meconopsis napaulensis - Red Form (Grown from Seed Collected on the Milke Danda)

Prunus rufa at 12,000 ft (Topke Gola)

Daphniphyllum himalense at 7,300 ft (Above Sedua in the Kasuwa Valley)

Embelia floribunda at 6,700 ft (Above Hatia)

Rheum nobile at 14,000 ft (Jaljale Himal)

governments. To Tibetans, Kangchengjunga is known as 'Five Treasures of the Eternal Snows'. They believe that the god of wealth lives there, storing on its five peaks the five treasures of gold, silver, copper, corn and sacred books.

The porters were still concerned about the snow so Morris, Beer and I shared our spare boots and plimsolls between them and we set off down the hill. It was not long before we cleared the snow-line and walked through the undergrowth. In these hills the dwarf rhododendrons carpet the ground like heather on a Pennine moor and our boots crunched through dense aromatic scrub. We splashed through shallow streams and torrents whose sparkling waters ran on smooth stones to leap headlong into space. It was one of those days when it felt good to be alive.

The track in places ran across grassy hillsides spangled with sky-blue *Gentiana depressa*, dark-blue *Aconitum staintonii*, yellow *Delphinium viscosum* and the lovely blue *Cyananthus pedunculatus*. Here also two dwarf junipers were rife. *Juniperus squamata* occurred as a dense, low spreading bush, some forms actually hugging the rocks, whilst a few individuals were more open, even scraggy, in growth. All however, had the characteristic orange-brown peeling bark and sage-green foliage on nodding shoots. The other species has been identified as *J. indica* which is the same as *J. wallichiana* though very different in habit from the columnar plants in cultivation of that name. Even more did it differ from the substantial trees of *J. wallichiana* found in other areas of Nepal and pictured in Adam Stainton's book, *Forests of Nepal* (Figure 149). Having said this, I must add that the plant whose description follows is also figured in Stainton's book (Figure 15) again under the name *J. wallichiana*.

J. indica reminded me of some forms of *J. sabina*, only without the characteristic savin smell. It too, like the accompanying *J. squamata*, was variable in habit, one form making compact mounds 2 ft high and several feet across, whilst others, more open in habit, reminded me of a small Pfitzer juniper. It differed most noticeably from *J. squamata* in its rich green colour and densely clothed, densely packed branches and branchlets which were straight rather than nodding at the tips. Leaves were a mixture of the adult-scale and juvenile-needle types. Both species bore ovoid, shining black, single-seeded fruits 0.375 in. long.

That evening we camped in a deep glaciated valley above a cold, still, alpine lake whose surface mirrored the progress of the sun across the sky until it passed behind the mountain, leaving a trail of gold and orange flotsam in its wake. The sky was overcast next morning as we packed bags and rucksacks. A visit to the lake flushed a pair of white-capped redstarts whose red tail feathers and creamy-white caps created a bright flash of colour in the cold grey dawn. We climbed out of the valley as snow began to fall and were soon on the ridge where we found a small lake partially covered with thin ice. The height was 14,000 ft and we were surprised to see a dipper swimming on the surface of the water, looking like a miniature waterhen with a white breast. A shallow layer of snow covered the ground, punctuated by tiny stains which on close examination proved to be nodding flowers of *Cremanthodium pinnatifidum* pushing through their chill blanket, like crocus and Soldanellas in the European Alps. *Swertia multicaulis* in seed with several depressed stems radiating from a basal rosette occurred both on the track and on the slopes above. Gradually the snow thickened and visibility decreased to a few yards but still the track was discernible as it threaded its way through a huddle of dark crags. Then we found ourselves in a narrow defile and looking up we perceived dim shapes, solitary or in groups, which seemed to be watching our progress like squat inhabitants of some alien realm into which we had stumbled. Some of the 'inhabitants' appeared on rock ledges near at hand and we discovered to our amusement that they were merely columns of the noble rhubarb — *Rheum nobile*. Another *Cremanthodium* was found — *C. ellisii*, with obovate leaves and nodding flowers on robust 6-8 in. stems.

About midday we stopped for lunch where a long low cliff afforded us shelter from the wind-blown sleet. The crevices of the cliff supported several interesting plants including *Tanacetum gossypinum* (*Chrysanthemum gossypinum*), a 2 in. tall, white, woolly plant with a tight terminal head of yellow flowers, also a fern which looked to be the parsley fern — *Cryptogramma crispa*. Another creeping willow carpeted the rock, its slender, interlacing, reddish stems closely following the contours in the manner of an ivy. Its leaves were small and narrow and already turning yellow.

At the base of a waterfall we discovered a group of *Primula capitata* ssp. *crispata* in seed, and a plant from this collection flourished in the peat garden at the Hillier Arboretum for seven years or more. Each year in July or August it sent aloft several 4-6 in. scapes bearing dense terminal rounded heads of blue-purple, yellow-eyed flowers. The leaves were liberally powdered with farina. On our climb up a long rocky gully we twice disturbed groups of the chukor, similar to, but larger than the partridge and more colourful. Usually when disturbed they launched themselves from rock or crag to fly rapidly downhill rather like the British red grouse. Another bird seen on several occasions by lakes and torrents was the Hodgson's pied wagtail, in general aspect similar to our native species and named for B. H. Hodgson of *Rhododendron hodgsonii* fame.

We suddenly came upon a large lake hemmed in by vast, steep, snow-covered slopes where several landslips had recently occurred. The track traversed one of these slopes and we all followed moving slowly and with great care. Some of our porters were still barefoot and seemed ill at ease, understandably so in these difficult conditions. Half way across, those in the lead stopped to allow everyone to catch up and I took the opportunity of distributing lavatory paper and tobacco amongst the porters, most of whom tucked their supply into their inner garment preferring to wait until they reached safer ground before enjoying a smoke.

Whilst sitting on a rock attempting to retie my bootlace I spotted a cluster of smokey-blue hooded flowers with coal-black anthers peeping from beneath the rock. They belonged to *Delphinium nepalense*, a choice alpine species which had only comparatively recently been named by the Japanese. The palmately cut leaves, as well as the 3-6 in. stems and 1-1.5 in. long flowers were densely and-softly hairy. It was a most exciting find which led to a successful search for further plants. Invariably they had chosen warm sheltered pockets beneath rocks and seemed quite unperturbed by prevailing conditions. Indeed it was amazing that plants not only grew but flowered in this seemingly hostile terrain. Sharing the slopes with the *Delphinium* we found a Himalayan version of the familiar edelweiss — *Leontopodium jacotianum* — and a tiny creeping shrublet forming dense tufts of stiff green rush-like stems 3-4 in. high which proved to be *Ephedra gerardiana* var. *sikkimensis*. As seen in the wild on these alpine slopes this is a most acceptable subject for the rock garden, especially when bearing its bright red currant-like berries. Unfortunately, like so many others, once in cultivation it grows fat in the fertile soil and benign conditions and grows into a coarse mound up to 2 ft high, rarely if ever fruiting as the flowers are unisexual — male and female born on separate plants.

On these same slopes we saw a party of rose finches, mainly brown females with a few rose-coloured males for company. Continuing our march we plodded up to the pass at 15,000 ft where a chorten of stones had been constructed to support a cluster of poles bearing white prayer flags. The driving snow and gathering mist, however, dissuaded us from resting here so we pushed on through an area of fallen rocks and down the other side. Soon we had left the pass with its cold grey slabs and walked down a steep hillside where the snow had almost cleared. Before us stretched a large green valley with a river and flanking forest. The entire north-facing side of the valley was covered by a dense tangled growth of *Rhododendron wightii* which would have presented a spectacular effect in May when the trusses of pale-yellow flowers appeared. We descended the hillside moving through a mixed deciduous and evergreen forest which was a relief after several days in the heights. We then broke into a large glade in the middle of which stood a small tent-like shelter made from a heavy black woollen material. From out of this emerged two small children, a boy, barefoot and urchin-like, and a girl; their black woollen garments, striped apron and long black greased hair showed they were Tibetans. They spoke to Pema who

Valley above
Topke Gola

Paul Chester

told us that their parents were away bringing their yaks down from the high pastures. The clearing was surrounded by tall firs whose heads seemingly supported the clouds, the lower branches providing both fuel and bedding for these nomads who wander in the high border regions with their herds of yak, sheep or goats until winter forces them into the valleys. The dense firs created beneath them a gloomy world relieved only by the colourful mounds of *Berberis* species whose foliage smouldered like so many bonfires.

Leaving the glade behind, we continued through an area of Rhododendron and juniper scrub in which many plants of interest caught our attention, but we were tired and hungry and anyway we could return here another day. The track surfaced on an open hillside and we saw below us a collection of dark wood and stone houses whose ragged occupants came out to meet us as we descended the slope. The village of Topke Gola consisted of 20 occupied houses plus a small stone gompa (temple) presided over by a lama. Our first contact however was brief since our camp was situated some 500 ft above the village at a height of 12,700 ft. Wearily we plodded up a steep boulder-strewn slope to emerge at last onto a deep green pasture running gently down to a still lake. A hundred yards above the water's edge our first base camp had been established and with renewed energy we strode towards the orange tents to be greeted by Dawa and Da Norbu. A large meal was prepared and after much talking and consumption of chang (mountain beer) we retired to our tents for a long sleep.

Yak Cow and Calf — Topke Gola

6   TOPKE GOLA AND THE SACRED LAKE

The lake below our camp was believed by the Lama and villagers to contain a beautiful goddess, and in deference to their beliefs we had promised not to wash or swim in its waters, nor to camp within 100 yards of its shore. A Rhododendron-covered knoll by the lake's edge supported a small temple to the goddess and each morning the Lama would toil up the hill from the village to conduct a lone ceremony during which he rang various bells and sang lamentations. A trident protruded from the water close to the shore and a small metal dish attached to its stem was a repository for money and food offerings to the goddess. Each morning in the village small heaps of dry juniper twigs and foliage were ignited on several bird-table-like structures, the air carrying the resultant incense up the hill to please her.

The villagers, all of Tibetan origin, spend the summer months above the village grazing yak, sheep and goats, from which they obtain milk and wool. The wool is woven on crude wooden looms to make various articles of clothing including a poncho-style garment which is worn by shepherds. It is thick, oily, warm and virtually waterproof. When winter threatens they migrate down the Mewa Khola to villages where the snow does not reach, leaving the Lama to keep a long lonely vigil.

We arrived at Topke Gola on 15 October and stayed for twelve days, during which time we explored the forests, valleys and hillsides around, finding innumerable plants and collecting a great deal of valuable seed. The seed we generally dried in the sun on plates and in dishes before cleaning and bagging. Linen bags were used for the final drying process, these being hung on a line stretched between the various tents. Small collections of dried seeds were placed in stout paper envelopes and stored in wooden crates or polythene-lined kitbags. We found cleaning of the various seeds the most tedious business and were delighted therefore to find that the Sherpas and porters, especially the women, had a natural ability in this often delicate operation. Obviously their dextrous hand movements had been perfected when as children they had helped their fathers to sort and clean the year's grain supply. It was fascinating to watch the way they shook the dish with trembling movements causing the chaff and debris to leap over the edge, leaving the seeds behind. Supervision was however required when changing seed batches. It was no use leaving them alone with several separate collections to clean and we gave them one collection at a time taking care not to produce the next until the last was safely bagged or packeted and labelled with its collection number.

Pressing of specimens continued and Beer had long since organised the porters into drying teams, the damp drying sheets being held over the campfire to dry or laid out on the grass when weather permitted. Our arrival at Topke Gola signalled the end of unsettled weather and the majority of our days there proved warm and sunny, much to our delight and relief. Our duties fell into three main categories. Beer assumed responsibility for the pressing and recording of specimens, whilst I compiled the field notes to accompany each seed collection. I also kept a plant diary into which all interesting information concerning plants found but not necessarily collected was entered. Morris was responsible for the seed cleaning and bagging as well as the overall camp organisation, for which he possessed just the right mixture of patience, authority and common sense.

During the reconnaissance, Beer had built a little nursery garden at Topke Gola to accommodate some of the interesting plants he had brought from further afield. Unfortunately little now remained due to the ravages of yaks and goats. The yaks and their calves shared our campsite having been brought down from their summer grazing at 16,000-17,000 ft. One night we were woken by the ground vibrating and heard the sound of many running hooves. Morris and I threw ourselves out of the tent, still in our sleeping bags, and crawled to the nearby slope where Beer and some of the others had already gathered. At that point stampeding yaks reached the camp knocking things over, including our tents, and rushed on to the lake. Apart from this, we co-existed with them until they were moved on down the valley to pastures new.

The hillsides above the village and lake were steep and clothed with fir, juniper, rhododendrons and various deciduous shrubs in autumn colour. They presented a vast rolling tapestry of green, brown, red and gold, far richer in colour than anything I had ever seen before.

All around on slopes, paths, amongst bushes and beneath rock over-hangs occurred the over-wintering rosettes of the fabulous Himalayan poppies – *Meconopsis* – and we found a total of six different species within an hour's walk of the camp. By far the most common was *M. paniculata*, whose dense rosettes measured as much as 20 in. across. Its leaves were deeply and pinnately lobed and densely covered with golden bristles which caught and held drops of dew or rain, making of them mirrors to reflect the sun into one's eyes. This is a monocarpic species, the plant dying after seeding, and there were many seeding panicles 5-6 ft high clothed, like the leaves, with golden bristles which came away in clouds like fibreglass. It made seed collecting an uncomfortable task. Occasionally we saw a few late yellow flowers 1.5-2 in. across. However, Beer told us that during his previous visit in July, this poppy was at its peak and coloured the hillsides as far as the eye could see. Although in full sun, these poppies received their share of underground moisture, and judging by the number of lush rosettes growing on and by tracks, the amount of running surface water during the monsoon must be beneficial if not essential to their well being. The young shoots are sometimes eaten by the Tibetans and Sherpas.

Meconopsis napaulensis, by comparison, produced pale or lime-green rosettes with paler bristles. Late flowers all proved to be in the blue-lilac range, though from seed of B. L. & M. 37 grown at Longstock Gardens near Stockbridge in Hampshire, a plant with breathtaking ruby-red flowers has been produced. It is being maintained by careful seed selection as this species also is monocarpic. By contrast the stout clumps of *M. grandis* which we found in the vicinity of the lake were perennial with oblanceolate, dark-green, bristly leaves to 12 in. or more in length. Beer described having seen in July the single purplish-blue nodding or inclined flower atop a 3-4 ft stem, a well-flowered plant creating a striking splash of colour amongst its native scrub and boulders.

Under a large boulder on the hillside at a height of 14,500 ft we found the monocarpic *M. discigera* forming a dense tuft of oblanceolate leaves slightly lobed towards the tips. The seed capsules were barrel-shaped, 1 in. long with a conspicuous club-shaped style projecting for 0.5 in. They were borne in a few branched panicles 12 in. tall and the whole plant was clothed in silky brown hairs. This is a handsome species when sporting its blue flowers and is well-worth growing in one of its better colour forms. *M. sinuata*, another monocarpic species, we found only once on a rather wet patch of hillside. From a tuft of withered leaves arose several 2 ft stems each bearing a single, elongated, bristly capsule. There were several plants in a limited area, and like so many of these hillside plants, it enjoyed having its 'head' in the sun and its roots in a well-drained medium, suitably supplied with water at the critical time of growth and flowering. During his previous visit to Topke Gola, Beer had found a single plant of *Meconopsis simplicifolia* growing beneath a rock face close to our campsite.

Potentilla peduncularis formed extensive patches on the hillside. It looked very much like our native silverweed — *P. anserina* — with pinnate leaves, silvery silky (especially beneath), turning a rich reddish-brown in autumn. The flower too, according to Beer, resembled those of the familiar species being yellow, 1 in. across, borne several together at the top of a 9-12 in. stem. Another species *P. cuneata* was equally common on grassy banks and by streams, often on moist ground. Compared with the other this was a diminutive creeping plant forming pads of tiny trifoliolate leaves, the leaflets three-toothed at the apex. The yellow flowers too were smaller, 0.5 in. across, but produced in sufficient numbers to make the whole plant conspicuous, which is why it is a favourite with rock gardeners in Britain. Under a large boulder above the camp we found a peculiar withered plant with fruits that resembled small green tomatoes, except that they were almost enclosed by the five-lobed calyx and borne singly on an elongated fleshy stalk. Beer remembered having found it in July when it bore small greenish flowers. It later proved to be a Himalayan mandrake — *Mandragora caulescens*. Growing in some quantity on these slopes was *Primula calderana* ssp. *strumosa*. In July Beer had found it covering our campsite in full flower, when it presented a heartening sight, the orange-eyed yellow flowers, 0.5-0.75 in. across, borne in a many-flowered umbel atop a stout 10-15 in. scape. At the time of our visit, however, the stems and leaves were withered and all that remained to indicate a living plant was a large, plump, pointed, green bud. We gently teased aside the outer scales to reveal the inner scales covered with a bright yellow farina. It resembled more a bulb than a resting bud.

Anemone polyanthes was frequent amongst the boulders strewn about the hillsides and Beer told us that in July he had found both white and apple-blossom-pink flowered forms of this desirable perennial. Many of the banks by tracks and above the river which fed the lake were clothed with the creeping carpets of *Gaultheria trichophylla* and the carpeting stems of *Cotoneaster microphyllus* var. *cochleatus*. The two were often mixed and the comparatively large sky-blue fruits of the former contrasted with the red fruits of the latter to create a colourful, almost jewel-like, effect. Lots of *Primula capitata* was found in seed, and in wet ground by the lake and along the river banks two other species were fairly plentiful. The first of these, *P. hopeana*, seemed happy in either sun or shade and formed dense rosettes of oblanceolate, toothed, green leaves 6-10 in. long. The scapes were 12-18 in. high and at the time of Beer's arrival at Topke Gola in June bore umbels of nodding, bell-shaped, creamy-white flowers. This is closely related to *P. sikkimensis* and is regarded as the same by some

75

authorities. It was named after J. Hope (1875-1970), a Yorkshireman who began his career at the University Botanic Garden, Cambridge, moving to the Royal Botanic Garden, Edinburgh before joining A. K. Bulley as gardener at Ness in Cheshire. In one area *P. hopeana* formed drifts, even entering the shallow water at the edge of the lake. Accompanying the above species and sharing its sunnier locations was *P. megalocarpa* (*macrophylla* var. *macrocarpa*), its stout clumps of lanceolate, fleshy, finely toothed leaves 6-10 in. long, covered beneath with a white farina. Beer described the flowers as being 1 in. long, lilac in colour with a conspicuous calyx borne in erect umbels, terminating a 9 in. scape in June and July. In the same boggy areas as the primulas grew a delightful little alpine lousewort — *Pedicularis longiflora* var. *tubiformis* — whose tiny tufts of deeply cut leaves gave birth to the most delicate yellow, two-lipped flowers with corolla tubes 1.5 in. long.

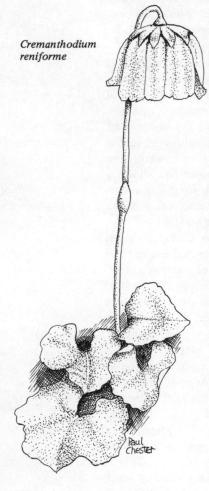

Cremanthodium reniforme

It is an everlasting pity that the lousewort tribe are semi-parasites and difficult if not impossible to grow in cultivation. Our two British species give no clue to the immense variety to be found in the mountains of Europe and Asia.

When Beer had left Topke Gola in July the banks of the river above the lake had been lined with a deep-pink frothy cloud of *Myricaria rosea* in full flower. This dwarf shrub, a relation of the tamarisk (*Tamarix*), formed dense clumps and mounds of slender plumose stems, the tiny leaves densely clustered along the purplish shoots, turning from summer green to red then rusty-brown. As far as I am aware this species is not in general cultivation and although we collected abundant seed I have not heard of any success with its germination. Maybe, like the willow, its seed is of short duration and needs to be sown immediately on ripening. It would certainly repay someone to introduce a living plant into cultivation where it would surely be hardy and an excellent dwarf flowering shrub for exposed places, especially by the sea.

On grassy rock ledges above the lake we found a dwarf tap-rooted member of the carrot family — *Umbelliferae*. No more than 8 in. high, the many radiating branches terminated in a dense cluster of fruits with a ruff of conspicuous bracts. The whole seed-head was dome-shaped and several inches across, whilst the pinnate leaves formed a basal rosette. The entire plant possessed a strong smell of fennel and we were delighted to learn later from the British Museum (Natural History) that this plant was *Pleurospermopsis sikkimensis* and new to Nepal.

In the shelter of the deciduous forest beyond the lake grew large quantities of *Cremanthodium reniforme*, its nodding daisy heads seeding on 6-12 in. stems above the long-stalked, boldly toothed, kidney-shaped leaves. The monotypic *Megacodon stylophorus* also occurred here, its bold Hosta-like basal leaves supporting a 3 ft leafy stem. A member of the gentian family, it bears a 10-12 in. raceme of eight to ten pendant, yellowish-green flowers in July. This rare species would be much in demand if it were in cultivation, its foliage alone being worthy of inclusion in the woodland garden or herbaceous border.

Berberis angulosa

The shrubby flora of these hillsides mainly consisted of *Spiraea*, juniper, *Berberis* and *Cotoneaster*. *Spiraea arcuata* reached 6-8 ft, its arching, angled stems, densely clothed with obovate leaves, toothed in the upper half. The pink flowers which Beer had seen in June were now brown seed capsules borne in tight corymbs all along the upper sides of the branches. It was common in scrub, and plants are now established in the Hillier Arboretum and elsewhere. Its most frequent companions were *Berberis angulosa* and *Cotoneaster acuminatus*. The former shrub, with its erect reddish, ribbed stems and dark green clustered leaves, is not one of the most desirable species except in autumn when the deciduous leaves turn a brilliant crimson, creating an effect of flames on the hillsides visible for some distance. I have since seen numerous pictures taken of autumn scenes in the Himalaya and the rich colour of this *Berberis* can be detected on most if not all of them. Unfortunately it rarely colours as well in English cultivation where it remains an uncommon shrub, mainly grown for its comparatively large orange-yellow flowers and scarlet fruits. In Nepal these fruits vary in shape from rotund to oblong and are eaten by Sherpas and Tibetans. The erect branches of the *Cotoneaster* attained greater heights — 6-8 ft — with hairy, elliptic, pointed leaves to 2 in. long. The oblong red fruits 0.66 in. long were borne singly in the axils of the leaves. Although *C. acuminatus* was first introduced to England as long ago as 1820, it is rarely cultivated because it is less ornamental than the Chinese species.

A small shrubby honeysuckle — *Lonicera myrtillus* — formed occasional mounds of tangled branches 3-5 ft high with small narrowly oblong leaves, turning bright yellow. The red fruits, though freely produced, were rather small. *Ribes luridum* was in the same category, its small red currants being no compensation for the untidy habit and small three to five lobed leaves. It was, nevertheless, common in mixed scrub in sun or shade.

The junipers, however, were the most noticeable members of the hillside community. Three species were involved — *Juniperus recurva*, *J. squamata* and *J. indica*. The first of these made a tree with a single main stem up to 25 ft high, though there was evidence that larger specimens had been felled in the past and there remained on one hillside a few decrepit trees of large girth. It varied enormously in appearance, some specimens being open branched and gracefully drooping, whilst others were as dense and compact as many Lawson cypresses seen in cultivation. All forms had brown flaky bark and the characteristic nodding or drooping branchlets. The colour too, was variable and we found forms with rich-green, sea-green and silvery-green foliage. The black fruits, 0.5 in. long, contained a single seed. As seen at Topke Gola, this juniper is a variable species with many forms of high ornamental merit, far more so than the tree one normally encounters in cultivation in the British Isles. *J. squamata* seems closely connected in the field with *J. recurva*. Both species showed similar variations in foliage, form and colour. However, even in young specimens, the latter possessed a single leader whilst the former was multi-stemmed and bush-like.

J. squamata in the Topke Gola area encompassed a wide assortment of forms. There were those of low, dense and compact habit, similar to certain named forms in present cultivation, whilst at the other extreme were those taller, often gawky forms of less ornamental merit. The majority had ascending branches, developing a vase-shaped habit similar to the Pfitzer juniper (*J.* 'Pfitzerana'). Foliage varied in colour through several shades of green to grey and 'blue'. Some forms had long slender branchlets, others were short and congested. Seed of many forms was collected and resultant plants are now established in many collections including the Hillier Arboretum. In some locations these two species were present in such great numbers that the spectacle would have daunted or delighted most taxonomists. In contrast, *J. indica* formed dense low patches of rich deep-green foliage. It rarely mixed with the other two.

Abies densa grew to a large size in the valley above Topke Gola. One venerable specimen had a huge bole containing a hole large enough for a man to pass through, caused no doubt by fire. An unfortunate habit of the hill people, especially herdsmen, is the lighting of fires at the base of large trees. The tree, of course, offers a measure of shelter, but it was distressing to see the number of trees so effected. One day I climbed up a small specimen of this fir in order to pick the cones from the upper branches. Later that same day I wandered beneath a grove of superb giants well over 150 ft high, their boles clothed with moss and polypody ferns. Some large specimens had been felled using the fire method and we were able to pick cones in some quantity. Despite the intentional and accidental destruction of these firs it was gratifying to see a great deal of regeneration taking place, the young saplings forming dense thickets in some places.

Rhododendrons occurred in quantity especially *R. campanulatum* which formed dense thickets, often with *R. wightii*, whilst *R. campylocarpum* and *R. cinnabarinum* were nearly as common. The large leaved *R. hodgsonii* was conspicuous though only as scattered large individuals.

Clematis montana was in fruit, its silky seed tassels flaunted all along the stems as they scrambled into trees and over shrubs. *Aconitum spicatum* was present in several clearings in the fir forest, and on our way back to the camp one day we found the seeding capsules of *Parnassia nubicola* scattered through a lakeside bog.

The villagers were most inquisitive and looked upon our presence as something the gods had arranged. They regularly visited our camp simply to stand and stare. Predictably the children were the least inhibited and they followed our every move, sometimes to our embarrassment. The Tibetan child is expected to take its share of the family chores just as soon as it is able to walk. Little girls carried even younger brothers and sisters on their backs, and every day a small band of urchins of both sexes would stop off at the camp on their way to collect firewood in the hills. Several carried sharp kukris tucked into their cummerbands and a coil of rope over their shoulders. They looked sticky and dirty but were possessed of the most disarming smiles. One small boy helped milk the yaks each day by binding the yak's front feet together so that it could not move away.

One day we were invited to visit the panchayat leader at his home in the village, and this was our first social contact with Tibetans. The night before had witnessed a storm in the hills to the south, and although we caught only the edge of it, the campsite was running with water and the kitchen tent had blown down. We arrived in the village in good time anxious not to displease the panchayat leader. Our host bade us climb up the steps of his home and we immediately entered a dark passageway full of pungent and unfamiliar smells. We moved slowly forward stumbling over pigs, goats, cats, dogs, chickens and children, in that order, all intent on leaving. Finally we sensed ourselves in a much larger space and our fingers searched urgently for signs of contact until at last they touched and were held by a warm hand. The hand belonged to our hostess who then led us gently to a place where a fire spluttered on a stone flag set into the wooden floor.

We sat down with our backs against the planked wall and as our eyes strained to take in our surroundings we saw faces gradually materialising from the shadows around. There were long faces, fat faces, old faces, young faces, faces etched with experience, faces with the shine of innocence. Yet all the faces had one thing in common — they all smiled and nodded as if to reassure us that we were among friends.

We were handed tompas (wooden containers like steins without handles) and urged to drink the contents — chang or mountain beer. This we did by sucking at a wooden 'straw' which entered through a hole in the lid of the vessel. The warm milky-white liquid seemed immediately to enter the blood stream and all memories of the recent storm receded to be replaced by an increasing desire to laugh and sing. The faces smiled encouragingly and our hostess immediately topped up our tompas from a hot kettle, ignoring our mild protestations.

Chang is made by fermenting any one of several grains, mainly rice, maize or millet. Our current brew originated from the latter source and each draw on the 'straw' filled the mouth with a myriad of tiny seeds which, if one was not to offend, had to be swallowed without trace of displeasure. Those westerners who do not like caraway cake would not have enjoyed the experience.

Whilst we sat thus, drinking and smiling, my eyes wandered around the room taking in the shadowy corners, the corn-cobs hanging from the low ceiling and the dull glow of pans and containers. They then came to rest on the fire which struggled beneath a heap of green juniper wood and leaves. This unhappy combination gave off a dark acrid smoke which spiralled to the ceiling where, unable to escape, it billowed out in an ever-threatening blanket. It then occurred to me that this chimneyless abode contained no windows either, and, as a result, the smoke and occupants were prisoners together. I looked again at the ceiling and realised to my horror that the smoke was fast descending in an all-enveloping cloud. We shrank to the floor as the smoke settled and then we were struggling to our feet, shaking numerous hands, gasping sounds of thanks. Down the passage we staggered, pursued by the smoke, stumbling over children, chickens, dogs, cats, goats and pigs all trying to get in. Down the steps we tumbled, eyes streaming, chests heaving, gulping the cool mountain air.

When we were still in the foothills at Side Pokhara and had already tasted several meals in which dried potato had formed the main ingredient, Pema had met our complaints with the solemn promise 'when we get into the mountains Sahib, where it is cold and they grow many potatoes, I will make you chips'. Somewhere he had been given the impression that Englishmen liked chips. Accordingly, when we reached the mountains at Topke Gola where it was cold, Pema was despatched in search of potatoes. He returned one afternoon with a small basket of them, each no bigger than a pigeon's egg. To a Sherpa, however, a promise is a promise and he peeled each and every one and we had chips with our evening meal. The main course was a kind of pasty called moma by the Sherpas. It was a pastry case stuffed with chopped vegetables and a meat which was far more tasty and tender than the scrawny chickens we had been used to. It was not until we had eaten the last pasty that Pema told us that the source of the meat was the lovely blood pheasant, a brace of which he had purchased from a villager. Fresh yak milk is rich compared with cow milk but was welcome after the dried milk we had been using. But, pheasant and chips apart, far from living on local fare, we found that few villagers were in a position to sell food, let alone share it, and we relied on our dried meals, though sugar and rice were two commodities in reasonably plentiful supply and on two occasions Dawa and two assistants were sent down the Mewa Khola on shopping expeditions.

On our arrival in the camp at Topke Gola we had found two new Sherpa porters, both girls in their late teens. Berma was a plump girl with an active imagination and a tongue to match. Mile was by contrast slender and of shy disposition. Both came from the village of Sedua in the Upper Arun Valley and had accompanied Beer on his reconnaissance. Berma and Mile were sisters of Dorje and Tende respectively, both of whom we had engaged as porters in Dharan. Apart from these Sherpa porters, all others had been paid off and had returned to their villages in the valleys.

One day Morris and I decided to explore the valley which we had travelled down on the day we entered Topke Gola. On our way to the village with Da Norbu we encountered the Lama on his way to the temple by the lake. He possessed a wonderful face, as brown as a fig. His long black hair he had plaited into a pigtail and he wore a long claret woollen gown. We exchanged pleasantries for a while before continuing on our respective journeys and he extracted a promise from us to visit his gompa the next day, which we were only too ready to accept.

A family group were sitting outside their village house spreading plant material on a bamboo mat to dry in the sun. The man of the house told us that the plant was collected in the mountains and was a powerful medicine against stomach troubles. On closer examination it proved to be *Picrorhiza scrophulariifolia* (*kurooa*), a humble member of the *Scrophulariaceae*. It is a creeping plant forming tufts of spoon-shaped toothed leaves 2-6 in. long and dense racemes 4-6 in. long of small pale-blue flowers with conspicuous protruding stamens in July and August. According to B. O. Coventry, *Wild Flowers of Kashmir*, the root and rootstock contain a bitter substance called 'picrorhizin'. The crude drug appears on the market in the form of short dry pieces of root and is used medicinally as a stomatic tonic and as a febrifuge in cases of fever.

We left Da Norbu to wash the expedition laundry in the village

Village Girl
from Topke
Gola

Paul Chester

stream and proceeded up the valley and into the trees which were a glorious jungle of fir, juniper and birch. We first found a plant which reminded me of our native golden rod — *Solidago virgaurea* — with its narrow elliptic leaves and slender raceme of widely spaced, nodding, yellow flowerheads. It turned out to be *Youngia racemiflora*, presumably named after Alfred R. Young (1841-1920) who collected plants in Kashmir. We reached the open hillside at a place where a long narrow landslip had recently taken place. Here several trees attracted our attention beginning with *Acer papilio* (*caudatum*), a small tree with a handsome grey or brownish-grey flaky bark. Several of these trees had been damaged by fire at some stage in the past and strong basal sucker growths were already well developed. The deeply five-lobed irregularly toothed leaves were a rich green in colour and carried on rhubarb-red petioles which, like the young shoots, were finely pubescent. There were tufts of greyish hairs in the axils of the main veins beneath. The bunches of red winged fruits were mostly empty of seed and as far as I am aware only one seedling resulted from this collection. *Sorbus ursina* was our next find, a small spreading tree 15 ft high with pinnate leaves, the leaflets covered beneath with a grey rufous-tinged tomentum. The few fruits which remained were coloured a dark crimson.

Several trees of *Betula utilis* were conspicuous by their rich orange-brown peeling bark and we collected the seed of a particularly fine specimen. Accompanying these trees was a small cherry up to 18 ft high with a spreading head of branches. The leaves were elliptic, toothed and long acuminate, 3-4 in. long, rounded at base and with glands on petiole and leaf base. It was the bark however that caught our attention, varying between individuals from blackish-brown to a warm amber and peeling in the best *Prunus serrula* tradition. It was as ornamental as this well-known Tibetan cherry, having the same polished shaggy appearance. Some trees were single stemmed, whilst others had several stems from a common base. Only a few small fruits could be found on the branches. These were ellipsoid, 0.5 in. long, green at first turning to red and finally shining black, borne singly on a 1-2 in. drooping stalk. We scratched around in the debris beneath several trees without success and came to the conclusion that the fruits are eaten by birds before they have chance to fall. We argued about the identity of this cherry for the rest of the expedition, but not until the British Museum (Natural History) examined our specimens did we hear that it was *Prunus rufa*. This species is present, though rarely, in cultivation and has been grown by Hillier's Nursery for many years but with a close unimpressive bark. According to Bean, the Nepalese tree is the form *trichantha*. From the few seeds we collected only one germinated. This now grows in the Hillier Arboretum, whilst plants grafted from this specimen have been sent to Wakehurst Place, Sussex, and to Maurice Mason's collection at Fincham in Norfolk. As we stood admiring the cherries on the hillside we saw a flash of white and looked up just in time to see a flock of snow pigeons coming in to land on the cliffs above, their white underparts sharply contrasting with the dark upperparts.

The next day was a lovely sunny morning which augered well for our collecting on the screes. These vast seas of broken rock and rubble seemed almost to be moving beneath one's feet. From the high crags which gave them birth they stretched for almost a mile before emptying into the belly of the valley. It was surprising that plants survived in this terrain let alone flourished. The cruel winds from Tibet came howling over the fanged ridges to pounce on animal and plant alike. They swept across the screes cutting down to size anything that dared to rise above a certain height. Within the body of the scree ran long sunken rivers of larger rocks where plants had managed to establish themselves and live what was at best a precarious existence.

Leontopodium himalayanum was fairly common here and seemed little different from the edelweiss of Europe. *Soroseris pumila* was another composite but very different from the last. Its leafy stem, 3-4 in. long, was concealed by the dust and grit in which it grew so that the slightly domed inflorescence, 1.5-2 in. across, rested on the ground and appeared stemless. The inflorescence was surrounded by greyish-brown hairy leaves, and when not in flower was difficult to distinguish from the surrounding ground. The individual flowers possessed four yellow-ray florets each with a single style. They opened first along the margin, gradually moving in towards the centre. It was a peculiar plant, not without merit, but probably not worth cultivating. Our old friend *Saussurea gossypiphora* turned up again and we were later told that it was collected and dried by the Lama at Topke Gola who burned it on special occasions in honour of the lake goddess.

A tiny catchfly – *Silene setisperma (Lychnis inflata)* – grew very commonly between the stones, a delicate plant for such a hostile place as this. Its slender 3-4 in. stem bore a terminal nodding flower 0.66 in. long. This consisted of an inflated calyx, parchment-white and slightly transparent, with ten narrow brown ridges. The tips of the five free purple petals protruded from the mouth of the calyx and were similarly coloured.

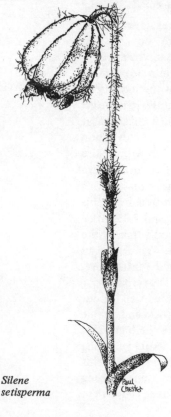

Silene setisperma

Tanacetum gossypinum (Chrysanthemum gossypinum) occurred in some quantity, growing with the slender-stemmed white-flowered *Arabidopsis himalaica*. In an area of shifting grit we came upon *Delphinium glaciale* forming tufts of deeply cut palmate leaves, from out of which the comparatively large blue-purple flowers protruded. It looked very similar to the *D. nepalense* we had previously seen, and we were still debating this similarity when a wind swept across the screes bringing with it a blinding sleet. We were so caught by the suddenness of the wind that we could only crouch close to the ground in a huddle and wait for it to pass. We waited no more than ten minutes and when we rose to our feet the entire scree was white with powdered snow. We continued on our way across the shattered boulders and rocks until a long deep depression opened up before us. The first thing to attract our attention was an animal the size of a hare and dark bluish-grey in colour. We saw only the back-end of it as it darted out of sight beneath a large boulder. This sudden disturbance flushed an Impeyan pheasant from its hiding place and as it glided on outstretched wings down the depression we had an excellent view of its upper parts. The irridescence of its purple wings and cinnamon-coloured tail were breathtaking, and with the distinctive snow-white patch on its back it is one of the Himalaya's most beautiful birds.

Delphinium glaciale

Paul Chester.

A stream ran along the depression, tumbling in miniature waterfalls down steep rocks. Colonising the streamside for a considerable length was a most striking and unusual perennial which we later identified as *Saussurea obvallata*. Although it thrived by the streamside we also later found it established on the open scree where, however, its stems were

85

invariably broken and shattered. It begins life as a stout basal clump of lanceolate to oblanceolate toothed leaves 12 in. or more long. From the centre of the clump emerge several stout leafy stems 1.5-2 ft tall, each bearing at its summit a dense cluster of large shell-like creamy-white bracts which collectively formed a hemispherical cocoon around the cluster of thistle-like flowerheads. What an intriguing species this is, related to the cottonwool plant *S. gossypiphora*, having the same basic thistle flowers yet in totally different guise. We collected lots of seed and though much of this germinated I never heard that plants had successfully flowered in cultivation.

The depression proved rich in species, because of its comparatively sheltered and stable condition. Stout 4-5 in. clumps of the small leaved *Rhodiola quadrifida* occupied moist shady pockets, and the terminal clusters of red flowers shone in the darkness. This species would enjoy similar places in the garden as our native roseroot *Rhodiola rosea*. A charming find was *Thalictrum elegans*, a delicate plant with finely divided glaucous green leaves and 3-6 in. panicles of tiny purple fruits. The desirability of this plant in fruit is misleading as the flowers are small greenish-purple and worthless. Crowding the streamside for as far as the eye could see was a saxifrage with clumps of erect fleshy stems 6-8 in. high, clothed with obovate fleshy leaves 1.5-2 in. long turning purple or red as winter approached. The flowers were yellow, 0.5 in. across, each petal with two orange spots on its inside base. It was identified by the British Museum (Natural History) as *Saxifraga moorcroftiana*, named after William Moorcroft (1765-1825), a Lancashire man and a veterinary surgeon in the East India Company who collected plants with Nathaniel Wallich in Nepal.

On many parts of the scree we encountered large patches of cotton-wool which looked from a distance like dead and decayed sheep. On closer inspection they proved to be prostrate willows in fruit. In certain exposed stony areas we discovered groups of the delicate *Primula buryana* with rosettes of ovate, toothed, hairy leaves 1-2 in. long. The 3-4 in. stems carried white flowers 0.75 in. long. We grew a few plants at the Hillier Arboretum from this seed but they did not thrive.

The depression developed into a narrow gully which we climbed down disturbing at one point a pair of sooty wrens who flew further down the gully and out of sight. After a while we encountered dense scrub in which *Rhododendron campanulatum* and *R. wightii* predominated, and feeling too tired to retrace our steps, and with the light diminishing, we were obliged to force our way through the thicket for several hundred yards before reaching the valley track, along which we trudged wearily back to camp.

We spent the next morning sitting on the hillside above camp collecting seed and writing up our notes. Da Norbu had been down to the village and returned with small blocks of stone-like material which he assured us was Tibetan cheese. It was yellow-brown in colour and appeared remote from my favourite creations from Caerphilly, Wensleydale and Lancashire. In fact I have several times since shown a piece of this material to audiences describing it as a dinosaur's toe-nail and many have believed me until told the truth. The cheese is made from yaks' milk and when first formed is packed into linen bags and strung up under the rafters in the main living area. In time, and influenced by warmth and smoke, the cheese solidifies and when required needs to be chopped into pieces with a kukri. Small pieces are popped into the mouth and sucked rather like a caramel but harder and longer lasting. I remember my grandfather telling me how, in Mesopotamia, as a soldier on the march, he would suck a pebble or small smooth stone to keep the saliva active. Tibetan cheese was used similarly by travellers in the hills, and we found it quite refreshing once we had grown used to the idea. There was very little taste and if I had been given a piece to try whilst blindfolded I would have imagined I was sucking a piece of flint.

On the lake we could see a family group of six surface-feeding ducks. They had been there for several days and occasionally called to each other in a goose-like manner. Once, when they flew we saw their striking pattern, consisting of a pale biscuit-coloured back and under-parts, creamy-brown head, white upper wings and black tail and wing primaries. They were ruddy shelducks and seemed quite at home in their mountain fastness, very different from the maritime habitat of the common species.

Da Norbu helped me clean seed and talked in a slow uncertain English, using his hands and facial expressions to emphasise a particular point. He was a short, strong, stocky fellow and I was surprised therefore to learn that some years ago he had damaged his back in a climbing accident and had spent much of the time since then in various hospitals in Nepal and India. This was his first expedition since his recovery and I had many occasions on which to ponder this fact with amazement and disbelief. Da Norbu's father, Ang Norbu, had been a high altitude porter for several expeditions including the Swiss Everest Expedition of 1952 and the successful British Everest Expedition the following year. Twice for the British he carried to the South Col, 26,200 ft, and was awarded a Coronation Medal by the Queen. Sadly he died in an avalanche on Cho Oyu (26,000 ft) whilst with the British Women's Expedition to Nepal in 1959.

Morris had headed towards the ridge above and after lunch I explored the cliffs on the same hillside. I disturbed a variegated laughing thrush whose plumage appeared mainly greenish with a black and white face. It called continuously and seemed in a bad humour, belying its common name. I felt the sun warm on me and lay on the ground staring at the sky. A noise of birds calling came to my ears and twisting my head I saw a flock of alpine choughs floating and wheeling in the air currents above the cliffs. They behaved like a troup of clowns, flying first in formation then breaking up and weaving about, all the time calling as jackdaws do. Occasionally two would break away and a mock battle would ensue as they tumbled through the air always disengaging and sweeping to safety just above the ground.

Scents both sweet and earthy drifted up to me from the pastures, and far below in the valley I could see the orange tents of our camp, and below that the village houses blurred every so often by whisps of smoke escaping through the many cracks. I must have lain thus for some time because I was suddenly aware of the temperature cooling and a change in the light intensity. Climbing to my feet I followed a circuitous route back to camp collecting on my way seed of *Fritillaria cirrhosa* and *Morina nepalensis*.

Beer had returned from a seed-collecting trip in the village area where he had previously marked several plants in flower. These included a pale-yellow flowered form of *Rosa sericea* and a prostrate member of the *Leguminosae* called *Gueldenstaedtia himalaica*. This pretty little alpine formed mats of tiny pinnate leaves plastered with purple pea-flowers 1 in. long borne singly on short erect stalks. *Aster stracheyi* was another of his finds, a tufted perennial with long-stalked, elliptical basal leaves and 2-4 in. hairy reddish stems bearing a single purple-rayed flowerhead 1 in. across. The name commemorates Sir Robert Strachey (1817-1908) of the Bombay Engineers who collected in NW Himalaya and adjacent Tibet. On the way up the hill Beer had collected a large amount of small shining red berries 0.25 in. across which belonged to *Hemiphragma heterophyllum*, a perennial member of the *Scrophulariaceae*, whose loosely trailing pubescent brown stems were to be found throughout the Topke Gola area. The opposite, ovate to rounded leaves 0.25 in. long were toothed and very different from the tiny linear leaves which occurred in bunches on the numerous axillary shoots.

Cotoneaster microphyllus var. *cochleatus*

7 THE GOLDEN EDELWEISS

Many times during our march across the Jaljale Himal we had listened to Beer's stories of the plants he had seen on his reconnaissance. One of these, the giant lily — *Cardiocrinum giganteum* — he had found amongst boulders and trees in the Mewa Khola, a day's march below Topke Gola. It was then in full flower with 5-8 ft sturdy leafy stems bearing a terminal raceme of six to eight large, pendant, creamy-white trumpets. It was because of this and other finds that Beer and I decided to spend a couple of days seed collecting in the Mewa Khola. Leaving Morris and the others in camp, and taking Da Norbu with us only, we climbed down the hill to Topke Gola and followed a track leading from the village into a wooded valley. It was a gorgeous morning and we were in high spirits singing our favourite melodies in between discussing the interesting plants we might see. The river tumbled and crashed a few yards below us and its sound was a constant companion as we followed the track through Himalayan silver fir and birch and beneath archways of rhododendron. Passing between two steep banks we found *Cotoneaster microphyllus* covering one side and its variety *cochleatus* equally common on the other. Further on we found both forms growing together in a tangled carpet. The authority G. Klotz has given the above variety species status under the name *C. meuselii*.

A *Berberis* species was frequent, its leaves just beginning to turn orange and red. It was a robust shrub with erect stems 8-10 ft high, the young shoots bearing obovate, slightly spinose leaves 1-1.5 in. long. The

89

Rubus nepalensis

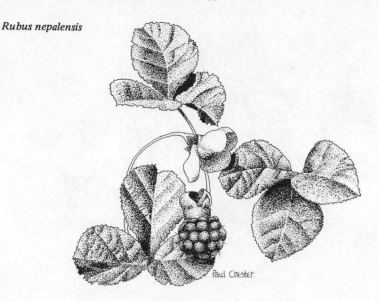

Paul Chester

dark red oblong fruits were borne in long clusters. Which species this was I have been unable to discover and all attempts to have the herbarium specimens named have so far proved futile. It would seem that the very mention of *Berberis* defeats most botanists. There is a story told by horticulturists about one of their kind who marched into a well-known herbarium on a busy midweek morning clutching a bagful of unnamed *Berberis* specimens collected from his garden. Unfortunately for him he made the mistake of announcing the reasons for his visit in a loud voice, at which the department became deserted as a dozen athletic botanists sought out those corners and hideaways so plentiful in such places, and for which all experienced herbarium and museum architects make provision.

To be fair, it is well known that *Berberis*, like willows, are promiscuous, and cultivated *Berberis* can be a nightmare even to one familiar with their goings-on. I remember Harold Hillier telling me about a visit paid to his nurseries many years ago by Camillo Schneider, the German botanist who named and described many of E. H. Wilson's Chinese *Berberis* introductions. Schneider had asked permission to collect specimens in the Hillier nurseries and, aware of the reputation of both botanist and *Berberis*, Hillier was puzzled therefore to see Schneider cutting specimens he knew to be seed grown from cultivated sources. At the end of the day Schneider thanked Hillier profusely for his generosity and left carrying a large hamper stuffed with *Berberis* specimens of as mixed an origin as could be devised. What became of the specimens no one seems to know. Hillier heard no further from Schneider who died in 1951 and his manuscript of the genus *Berberis* has never to my knowledge been published.

Ribes himalense

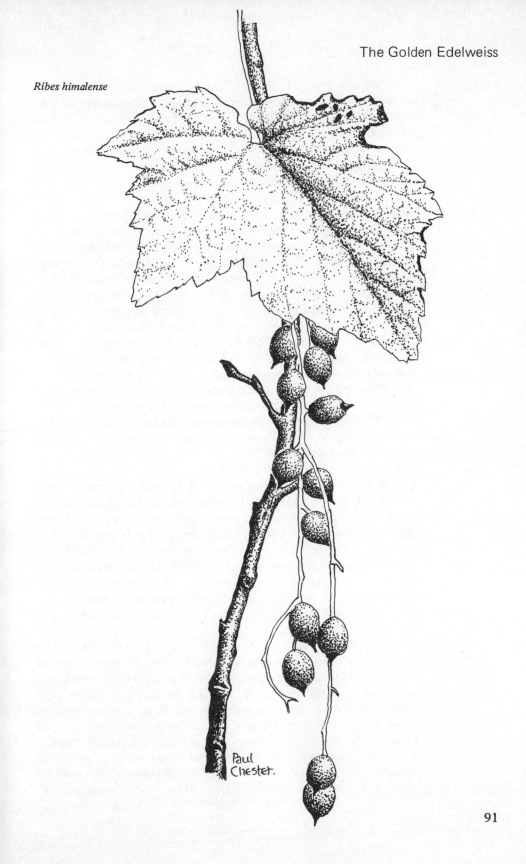

Paul
Chester.

Prunus rufa occurred in the valley as scattered individuals, its dark burnished peeling bark contrasting with the orange-brown peeling bark of *Betula utilis*. Some of the firs — *Abies densa* — reached heights in excess of 150 ft, most of them clothed with epiphytes. Lower down the valley the branches of old firs were almost entirely encased in a yellowish-green, cushion-like moss, whilst several burned-out shells remained as evidence of indiscriminate burning. Da Norbu told us that in the Solo-Khumbu region, this habit is prohibited, fines of R100 being exacted from proven offenders. *Sorbus microphylla* was quite plentiful above the river, its canopy a cloud of orange and yellow as the leaves turned. *Viburnum nervosum* (*cordifolium*) occupied similar locations, forming a large multi-stemmed shrub 18-20 ft high with stellately hairy young shoots and buds. On several specimens the heart-shaped, toothed, hairy leaves, 4-7 in. long, had turned a deep crimson, whilst the shining black fruits were borne in dense corymbs. Clambering 18 ft into the branches of a cherry were the rope-like stems of *Clematis connata*, with its large trifoliolate leaves. The leaflets were ovate-acuminate, rounded at base, three-lobed and sharply toothed, each on a long stalk. It was then in seed but a month or more earlier it would have been showing its bell-shaped soft yellow flowers in panicles, rather like a larger edition of the Chinese *C. rehderana*. Few alpine currants are decorative enough for gardens but *Ribes himalense* looked most becoming on the rocks above the river. It reached 6-8 ft in height with palmately lobed leaves 2-3 in. across and long pendulous 'strings' of red currants which glistened in the sun.

Acer papilio became frequent, especially in the several clearings through which our track ran. In these clearings the Himalayan bird cherry — *Prunus cornuta* — had been planted as orchards, some trees quite old with rounded crowns and gnarled trunks. In one such place we found a wooden house occupied by a family from Thudam. We decided to have lunch here and whilst Da Norbu was preparing a fire we watched a colourfully dressed old woman spinning wool so fast that the eye could scarcely follow. She sat on the grass surrounded by heaps of variously dyed wools, including some of a beautiful deep blue which had stained her hands.

Over lunch we followed the activities of a pair of white-capped redstarts that flitted about on the rocks below us. After lunch we continued down the valley which now became deeper and narrower and more of a steep-sided gorge, into which the vegetation crowded in dense masses. *Rhododendron hodgsonii* and *R. campylocarpum* were joined by *R. barbatum*, and the giant fir was now replaced by the equally giant Himalayan hemlock — *Tsuga dumosa*. It is a pity that this conifer is tender in the British Isles as it makes such a lovely symmetrical tree, quite the equal of the hardier American *T. heterophylla*. There was a zone, around 10,000 ft, where both fir and hemlock mingled before separating into their respective territories.

The large-leaved *Berberis insignis* appeared by the track carrying axillary clusters of ellipsoid black fruits 0.33 in. long, and many ferns now occupied the banks and other shady places above the river. We could tell from the gradual change in vegetation that conditions were becoming more amenable and we were not surprised to find *Rhododendron arboreum*, *Acer pectinatum*, *Osmanthus suavis* and an evergreen *Symplocos* making an appearance. *Carpinus viminea* was frequent here. If ever there were a tree I should like to introduce into cultivation it is this beautiful Himalayan hornbeam. Its leaves are attractively toothed, parallel veined and coppery-red when newly emerged. I have seen it several times since in Nepal and Kashmir but never in fruit, and any plant collector heading for the Himalaya should try to bring this tree back alive, preferably from the upper limits of its distribution, as collections from lower altitudes would doubtless prove tender.

At one point the track skirted the foot of a wet moss-covered shady rock-face on which a colony of *Primula geraniifolia* was well ensconced. The long-stalked, rounded, hairy leaves 3-3.5 in. across were sharply toothed and bore numerous small pointed lobes. Although now in seed, when Beer had passed this way in June the rosettes had carried 9-12 in. hairy scapes bearing loose umbels of mauve-purple flowers 0.5-0.75 in. across. The rock-face at that time must have presented a pretty sight. On the damp banks alongside the track we were surprised to see *Primula glomerata* still in flower. The blue-purple flowers were densely crowded into globular heads, unlike the flat-crowned heads of the related *P. capitata*, and some particularly fine specimens approached in size those of the drumstick primula – *P. denticulata* – a species we had seen only once on the Jaljale Himal.

The track meanwhile crossed a log thrown over a narrow gully and along the margin of the stream below grew a giant perennial. The huge thrice-divided angelica-like leaves and tall 6 ft panicles of crowded brown seed capsules announced the presence of *Astilbe rivularis*, whose appearance in cultivation is an all too rare occurrence. It is a stately plant which requires a sheltered streamside or woodland site, and I remembered having seen a well-established specimen in the garden of Tom Spring-Smyth's parents at New Milton, a plant collected by Spring-Smyth in E. Nepal.

Eventually at around 9,000 ft we entered a small pasture by the main river and decided to spend the night here in a wooden shepherd's-hut with a thatched bamboo roof. Da Norbu soon had a fire going and whilst he busied himself cooking, Beer and I wandered about in the rocks by the river. Apart from a single specimen of an erect, red-stemmed, yellow flowered spurge – *Euphorbia pseudosikkimensis*, the only other plant to attract our attention was *Rubus nepalensis*. This small plant sent out long, trailing, hispid stems which covered a great deal of ground between the stones, bearing small, trifoliolate, hairy leaves with toothed leaflets. The single, slightly nodding flowers were carried on erect stalks. They measured 0.75 in. across and consisted of five white petals backed by a contrasting purplish calyx. These were succeeded by conspicuous raspberry-like red fruits which were rather insipid but pleasant enough to the taste. We collected two bags full and ate half as many in the process. Plants from this seed are now well established in cultivation, where they should be given a dry sunny situation to encourage plentiful flowers and fruit. In shady moist situations it becomes rampant and flowers sparingly. Although hardy on the whole, it can be damaged by severe frosts and young plants should therefore be held in reserve over winter in a frame or greenhouse.

In the early hours of the next morning I awoke with stomach pains. I blamed the raspberries but as they had not affected Beer I could only assume that I had a more sensitive stomach. All the rest of that day I felt rough and our return up the Mewa Khola was for me a slow and wearying experience. After breakfast, Beer slipped down the gorge to where he had previously seen the giant lily, returning shortly afterwards with a bag of fat seed pods and a few bulbils. He told me that the bulbs of recently flowered plants seemed exhausted and produced subsidary bulbs as a result. Whilst he was away I collected the fruits of the small evergreen shrub *Sarcococca hookerana* which grew in quantity around the hut. The rounded fruits, purplish-black in colour and 0.33 in. across, contained three seeds. I then found a Himalayan holly — *Ilex dipyrena* — a small tree of 15 ft with angled young shoots and ovate to elliptic or oblong leaves, entire or with a few spine-tipped teeth. The leaves of young or sucker shoots were more densely spine-toothed. The juvenile green fruits were rounded to oblong, slightly laterally compressed and borne in axillary clusters. Scrambling into a nearby tree were the blanketing growths of a climbing ragwort — *Senecio scandens* — with lanceolate, long-pointed leaves and large terminal panicles of yellow daisy flowers. This is sometimes encountered in cultivation but it is not normally hardy or persistent there. The most exciting find, however, was *Rhododendron grande*. Several specimens grew in the thicket above the hut, all loosely branched trees of 20-30 ft with stout, green and glabrous young shoots. The terminal bud was large and rounded with tightly adpressed scales contrasting with those of *R. hodgsonii* which are long-pointed with scales free at the tips. The huge leaves 10-18 in. long were elliptic to elliptic-obovate, acute, rounded at base, dark glossy green above, covered by a thin silvery indumentum below. They were carried on stout petioles 2 in. long, forming magnificent rosettes. I could only wish that I had been here in the spring to see the purple-eyed, ivory-white, bell-shaped flowers in dense terminal trusses. We later discovered that Spring-Smyth had found this very same

94

colony in 1961 and had introduced seed which is now represented as plants in several well-known collections. Sir Joseph Hooker, who first introduced this species from Sikkim in 1850 under the name *R. argenteum*, considered it a magnificent rhododendron, stating: 'I know nothing of the kind that exceeds in beauty the flowering branch of *R. argenteum*, with its wide-spreading foliage and glorious mass of flowers.' In cultivation it is best seen in the great woodland gardens of the western parts of the British Isles, though I have seen excellent examples at Borde Hill in Sussex and several other collections in the south.

We travelled slowly up the valley for several hundred yards where the vegetation was full of new and ornamental individuals. The curious were well represented and we again collected fruits of *Helwingia himalaica* and the yew *Taxus wallichiana* occurred as several large spreading specimens on the hillside above. Several maples appeared and we recognised *Acer sterculiaceum*, *A. campbellii* and *A. pectinatum* from previous encounters. A fourth maple was found growing above the river, a small tree of about 30 ft, its leaves three or occasionally five lobed, in the latter case the basal lobes small, each lobe doubly serrate and with a tail-like point. They measured 5-6 in. across, glabrous above, sparsely rufous pubescent on the veins beneath, petioles bright red. I believe it was *A. acuminatum*, which is mainly found in the Western Himalaya.

At one point a stream tumbled down a steep rock-face and the banks on either side proved particularly rich in shrubs. A bramble — *Rubus splendidissimus* — formed dense clumps of arching, silvery-hairy stems up to 6 ft. The leaves were made up of three, almost sessile, broad elliptic, long-pointed leaflets which were doubly serrate, green above, covered beneath with adpressed, silvery, silky hairs. The orange-red, raspberry-like fruits were borne in downy branched corymbs. A plant grown from this seed and planted in a sheltered place in the Hillier Arboretum later perished after a severe frost. Of similar size and habit was *Neillia thyrsiflora*, whose strong, non-flowering, rich brown shoots bore three-lobed leaves 4-5 in. long. The peculiar green fruits borne in terminal panicles, consisted of a bulbous based calyx, covered on the outside with gland-tipped hairs and containing a small capsule. In denser parts of the vegetation, often in deep shade, we found a *Hypericum* with slender arching stems 4-5 ft high, bearing opposite leaves 2-2.5 in. long, ovate tapering to a blunt point, green above, glaucous green beneath. The fruits were conical with an irregular surface, borne in threes. The calyx was two-thirds the length of the capsule with lanceolate sepals. Although we guessed this shrub to be in some way related to *H. hookeranum*, we were pleasantly surprised when Dr Norman Robson of the British Museum (Natural History) identified it as *H. choisianum*, our seed representing possibly the first

95

introduction of this species into cultivation. It is now well established in several collections and is a most elegant shrub with yellow cup-shaped flowers and nodding tips to the shoots.

The most exciting aspect of this location, however, was the preponderance of Ericaceous shrubs, of which the most interesting was an evergreen blueberry, *Vaccinium glauco-album*. It formed dense clumps and patches of branching stems 1-2 ft high clothed with elliptic, finely toothed leaves 2.5-3 in. long. These were tapered at both ends, dark green above and vividly glaucous beneath. The leafy-bracted racemes were produced on the previous year's wood and bore pruinose black fruits in great quantity. One often sees this species in gardens on acid soils and a most handsome evergreen it is, but the pink-tinted young growths are liable to damage from late frosts and the plant is best given light tree cover.

Another evergreen – *Gaultheria semi-infera* – produced clumps of arching, shortly strigose hairy stems 4-5 in. high, clothed with elliptic-lanceolate leaves 3-4 in. long. These were acuminate, cuneate at base, serrulate, dark glossy-green above, pale below. The small fruits, 0.25 in. across, were borne in dense racemose clusters along the previous year's shoots, varying in colour and on different plants from white to lavender-blue. *Gaultheria nummularioides* was also plentiful, creeping and forming dense carpets in the moss, its small, neat, double-ranked leaves carried on densely brown, hairy, arching shoots. I had only once before seen this species at Caerhays in Cornwall where a thriving colony occupied a low shady bank by the footpath. Plants raised from seed collected in Nepal died in the Hillier Arboretum after the 1976 drought and the following spring frosts.

Vaccinium nummularia formed clumps on the wet rock-face and to complete the representation we found *Gaultheria griffithiana*, a much larger species than others we had seen with robust, arching, green and glabrous stems 5-6 ft high. One individual sent its stems 9 ft into the lower branches of a tree. The elliptic to obovate leaves, 4-5 in. long, were serrulate, ending in a slender point, dark green above, paler below. The fruits were jet black 0.33 in. across, carried in dense axillary racemose clusters. This is a bold species quite unlike any other I know and is now in cultivation at the Royal Botanic Garden, Edinburgh. William Griffith, after whom this plant is named, was an assistant surgeon in Madras and one-time Superintendent of the Calcutta Botanic Garden. He travelled extensively in Bhutan and Afghanistan and accompanied Nathaniel Wallich in Assam. He died aged 35 in Malaya in 1845.

By the river grew a large spreading bush of *Stachyurus himalaicus*, its leaves beginning to turn orange and pink, its branches strung with short drooping clusters of small rounded yellowish seed capsules which we collected.

We crossed the river by way of a rough unstable arrangement of planks and slowly climbed the steep slope beyond. It was here above the track that we found our second *Magnolia* species — *M. globosa*. It was a small, few-branched, spreading tree 20 ft high by 30 ft across with obovate leaves 6-8 in. long. Both buds and the leaf veins beneath were densely covered with a pelt of ferruginous hairs. There was no sign of its having flowered and equally no sign of seedlings. Still somewhat elated by this find we progressed further up the gorge until a huge boulder some 25 ft high blocked our passage. Then we discovered that the track by-passed the obstruction, which was by no means a recent happening, and continued up the slope beyond. We made to follow the track but Beer suddenly pointed to a *Rhododendron* sitting on the mossy top of the boulder. It was a large clump with stems 5-6 ft high, the older stems with reddish peeling bark. The young shoots, buds and leaf undersurface were densely covered with small brown scales. The leaves themselves were elliptic, 2-3 in. long tapering to a blunt tip with a small mucro, cuneate at base, dark green above. The seed capsules were borne singly, or occasionally in pairs, shortly stalked (0.5 in.), oblong (0.66 in.) long with a short (0.25 in.) bent style, densely brown scaly. We later identified this species as *R. camelliiflorum* whose small white wide-open flowers I saw in the spring of 1973 on the Milke Banjgang. It is frequent in the moist woods below 10,000 ft and is invariably an epiphyte on rocks or trees.

Gradually we climbed the gorge, my stomach and legs still weak, and Da Norbu, as a result, carrying far more than he had expected to. A last stop was made to collect seeds of an extraordinary evergreen holly growing beneath trees above the track. It was a low growing bush up to 3 ft, its tough wiry branches forming a dense thicket sprinkled with elliptic, toothed leaves 0.33 in. long, glossy dark green above. The red fruits were none too plentiful, rounded 0.25 in. across, occurring singly in the leaf axils. It proved to be *Ilex intricata*.

All the way up the gorge we passed yaks and zobyaks browsing as they were driven down from the heights. The zobyak is a hybrid between a yak and a cow, differing mainly from the yak in its shorter coat and longer, more upswept, horns. It is a hardy beast and unlike the yak is equally happy at low altitudes. These herds are taken down to altitudes of about 7,000 ft until spring when the snows melt and recede, at which time the herds and herdsmen return to the heights. This usually takes place in March and is eagerly awaited by all concerned. During summer a yak will give between one and two litres of milk a day. It is a valuable beast, for apart from its milk, it provides a dense oily wool, a tough hide, good meat, and more important it is a tough and reliable pack animal. It is wilder and more unpredictable in its habits than the domesticated cow and it is unwise for a stranger to approach it too close. Generally though it is docile when handled or approached by herdsmen, but even they have been known to receive an unexpected kick so they tie its back legs together when milking it. When on the move a yak caravan plods along at a steady pace, the lead yak feeling out the track like a giant mountain goat. When confronted by diverging tracks the lead yak is encouraged one way or the other by a stone thrown to its left or right side by a herdsman. They often wear colourful tassels around their horns or tails, and most if not all wear bells around their necks. A lost yak is invariably located by the sound of its bell, and equally the sound of a yak caravan in motion is one of those unforgettable experiences of the high Himalaya.

As we stopped to allow the passage of a rather splendid shining black betasselled yak, we were overhauled by two small boys. They were returning from school at Dongan some twelve miles from Topke Gola and 4,000 ft lower down the valley. They stayed with us almost to Topke Gola, talking all the time, stopping when we did whether to collect seed or to take a breather. Due to my condition and slow progress we decided not to push ahead to the village that day and prepared to spend the night in the house in the clearing where the bird cherries grew. The women and children sat outside on the verandah watching our approach. The men were not at home but the women were quite happy for us to stay and one immediately began roasting corn for us. The grandmother, on being told of my upset stomach, gave me a mug full of dahl (curdled milk) from a wooden container. It tasted quite pleasant and had an immediate settling effect on my stomach, even giving me an appetite for supper. Just before dark the menfolk arrived driving their yaks before them into the clearing. They entered the house one at a time showing not the slightest concern at our presence. There were three brothers all in their twenties, one of whom had a small child and a baby. Eventually the whole family settled on the floor around the fire talking amongst themselves and occasionally asking Da Norbu questions about the sahibs. Soon their meal was ready, having been prepared by the grandmother and her daughter-in-law. First they ate roasted corn and then a huge pile of fresh green nettles were crammed into a small blackened pot of boiling water. This was constantly stirred and beaten into a kind of thick spinach soup. During its preparation the grandmother produced small green limes from the folds of her gown and these were sucked silently by the others. When the daughter-in-law began to breast-feed her baby, Beer and I retired to the far corner of the room to sleep.

Next morning, my stomach was back to normal, thanks to the dahl, and ever since I have had the greatest faith in natural yoghurt and similar stomach mollifiers. The family were up and about, engaged on various tasks which we watched over breakfast. The two older brothers moved off down the valley whilst the small boy tugged the yak calves to a tying-up point, which allowed his mother to milk the cows without interference. Her husband meanwhile struggled to cut wool from a

odododendron hodgsonii at 11,400 ft (Milke
nda)

Saussurea obvallata at 13,000 ft (On Screes Above
Topke Gola)

ussurea gossypiphora at 14,000 ft (Jaljale
mal)

Primula obliqua at 13,600 ft (Jaljale Himal)

◄ *Pinus roxburghii* at 5,500 ft (Above Dhan-kuta)

► Valley Above Topke Gola: A Botanists Paradise full of Firs, Junipers Maples, Birch, Rhododendrons, Poppies and Alpines

◄ *Abies Densa* in mist at 12,000 ft (Jaljale Himal)

► Valley Above Topke Gola Down which the Expedition Travelled to their First Base Camp

Acer sikkimensis at 7,000 ft (Hillside Above Hatia in the Upper Arun Valley)

Aster himalaicus at 13,500 ft (Jaljale Himal)

large black yak. Wielding his kukri he made several attempts, dodging repeated kicks, before being caught on the ankle by a crafty double-kick. In retaliation he struck the animal between the horns with the back of his kukri blade and followed this by tying its back legs together with rope. This done he quickly set to work slicing away great chunks of wool from the yak's ample coat. The baby then starting crying, at which the mother casually tipped a ladle of cold water on its head, bringing an immediate end to its tears.

The house in which we slept was typical for these parts, consisting of a rough stone base with a wooden superstructure, usually Himalayan silver fir — *Abies densa*. Neither mortar nor nails were used, and as far as we could judge these structures stood for many years with just the occasional patching and repairs.

On our return to Topke Gola we were greeted by Dorje and his sister Berma and Tende's sister Mile who brought large tompa's of cold chang to quench our thirst. From the folds of her tunic Berma withdrew a bamboo comb and proceeded to attack Beer's hair and ended by plaiting a little pigtail in his beard to the accompaniment of much laughing from the others. The last 500 yards up the steep hill to camp was, as always, the most tiring and we arrived wheezing and panting.

Having long since paid off the porters, we had to hire yaks to carry our gear, and this needed time. Morris agreed to stay on another day whilst the yaks were rounded up, and so the next morning, Beer and I climbed up the side valley above Topke Gola on the track to the village of Thudam which lay two days distant to the north. After a stiff climb we found ourselves in a flat valley bottom with high cliffs on either side. A small group of men caught us up and we were pleased to see Pema the cook accompanied by Da Norbu, Namgyal and Dorje acting as porters. By the streams grew clumps of *Meconopsis grandis* in vast quantities, and we promptly filled many bags with its seed. Beer told us how, on the reconnaissance, he had seen the many streams in this area coloured by primulas of several kinds but especially *P. megalocarpa*. Their myriad rosettes remained as evidence of his story, those of the last mentioned often sitting in the shallow water. Our track continued upwards across a steep rock-strewn slope, most of which was snow covered. Before reaching the snow, however, we stopped to examine a new poppy which occupied the banks on either side of the track. The many rosettes were in seed, the capsules borne on several erect stems 6 in. high. The entire plant was armed with prickly bristles giving rise to the most apt name *Meconopsis horridula*. Beer had seen it earlier in flower, when it looked most becoming with comparatively large blue crimpled flowers. It is yet another monocarpic species, fortunately easily grown from seed.

We were now approaching 15,000 ft and having slowly negotiated a narrow stream gully we rested ourselves whilst contemplating a thousand-foot snow slope leading up to a col at 16,000 ft. Having decided that contemplation would not make our climb any easier, we set off on a zigzag course, making slow and laborious progress interspersed with numerous stops. Eventually we reached the col and lost no time in pushing down the other side. A huge valley opened before us and we saw many great screes and hanging glaciers. It was almost as hard plodding down through the snow as it was going up and we spent more time on our backs than on our feet, but finally we made it to the open stream, and after another mile of clearer walking located a suitable campsite for the night. It was still mid-afternoon and Da Norbu, Dorje and Namgyal set off on the return journey to Topke Gola. Beer and I climbed to a vantage point where we could watch the Sherpas' progress and by late afternoon they could be seen, ant-like, plodding through the snow towards the col. Soon after they had disappeared we returned to camp for a hot meal prepared by Pema.

Meconopsis horridula

Paul Chester.

Next morning after an early breakfast we climbed up the steep slope above camp making for a high crag. The main woody vegetation on these slopes consisted of *Rhododendron setosum*, *R. anthopogon* and *Potentilla arbuscula*. The last named was a dense twiggy little shrub 9-12 in. high with relatively thick, short branches densely clothed with large brown, grey-hairy, papery stipules. The leaves, though fallen and brown were composed of five leaflets. This species is sometimes treated as a variety under the name *P. fruticosa* var. *rigida*, but whatever its status, it remains an excellent dwarf flowering shrub for the small garden and is especially pleasing during summer when its hummocks are plastered with the comparatively large yellow flowers of good substance. Nowadays, although uncommon in cultivation, its 'blood' may be seen in several first-rate hybrids, including 'Elizabeth', 'Dart's Gold Digger' and 'Hachmann's Giant'.

Both *Saussurea obvallata* and *S. gossypiphora* occurred, the latter in seed, the cottonwool ball opened revealing a tuft of thistledown.

Soon we were negotiating a large scree and we needed all our concentration to prevent ourselves from sliding down the surface. *Eriophytum wallichii*, a relation of the common bugle (*Ajuga*) grew here, its large, dry, flannelly bracts being its main claim to fame. Most plants, having detached themselves from the ground, were blowing about like tumbleweed. We left the scree just below the crags and crossed an awful desolate area of broken rocks laced with snow. Here we found a plant as rare and as desirable as Jason's fabulous fleece. Growing amongst the rocks, forming mats and cushions was the golden edelweiss — *Leontopodium monocephalum* — a boring name for one of the most lovely and fascinating alpines imaginable. I had read somewhere about the elusive nature of this species and though I had momentarily wondered whether we should find it, the idea was quickly forgotten in the hurly-burly of preparations. Now I could hardly believe our luck and I took several photographs as proof to non-believers. Each mat was made up of pale green, densely woolly rosettes topped by a 2 in. stem bearing a golden, woolly inflorescence. Seed was in abundance and we quickly filled a linen bag. Although we produced two dozen seedlings in pots at Hillier's, they one by one wasted away within the space of a few weeks. I have never heard from any other shareholders about the fate of other seed or seedlings. To grow a flourishing pan of this species for exhibition at an Alpine Garden Society Show would be a highlight even in that eminent Society's year. Perhaps careful drainage in the correct medium might succeed where all else has failed, but even then it would require the protection of an alpine house and the luck of the gods maybe.

Several other plants occurred on the sheer walls of the crags above and included the delightful *Primula tenuiloba* which formed small pads on the moss- and lichen-covered rock as well as on the grit at the edge of the screes. Beer described how, during the reconnaissance, he had seen this delicate species showing its pale blue, or occasionally white, flowers on 0.5 in. stalks above the minute leaves. In the same area he had found *P. concinna*, its small, yellow-eyed, mauve flowers borne in umbels above cushions several inches in diameter. On a grassy ledge we found an umbel, its domed heads of fruits 2-3 in. across actually sitting on the ground, the leaf rosette having withered. It proved to be *Cortiella hookeri* (*glacialis*).

Back on the screes again we found a small saxifrage — *Saxifraga pseudopallida* — forming tufts between the stones. Beer had seen it previously in flower, each white petal with two yellow spots, five to six flowers in a cluster atop a 4-5 in. stem. *Potentilla argyrophylla* var. *leucochroa* was found with its silvery, silky, trifoliolate leaves and erect 6-9 in. stems bearing comparatively small yellow flowers. We had this plant successfully established in the Hillier Arboretum where it was admired for its foliage rather than its flowers. On the cliffs grew *Potentilla eriocarpa*, its 4-6 in. stems, with 'fingered' leaves, hanging in tufts from sunny crevices.

When we at last attained the exposed summit of the hill, all around us rose the peaks and ridges of the Lumbasumba Himal. We could see the valley of the Syamjung Khola, in which lay our camp, curving in a great arc to Thudam. Looking north across range after range of mountains glistening white in the sun we could see an enormous high plateau with brown dry-looking hills and my heart skipped a beat as I gained my first sight of Tibet.

A fall of stone beneath us diverted our attention and we looked to see Pema climbing towards us with flasks of tea and still warm chapattis. Happily munching our food and drinking the hot beverage, we gazed south, over and above the col, to the farthest distant ridge where our march had first begun over a month ago. We remembered our flight from Kathmandu to Biratnagar and our first sight of the white wall. Now we were sitting on the same wall and our minds dwelt silently on all that had happened in between. The rocks on which we sat we estimated to be at 17,000 ft, and it was the highest point either of us had ever achieved. The only sign of vegetation here was *Potentilla microphylla* var. *depressa* which formed dense, hard hummocks, 6 in. high and 2 ft across of tightly packed rosettes. We scraped the hummocks with a knife to fill a bag with seed.

Eventually we made our way back down the hillside trotting and jumping in the wake of Pema whose rapid passage over the rocks and broken ground would have done a goat proud. We were expecting the arrival of Morris's yak caravan, but although we waited for several hours there was no sign of them and when darkness crept quietly into the valley we retired to camp for our supper. Being well above the tree-line Pema simply gathered heaps of dwarf rhododendrons with which to make a fire and the heat and sparks given out by this aromatic fuel kept us well at bay until supper was served.

House and
Yaks in the
Village of
Thudam

We were filling bags with *Potentilla arbuscula* seed the following morning when Dawa arrived to tell us that the yak caravan was less than an hour behind. They had left Topke Gola at 11 a.m. the previous day after spending two hours rounding up and loading the yaks. Unable to make the col before lunch they had decided to camp at the foot of the snow slope and wait until morning.

After an hour we were on the move again and what a sight and experience it proved to be. The yaks charged along the valley bottom, their tails curled over their backs like chows, urged on by the yak-men who whistled, shouted and clapped their hands. After a while we allowed the yaks and yak-men to press on whilst we made a more leisurely progress in order to look at the plants and collect seed.

Many streams converged on the river and between their courses large areas of shingle and stones contained several interesting plants including *Waldheimia glabra*, a perennial plant of the daisy family with prostrate stems clothed with small obovate fleshy leaves, deeply lobed at the tips. The flowers, 1 in. across, had a yellow disc surrounded by reddish purple ray florets. It grew in the grit close to the water's edge where also grew *Myricaria rosea*, forming long thin bands of rust-coloured plumes, marking the routes of the water courses for mile upon mile. In

103

a small grassy pasture by the river we discovered a tiny monkshood —
Aconitum hookeri — with creeping stems ascending 2-3 in. at their tips.
The leaves were palmately lobed and each slender stem carried a downy
seed capsule 0.5 in. long. It was abundant over a limited area. An hour
later we were passing through a deep gorge, the cliffs so high that they
blotted out the sun and everywhere was dark and cold. Beer and I
were happy to press on but Morris dragged his feet looking longingly at
the splendid precipices, no doubt wishing there was time to do a real
rock-climb.

The track we were following now ran downhill and we found ourselves in a wooded area where birch, fir and rhododendrons of several
species flourished. We then broke through the trees to find ourselves
face to face with Thudam, a collection of houses huddled at the foot
of a steep hillside and a few feet above the river.

A Young Goral

Paul Chester

8 LAND OF THE GORAL

The village was situated above the confluence of the Syamjung Khola and the Lhesa Khola at a height of 12,500 ft. Our camp had been set on a fairly level piece of ground on the opposite side of the valley, and to reach it from the village a series of three bridges had to be crossed. These were no more than bundles of slender logs tied together and renewed when each melting snow flood swept them away.

The following day was quiet and we did our washing and seed drying, Morris again draping the tents with long strings of seed bags so that the camp appeared to be festooned with bunting.

The campsite was more or less covered in scrub, consisting of the red hipped *Rosa sericea*, *Berberis angulosa*, *Cotoneaster sanguineus* (similar to *C. acuminatus*), *Juniperus recurva* and *J. squamata* and a willow — *Salix disperma* (*wallichiana*) — a handsome shrub of 8-10 ft, its white woolly catkins borne in some profusion along the erect twigs. The synonym commemorates Nathaniel Wallich (1786-1854), one of the most famous superintendents of the Calcutta Botanical Garden, who made an extensive collection of both herbarium specimens and living plants including many from Nepal. He was a man of tremendous energy and played host, friend and adviser to numerous botanists and gardeners arriving from England wide-eyed and full of wonder and apprehension.

Wallich developed his own technique of establishing collected seedlings and cuttings in the Calcutta Botanic Gardens prior to shipping them to England, and such was his authority on the preparation,

105

packing and transporting of living plants by sea that a paper which he submitted on the subject was read to the Horticultural Society of London (now the Royal Horticultural Society).

Abounding on a grass bank above the river was a peculiar saxifrage — *Saxifraga brunonis*, with small rosettes of narrow green leaves and numerous slender thread-like stems (stolons) reminding me of a small, well-ordered dodder (*Cuscuta* sp.). The small clusters of yellow flowers on 2-3 in. stems, Beer had seen previously. *Primula glomerata* was again plentiful on moist slopes on both sides of the river and accompanying it in one place, near to the camp, was a rather lower-than-normal form of *Polygonum amplexicaule*, its flowering stems reaching no greater than 18 in., the slender spikes of red flowers drooping attractively. This plant, from seed collected at the time, has proved popular and distinct in cultivation, so much so that, in answer to several requests, I gave it the cultivar name 'Arun Gem' in recognition of its habit, flower colour and location in a branch of the Upper Arun valley. It appears to relate to the variety *pendulum*.

Across the river from the camp and around the village grew a large branching plant which appeared to be annual. The flowers, as described by Beer, were bell-shaped, greenish and produced singly in the axils of the large leaves. The rounded fruit capsules contained numerous small seeds and were themselves enclosed in a large bladder-like ribbed calyx. Pema told us that it was used as yak fodder. We have since identified the plant as *Scopolia stramonifolia* a member of the potato family *Solanaceae*. Both birch — *Betula utilis* and the peely-barked cherry *Prunus rufa* — were plentiful on the surrounding hillsides, though many of the cherries had been mutilated in the search for firewood. The birch too was much in demand for occasional building, especially yak pens and temporary supports. Our Sherpas had used it for several structures in camp including supports for the kitchen tent and as props for the clothes line and it certainly lived up to its Latin name, *utilis*, meaning 'useful'.

For more permanent structures fir had been used, and of the remains of fir forest in the vicinity of Thudam much was mutilated, as was the juniper — *Juniperus recurva*. The latter, however, was regenerating to a surprising degree and amongst the masses of seedlings and saplings we found several large old trees heavy with fruit.

Behind one of the village houses Beer and I found a superb specimen of *Rhododendron campylocarpum* 15 ft high growing with an equally impressive *R. hodgsonii* of 18 ft. Other Rhododendrons occurred in the vicinity but by far the most noticeable was *Rhododendron cinnamomeum*. It appeared as dense mounds 4-6 ft high scattered across the hillsides. The leaves, on being turned, exhibited a rich rusty pelt of woolly hairs which could be scraped away with the fingernail. This Rhododendron is, by some authorities, regarded as a sub-species of

R. arboreum, and it would appear to represent this species at high altitudes. The flowers are usually white, though they may also be pink or crimson.

Looking up the valley above the village we could see the fiery red splashes of *Berberis angulosa*, whilst closer to hand we collected seed of *Piptanthus nepalensis*. Sometimes called the evergreen laburnum, this robust shrub formed specimens 6 ft high by 12 ft through, the sprawling branches draped with flattened pods which rattled each time the wind blew. Three other shrubs were common on the hillside above Thudam and these were *Aster albescens*, *Spiraea bella* and *Potentilla fruticosa*. The last named was a small shrub 2-3 ft high, the leaves with five leaflets. It is now well established in cultivation and produces the typical yellow flowers of this group. The *Aster* also was a small shrub but of sprawling growth with grey-backed toothed leaves and flattened clusters of seed heads. In cultivation this shrub is only suitable for warmer areas but at Wakehurst Place in Sussex it has proved most successful in the wall garden where its grey-green foliage and wide heads of lavender daisy flowers are a familiar sight from summer into autumn. It is still to be found in a few nursery catalogues usually under the generic name *Microglossa*.

On descending the hillside to the village we came across a huge moss-covered boulder on which grew a *Pleione* sp. quite different from that which we had previously seen on the Milke Danda. Here the pseudo-bulbs were nice and plump and varying in shape from almost round to ovoid. In colour they were a lovely shining rose-madder turning to green with age. Neither leaves nor flowers were in evidence. Like the Milke Danda species this was in a dormant state, the moss in which it grew quite dry, yet during the monsoon period it would enjoy a thoroughly wet condition. Thudam is at approximately 12,000 ft and is covered in snow during winter which suggests that this *Pleione*, whatever its identity, is a hardy species and worth introducing into cultivation. This was probably *P. hookerana*.

There was another plant which caught the eye amongst the rocks of the hillside. This was an unusual small sub-shrub with a big name *Boehninghausenia albiflora*, a member of the buttercup family *Ranunculaceae* but most resembling a white flowered shrubby meadow rue – *Thalictrum* sp. It is a charming plant for a border with its elegantly divided leaves and rather fluffy flower clusters, but it is unfortunately of borderline hardiness and those plants which we grew from seed in the Hillier Arboretum have long since perished.

As we made to leave the village our attention was caught by a man who appeared from the darkness of a doorway and called to us. It was the Lama we had met at Topke Gola and who served both communities. He led us towards a new gompa built of stone with a wooden roof, barely two months old and we followed him through a bright-blue painted door into the dim interior. Before us stood a large cabinet packed with old books, and on either side a large prayer wheel — tall drums made of parchment colourfully painted and inscribed with Tibetan script and motives. These the Lama spun for our benefit and as they whirled around, a stick attached to the top of each drum struck the clapper of a bell positioned above. The rest of the room was bare save for a few tapestries on the walls.

Back in camp Tende produced a tall wooden churn which he had borrowed from the village and announced that he would prepare for us Tibetan tea. Into the churn he placed yak butter which is white and tastes like a weak margarine, black tea, yak milk and salt. He then beat the ingredients with a long wooden pestle before pouring the liquid into a large kettle which he then placed on the fire to boil. The resultant 'tea' looked and tasted like a slightly salty soup which we found unusual but not immediately enjoyable.

The following morning at breakfast a group of nine men arrived from Baracula, a village in the Arun Valley near Sedua. They had carried for Beer on his reconnaissance and had remembered that he would be returning this way. They were happy to wait until we were ready to leave Thudam in eight days' time and moved off to find food in the village.

Beer decided to climb up a steep gully above camp and took Da Norbu with him whilst Morris and I wandered downriver from camp to look for seed. It was a bright sunny morning and everything looked at its best including the snow cone of Makalu which we could clearly see from the camp. I was particularly impressed by the stems of the maple — *Acer papilio* — trees of 25-30 ft with deeply etched and furrowed brownish-grey bark. Lower down *A. pectinatum* appeared and flourished to where an old man stood in a clearing. He was busily beating milk in a churn and smiled a welcome as we arrived. Behind him stood a pile of neatly stacked newly cut planks. Our attention, however, was taken by a superb specimen of the same maple, a tree some 50 ft high, the young shoots as brilliantly coloured as the popular red twigged dogwood — *Cornus alba 'Sibirica'*. The spreading branches were draped in long clusters of red-winged fruits, whilst the leaves had turned a clear yellow. This is a most handsome maple, lacking the attractive bark of *A. papilio* which replaces it at higher altitudes but superior in every other department. The tree in the glade rivalled anything I had ever seen at the Westonbirt Arboretum, and in this setting with the crashing of the river in our ears and the paddling of milk in the churn it gave us a lasting memory.

Of other trees that day, rowans, mainly the white fruited *Sorbus microphylla*, and the dark firs, were the majority. On our way back to camp we found a parasitic plant *Xylanche himalaica* growing on the roots of *Rhododendron arboreum*. The brown fruiting spikes of this member of the broomrape family — *Orobanchaceae* — came straight from the ground and occurred singly or in clusters. Previously we had seen it on the roots of *Rhododendron hodgsonii, R. campylocarpum, R. wightii* and *R. lepidotum*. By the river below camp we found a lone specimen of *Lyonia villosa*. It was a small tree, 15 ft high, with smooth, polished reddish-brown shoots. The leaves were ovate to elliptic, 2-3 in. long, unequal at the base, obtuse to rounded at the tip, green above whilst pale green to sub-glaucous beneath. The small seed capsules were carried in short leafy terminal racemes. At this season I could see little difference between this species and the closely related *L. ovalifolia*. The latter species has a wide distribution from Kashmir eastwards to Taiwan and Japan. Bean comments on the tender nature of the Himalayan plant which is rare in cultivation. *L. villosa*, favouring a higher altitude may well be a more worthwhile introduction.

On our return we found that two surprises awaited us. First of all Dawa, after several attempts, had finally persuaded a jelly to set, no easy matter at altitude. Pema meanwhile, in answer to our request, had decided to bake a loaf of bread. To achieve this he first set a large pan on the fire. Into this he placed three stones to support a smaller pan containing the mixture. Replacing the two lids he then heaped on the top lid hot ashes from the fire. In two hours the bread was ready and it tasted delicious, crisp on the outside, warm and soft within, far better quality than Pema's previous effort — a cake which, when accidentally dropped, had shattered into a thousand pieces.

We had discussed the desirability of travelling up the Lhesa Khola to see if a more northerly valley might bring us a different range of plants. The Lama was leaving the next morning to visit Wallungchung Gola further to the east and it seemed a good idea to accompany him for a little of the way. We left late morning accompanied by Dawa and Pema, with Dorje, Namgyal and Tende acting as porters. Da Norbu remained in camp to keep an eye on things until our return in three days. The weather was fine and sunny as we climbed away from the village and followed the river which tore over the rocks through a ravine below the track. The whole of the far north-facing hillside was covered by a dense growth of *Rhododendron wightii* which, beginning above the river at 12,800 ft, surged upwards like a deep-green tide to the crest of the ridge at 14,000 ft. By contrast the south-facing hillside, across which lay our track, was covered by a mixture of birch, fir and juniper above a crowded undergrowth of *Rhododendron, Cotoneaster* and *Berberis* with *Rosa sericea* providing a thorny connection. Rhododendrons *campylocarpum, cinnabarinum* and *campanulatum* occurred in some numbers up to 13,000 ft, at which point *R. hodgsonii* and *R. thomsonii* took over. *R. campanulatum*, however, appeared as scattered individuals up to 14,000 ft, whilst 300 ft higher we discovered a lone stunted *R. campylocarpum*.

The Rhododendron population above 13,000 ft was dominated by the dwarf species *R. anthopogon*, *R. lepidotum* and *R. setosum* which formed a continuous carpet, shared in the lower reaches with *Spiraea arcuata*, *Cotoneaster microphyllus* and *Lonicera rupicola*, the last a dwarf shrubby honeysuckle related to the popular *L. syringantha* but inferior in merit. It was in this 'moorland' zone that we collected the dry seed capsules of a bulbous plant — *Fritillaria cirrhosa* — whose nodding green-based bells would have graced the scene in June and July. Eventually we came to the parting of the ways and the Lama took a track which moved north-east towards Wallungchung Gola, whilst we continued north in the direction of Tibet. The terrain became drier and more exposed and most plants seen were creeping or dwarf in nature and included the tiny green-stemmed shrublet *Ephedra gerardiana* var. *sikkimensis*. We made camp that evening by the river at a height of 14,600 ft. A short pre-supper foray turned up two gentians — *G. sikkimensis*, also called *Lomatogonium sikkimense*, a tiny annual with slender stems and pale-blue flowers 1 in. long by 0.5 in. across, and *Gentiana ornata*, a more substantial species with comparatively large Cambridge-blue trumpets.

We awoke early the next morning to find a cold north wind blowing down the valley. The river, which here flowed shallowly between rocks and boulders, was partially frozen. Dorje was the first to awaken and shortly afterwards we saw him quartering the ground above the camp filling a bamboo basket with hardened yak dung for the fire. After a quick breakfast we continued up the valley leaving Dawa and the others to break camp.

The waters reflected the sun which slowly climbed out of the east beyond the peaks of the Lumbasumba Himal. The river itself was bordered by the rust-coloured plumose growths of *Myricaria rosea*, a dwarf tamarisk which we had seen several times before. Some of the clumps and mounds had turned a rich scarlet and others a deep beet-root purple. Occupying shingle banks, sometimes in company with the above, was a dwarf sea buckthorn — *Hippophae tibetana* — its stout grey spiny branches forming dense low carpets 6-9 in. high and many yards across. The small grey oblong leaves had already fallen and as we could see no sign of fruits we assumed that these were male plants. Sea buckthorn carries its male and female flowers on separate plants and both sexes need to be in fairly close proximity to effect pollination. A colony of female plants massed with bright orange berries must present a striking picture in these dry, brown, autumn valleys, but we did not see a sign of one.

About an hour out from camp we spotted what we thought was a sheep standing by the river's edge ahead of us. On closer examination however we decided against this identification and realised that it was a young goral, a high-altitude Himalayan animal which looks like a cross between a sheep and a deer and is related to the latter. In colour it was grey and small straight horns protruded from its crown. It was reasonably tame and allowed us to approach to within a few feet before moving away, sometimes stumbling in doing so. We came to the conclusion that this was a sickly individual left behind by the main herd as the species is normally timid and fleet of foot and avoids contact with man.

Soon we were above 15,500 ft. The only sound was of a nearby river and the only movement was a flock of snow-pigeons clearing a dark-faced cliff above us. The only woody vegetation appeared to be *Rhododendron anthopogon* and *R. setosum* with an occasional patch of *Potentilla arbuscula* whilst large dark stains on the hillsides proved on examination to be patches of the juniper — *Juniperus indica*.

At the head of the valley was a chorten built on top of a large rock slab. Here the track curved to our left and followed another valley whose steep sides appeared bare of vegetation. We stopped to watch a lone hoopoe which suddenly appeared and perched on a nearby boulder, flexing its strikingly barred crest. Another movement then caught our attention and we saw on the opposite hillside several puffs of dust and stones tumbling down the slope. At first we could not detect anything and then, through his binoculars, Beer spotted a herd of gorals, some thirty or more, motionless, watching us. Gradually we began to pick them out with the naked eye and there began one of those frustrating schoolroom games, each waiting to see what the other would do next. After a quarter of an hour, however, we conceded victory as, impatient to be off, we turned away and climbed slowly up the track.

At a height of 16,000 ft we found ourselves looking along a wide shallow valley which travelled a mile or so to the foot of a steep slope whose crest almost certainly marked the border with Tibet. Two dark specks had appeared in the sky above the ridge and gradually loomed larger as they flew in our direction. They were ravens, and as though trained to do so they circled above our heads for a short while before returning from whence they came, having uttered no sound of alarm.

There was no sign of the Sherpas so we decided to wait for their arrival and having dropped our rucksacks in a pile on the track began to examine the nearby slopes. Beer and I were slowly searching on opposite sides of the river when we each found a new *Rhododendron* sp. Our shouts were simultaneous and I crossed the water carrying a small twig of my find to match that which Beer was busy photographing. It proved to be *R. nivale* and formed low mounds 6 in. high of tangled stems with reddish scaly young shoots clothed with tiny, greyish-green, scaly leaves 0.25 in. long. The whole plant was aromatic when bruised, in common with *R. anthopogon* and *R. setosum*, both of which accompanied it. Although we searched for some time these appeared to be the only woody plants at this height — 16,500 ft — and, apart from a few miserable shrivelled grasses, the only other plant to be seen was *Arenaria polytrichoides* which formed straw-coloured cushions up to 10 in. across. Each cushion was made up of numerous closely packed rosettes of sharp pointed narrow leaves and were hard enough to stand on without their breaking. These seemingly indestructible high-alpine cushions seemed a far cry from the little sandworts of Britain, and even further removed from that curse of fine lawns, the creeping pearlwort, to which it is also related.

We had waited for over an hour with still no sign of the others so reluctantly we picked up our belongings and retraced our steps down the valley. The sun was setting before we met Dawa coming up the track to find us. He explained that having had instructions from the panchayat man of Thudam not to go near the border, he had made camp some distance further down the valley and hoped that we would not be too angry. I was angry at having to return from what promised to be a fascinating region, but eventually acknowledged Dawa's good sense.

On 5 November whilst breakfast was cooking we found by the river *Polygonum affine*, a carpeting perennial with strap-shaped leaves and dense spikes of rust-coloured fruits. I was pleased to see this plant in the wild as it is such a garden favourite when its rose-pink flowers are present. This form was the same as that collected in Central Nepal by Colonel Donald Lowndes in 1950 and with its shorter, thicker spikes, far superior to the thin-spiked forms from the Western Himalaya of which 'Darjeeling Red', despite its name, is one.

After breakfast we decided to climb a steep hill above our camp and leaving Pema and Namgyal as watchmen, immediately set off. At a height of 16,200 ft we stopped for a rest. Above us a rock stack soared to 17,200 ft and we made this our next objective. The snow had frozen on the steep ground below the stack and we reached its base by cutting steps with our ice picks, the first occasion we had used them for this purpose. From the summit we could see Tibetan peaks covered in snow and to the north-west lay more snow-covered peaks, whilst to the west other ranges could be seen, their summits obscured by cloud. Whichever way we turned we saw mountains and valleys and hanging glaciers, a cold grey landscape whose black and white fangs carved a picture both beautiful and cruel. The cold winds dislodged us from our perch and we clambered down across a field of large rock slabs which lay strewn like a pack of giant cards in our path.

That night the Sherpas built a huge bonfire of juniper to which, to our shame, were added quantities of potentilla, tamarisk and dwarf rhododendrons, and having explained to them the story and tradition of the Gunpowder Plot, we started an exciting if childish game of leaping over the fire through the alternate licking of smoke and flame. The Sherpas joined in with gusto, yelling and catching the brushwood with their feet to send showers of sparks into the night air. To any watching herdsmen or travellers, the scene must have suggested a gathering of demons.

The following day we retreated down the valley as the weather deteriorated. Dense mist was dispersed by a freezing wind which in turn brought a fine hail. By the time we reached our campsite in late afternoon, snow was falling thickly and by the time we were all huddled in the kitchen tent, we were snowed in. Beer told us he had seen a snow leopard — pale brown with dark head and tail — whilst the only thing of note that I had seen had been a golden-leaved form of *Rhododendron setosum* which had stood out like a beacon in a patch of the normal kind. When we retired to our sleeping bags the snow was still falling but the situation changed during the night for the sun was shining next morning.

The snow had drifted against the stone walls of the yak pen in which we had encamped and we all set about clearing a passage to the track outside. The wind had gone, leaving in its wake a silent white world through which we slowly trudged. For several hours we followed a track which wound its way through birch and rhododendron, the peeling stems of which lent a warmth to the otherwise wintry scene. The antler-like branches of the silver firs were lined with snow, whilst at ground level the same snow held tall brown herbs and sedges in an icy grasp.

We reached Thudam at mid-day, by which time the weather had once again deteriorated bringing mist and snow. Four of the Wabak Khola porters turned up for work and we set them to cleaning seed in the jouster tent. One of them made great play of a cough and when we enquired as to his condition, he claimed to have developed pains in his chest and left foot. Morris promised him some medicine and left the tent to return five minutes later armed with a box of mixed pills and tablets to cure anything from headaches to dehydration. By this time the wracked porter was putting on a convincing show of suffering emphasised by contorted features and a low persistent moaning. The man's companions were also showing signs of developing pains and when Morris placed a quantity of pills into an outstretched hand, it belonged not to the man with the cough but to another who complained that his throat was on fire. Before we could retrieve them they had been swallowed and a second lot had to be given to the original porter to stop him strangling the usurper.

Dawa returned from the village to announce that there was to be a dance that night and we were all invited. Having first eaten we trooped along to the river where we spent some time negotiating the log bridges by torchlight. On reaching the far side we were met by a pack of mongrels who snarled and complained in their eagerness to cross the bridges to go scavenging in our camp which they did just as soon as we had left the area. Picking our way through the rocks we headed for a long wooden building from which singing and shouting could be heard. We bowed our heads to avoid hitting the low doorway and entered the candlelit living room where many people were gathered. Beer, Morris and I were given a place by the fire whilst the Sherpas settled themselves about the room. Four men and four girls were standing in a line, their hands clasping those of a second rank behind. Slowly they shuffled forward and backward occasionally stamping their feet hard on the wooden floor, all the while chanting and wailing. They performed several dances, all basically similar in steps, and Dawa explained that they were old Tibetan dances, some of which he knew well.

It was approaching midnight when Beer and I decided to dance our version of a Highland fling, a suggestion well received by the villagers who settled themselves on the floor. It is certain that no Scot would have recognised the dance that followed. We hopped and skipped, bounced up and down, leapt in the air with arms outstretched, clapped our hands, shouted, screamed and whistled, in fact we did whatever came to our minds. The crowd loved it and encouraged us with shouts and banging of boots on wood. We were just about to stop for a rest when everyone leapt to their feet and joined us in the dance. Even if we had wanted to stop there was now no hope as sundry bodies hemmed us in, preventing us from sliding to the floor. I shall never know for how long we danced thus, but much later when the dancing ended and the butter lamps burned dry, we stumbled from the room and returned to camp where we promptly fell asleep.

All the next day the snow fell half-heartedly and we spent the time cleaning seed and writing notes. In mid-afternoon we were called over to the village to witness the slaughter of a yak. When we arrived the animal had already been pinned to the ground and whilst one man held its head another plunged a long bladed knife into its heart. It seemed the yak died slowly with occasional kicks and trembling, and then the knife was withdrawn and the wound plugged with straw. A small bowl of water was then produced and poured down the yak's throat. In the water was a potion prepared by the Lama, supporting a superstition which claims that, if the yak accepts the drink, then the sins of the slaughterers are forgiven. The yak was dead. Several men set about skinning the animal and cutting up the carcass. Every part of the yak was utilised and even the blood which gushed from the main artery was caught in a large bowl.

The day of our departure dawned clear and sunny and all morning we busied ourselves with packing and preparations. Some of the villagers came across the river to watch us and to sell or barter goods. The tail of the slaughtered yak was sold to Beer for R25 and a Singapore nylon shirt. Hats, furs, beads, tompas and rings were produced in turn. Eventually we called a halt to the trading and gathered the Sherpas together for a discussion.

Our next destination lay down-river in the village of Chyamtang. The locals told us that our best route lay over the hills west of Thudam, a journey of about two days. Beer and I however, felt that there was much to be gained by following the River Bagang Khola which, on our map, appeared to join the River Arun below Chyamtang, Beer arguing that such a route might well reveal new plants including Rhododendrons. In the event we split the group; Beer and I and Da Norbu took the river route and Morris and the rest followed the mountain route. It was a decision we almost regretted.

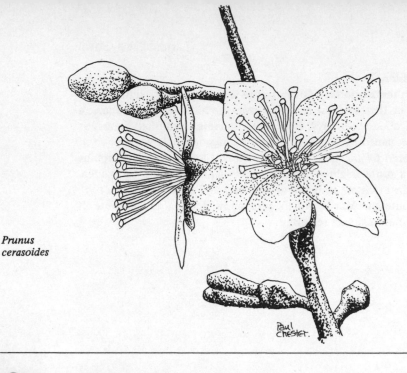

*Prunus
cerasoides*

9 DESPERATION VALLEY

It was on spring heels that Beer and I strode down the valley that day. The river threshed along beside us drowning our shouts as first one plant then another caught our attention. Da Norbu trundled in our wake. Metal pans and containers hung from his pack on bits of string, rattling furiously at every turn, and he reminded me of a travelling hardware man of gypsy origin who used to visit our neighbourhood when I was a child. Da Norbu, however, was no salesman and seemed to gain the greatest pleasure from assisting us in our collecting activities. He caught us up at one point festooned in a glossy leaved vine — *Smilax menispermoides* — whose prickly stems clamber over bushes and into small trees.

We collected seed from a particularly splendid birch by climbing into its crown and shaking its branches. Seed and scales showered down like so much confetti and a plastic sheet spread upon the ground was soon covered with the brown booty. *Rhododendron arboreum* and *R. barbatum* now formed trees up to 40 ft and 25 ft respectively, and the undergrowth consisted mainly of ferns including *Pteris biaurita*, a relative of the so-called finger fern — *P. cretica* — commonly sold as a houseplant in the West.

Around 11,000 ft we found a 20 ft specimen of *Hydrangea heteromalla* with large oval leaves and flattened terminal seed heads. Nearby stood a young silver fir with extra long leaves which reminded me of the tree, rare in cultivation, known as *Abies intermedia*. I have no

116

reason, however, to believe that it was anything other than a rather luxuriant young specimen of *A. densa* which grew all around.

We made camp that night in the dank, dripping darkness of the rhododendron forest, the three of us sharing the one tent. The glum atmosphere was relieved next morning by the sun filtering through the layers of leaves and branches and we were quickly on the move following the same track as the day before, collecting all the while. We found a bold bramble *Rubus treutleri* 4-5 ft high, the arching downy stems carrying downy, vine-shaped leaves 4-5 in. across, turning an attractive reddish-purple. The red fruits were set on large calyces and borne in terminal and axillary clusters.

Daphne bholua became increasingly common and we found an extraordinary specimen with a single stem rising to a height of 20 ft. *Tsuga dumosa* appeared, large trees with tall massive trunks. Beneath these giants *Rhododendron arboreum* formed a dense canopy, their moss-swaddled branches supporting large clumps of *Vaccinium nummularia* and various ferns. Here we found a single specimen of the Sikkim holly — *Ilex sikkimensis* — a small tree to 15 ft with grey bark, shallowly toothed leaves 4-5 in. long with purple stalks and midrib beneath. The axillary clusters of bold red fruits identified this form as the variety *coccinea* of Comber. This holly is occasionally seen in cultivation in Britain, but it is of borderline hardiness and is only successful in the south-west and west. According to Professor H. Hara of Japan, the name *I. hookeri* is a synonym of the above species, but plants I have examined under this name in British cultivation have always proved to be another Himalayan species — *I. dipyrena*.

The track we had been following suddenly took an abrupt turn and climbed the steep hillside to our right. A suggestion of a track meanwhile continued above the river and this we followed for several hundred yards until faced by a deep ravine across which there appeared to be no discernible route. We turned back and began a 3,000 ft climb up the valleyside through bamboo thicket and dense herbage, amongst which we found extensive colonies of a *Strobilanthes* sp., already flowered. This is a large genus of the *Acanthus* family but very different in general appearance from the familiar bear's breeches of western gardens. Like others I have since seen in Kashmir, it was a downy herbaceous perennial 2 ft high with sharply toothed, nettle-like leaves. The two-lipped flowers are invariably blue and are produced in clusters over a long period during late summer and autumn. I have seen plants in cultivation, possibly *S. alatus* which, given a warm border or bed, create a cheerful late splash of colour each year.

After four-and-a-half hours of climbing, we attained the rim of the valley at 12,800 ft. On the way we had passed through a scattering of the Himalayan juniper — *J. recurva* — large specimens up to 50 ft with stems almost rivalling those of the silver fir in size and girth. Most of these trees possessed an open-branch system with gracefully drooping branchlets and striking grey or blue-grey foliage.

The bamboo through which we had toiled was almost certainly *Arundinaria maling*, and looking back into the valley we could see a whole series of dome-shaped hills, their summits capped by the same bright-green bamboo.

A short walk along the ridge track brought us to a suitable place to make camp. Our night was disturbed by yaks crashing and blundering around in their attempts to reach the spring near our tent, but morning saw no damage to our belongings and we began climbing the ridge to where a huge rock outcrop barred our way. Following Da Norbu we scaled the obstacle, to be met with possibly the most breathtaking view of the journey so far. From our perch at approximately 12,800 ft we gazed over the lower Bagang Khola and across the Upper Arun Valley to the hillside where lay the village of Chyamtang — our destination. But it was not the intervening valleys and hills which drew our attention, but the magnificent show of mountains on the western horizon. Occupying the centre of the stage was the conical mass of Makalu with Nepal to the south and Tibet to the north. We were looking due west along the very spine of the Greater Himalaya — the roof of the world. For some time we sat on our rock fascinated by the panorama which lay before us, and watching a slender winged lammergeyer gliding far below until I saw the valleys rapidly filling with mist.

The ridge on which we found ourselves was a haven for rhododendrons, which formed dense carpets or thickets. *Rhododendron thomsonii* and *R. hodgsonii* were the two most common, whilst *R. cinnabarinum*, *R. campylocarpum* and *R. campanulatum* were in lesser numbers. Our excitement was complete, however, when we found another species — *R. fulgens* — for the first time. It formed a large shrub 10-12 ft high with attractive pink-tinged cinnamon and grey peeling bark. The leaves were 4-5 in. long, elliptic, polished dark green above and covered with a thin woolly fawn pelt below. Nearby, a grassy bank was scattered with the pale-blue trumpets of *Gentiana depressa* and the fruiting spikes of *Lobelia erectiuscula*, a relative of our native *L. urens*. Plants in cultivation from this seed however have proved of little merit.

Descending the hillside we followed a track which took us through a forest of *Rhododendron hodgsonii*, many of which had stems 25-35 ft high. These were covered with pink-tinted cinnamon bark which peeled away, sometimes in enormous sheets as in the canoe birch — *Betula papyrifera* — of North America. There was freshly fallen snow on the ground and this, heightened by the slanting shafts of a wakening sun, painted an unforgettable picture.

In the snow we found tracks made by a four-legged animal, probably a snow leopard. They appeared quite fresh, possibly two or three hours old, and followed the same track as us. For several miles we followed both track and leopard until the snow ended abruptly and the track, never clearly marked, now disappeared and left us staring into a deep ravine down which tumbled a foam-crested torrent. This we crossed and for the next fifteen minutes toiled up a steep incline to where the snow again covered all. To have lost the track at this stage would have brought us problems so we cast around at the edge of the snow until, to our surprise, we again found the snow leopard's tracks. They led us up and down the contours for close upon a mile before leaving the snow at exactly the same point as the re-emergent track.

On we trudged through rhododendron and juniper thicket until late afternoon when we found ourselves descending a gulley so steep that we slid down rather than risk falling head first. It was while negotiating a difficult piece of ground that we came across a large dense colony of the small-leaved holly — *Ilex intricata* — many bushes crowded with red berries. This was too good a harvest to miss so we spent the next hour stripping the twigs, filling two cotton bags with the swag. The delay, however, gave evening a chance to overtake us and we suddenly had to leave our temporary perch and continue our downward slide. Eventually we found ourselves in the rock-strewn belly of the gulley, and there, with darkness upon us, we spent the night wedged between two boulders, spat at by the torrent which passed within a yard of where we lay.

Long before the sun reached us we rose and packed, lingering just long enough to watch dawn fingering the summit of distant Makalu, which we could see through the western mouth of the gulley.

Once again we climbed steeply up the hillside through thickets of a common bamboo — *Arundinaria maling*. Himalayan juniper and silver fir provided a canopy, beneath which various shrubs and herbs flourished including *Jasminum humile*. This shrub is not commonly encountered in cultivation where its nodding clusters of bright yellow tubular flowers are borne profusely and over a long period in summer. This plant was sporting small shining black berries, and judging by the large number of its slender pointed leaflets probably belonged to the variety *wallichianum*.

Our track led us from the trees into an open area over which the mugwort — *Artemisia indica* (*vulgaris*) — was rampant. This strong herbaceous perennial is a common weed in Europe, including Britain, where it frequently occupies rail and roadsides, waste places and rubbish dumps. It seemed quite out of place here in the Himalaya, and no doubt, like the nettle, has followed man on his travels. Two small bushy-headed trees now caught our attention, one of which I climbed to retrieve a few dried red berries. This seed has since germinated to produce strong-growing shrubs with powerful stems. These are clothed with dark-green pale-backed leaves which colour richly before falling

119

in autumn, when, at the same time, the red fruits are borne in large drooping clusters. It seems perfectly hardy and to my mind looks to be typical *Cotoneaster frigidus*, but in the opinion of Mr B. Hylmo, a Swedish authority on the genus, it belongs to *C. gamblei*, a species recently named by his colleague K. E. Flinck. The second tree, an evergreen, was very different in appearance from the other. It reached approximately 18 ft with several branches forming a dense spreading head some 25 ft across. The leathery oval leaves measured 1-1.5 in. long and were prettily veined. No flower or fruit was apparent but I had no hesitation in naming this tree — *Euonymus tingens* — a rare spindle-berry which is represented in cultivation by plants collected as seed by Ludlow and Sherriff from Bhutan.

Leaving the trees behind we continued along a track which became progressively vague until eventually it disappeared altogether. Whilst Da Norbu cast around in the undergrowth Beer and I lay in the shade of a large bush which, when our eyes focused on its leaves, proved to be *Viburnum grandiflorum*, a huge specimen which must have measured at least 25 ft x 25 ft. After some time Da Norbu returned to tell us he had located a track and we climbed to our feet to follow him into the thicket. The next few hours were spent losing and finding tracks. It was amazing how a track clearly defined one minute could peter out the next and, as always, bamboo thickets proved the most confusing offenders. Casting around on one occasion we broke through the vegetation to find ourselves in a dried-up river gully which fell steeply down the hillside.

We agreed to make camp before dark. We were all tired and hungry, covered in sticky seed heads, scratched by rose and bramble and bruised from twanging bamboo. Lacking a flat piece of ground we found a depression in a large rock slab and there laid out our bedrolls. Da Norbu lit a fire and we located a water supply which at least enabled us to cook our remaining food — a bowl of rice and an Oxo cube! We had placed two stout logs across the base of the depression to prevent us sliding away in the night and it was with some relief that we awoke the next morning to find ourselves intact except for a kitbag which had rolled away and which we later retrieved some distance from our position.

In the light of the morning we were better able to appreciate our situation and, whilst Da Norbu was packing, Beer and I wandered about collecting seed of several interesting plants including two *Hypericum* spp. — *H. tenuicaule* and *H. uralum*, the latter with frond-like growths and pretty nodding buttercup-like flowers. *H. tenuicaule* was a shrub of some 4-5 ft with arching stems and narrow elliptic to narrowly ovate, wavy-margined leaves 1-1.5 in. long. The capsules were irregular in surface. This species is now in cultivation but is of little ornamental merit. *Boenninghausenia albiflora, Gaultheria semi-infera, Aster albescens* and several other small shrubs were common, and we discovered a particularly handsome colony of *Vaccinium glauco-album* in fruit. From the general thicket *Philadelphus tomentosus* threw its stems 6-8 ft high and *Elaeagnus parvifolia* reached even higher with its scaly stems flaunting narrow silver-backed leaves. We were excited to find another *Rhododendron* — *R. triflorum*, a straggling shrub to 5 ft with reddish-brown peeling bark. This is not one of the most striking species and I prefer its ornamental bark to the clusters of small pale yellow flowers in early summer.

Towering over these shrubs and forming living walls above the gully were the trees, mainly conifers — Himalayan hemlock, Bhutan pine *P. wallichiana* and silver fir. Broad-leaved trees such as *Alnus nepalensis* and *Populus jacquemontiana* var. *glauca* frequented the edges of the gully itself, whilst higher up we spotted the unmistakable presence of the Himalayan larch — *Larix griffithiana*, a single specimen some 40-50 ft tall, its needles already turning a tawny yellow. Uncommon and rather tender in cultivation, this graceful species is easily distinguished from all others by its large cones with conspicuous exserted bracts.

The rocks in the gully were borne in great slabs, their upper surfaces worn by monsoon torrents into channels and saucer-like depressions. In the crevices, grasses had become established, their bold tufts and plumes waving about in the wind which rushed from the valley below. Three species were mainly present of which the most common was *Calamagrostis emodensis*, its 3-4 ft stems bearing dense drooping plumes of silvery spikelets, most of which had already bleached to a cream or pale straw colour. An attractive contrast was provided by *Erianthus rufipilus*, whose dense, erect plumes of rose-tinted spikelets were just opening. I was particularly pleased to see *Miscanthus nepalensis*, with its silky fulvous spikelets borne in characteristic finger-like arrangements at the tip of a 2-3 ft stem. The leaves were turning a charming purplish shade contrasting effectively with the pale clear midrib. Whilst less spectacular than its Japanese counterparts, this species would be well worth a place in the garden for its small stature and elegance.

Our wanderings were curtailed by the sound of Da Norbu's voice and we descended the gully to where he stood packed and ready to leave. There was no discernible track so we simply cut our way through the undergrowth heading in a westerly direction.

Looking back on this day I believe it to have been the most wearying of the entire expedition. Our progress was slow and laborious, Beer and I taking it in turns to cut a path through the undergrowth which contained such shrubs as *Daphne bholua, Jasminum humile, Elsholtzia fruticosa* and *Philadelphus tomentosus*. I never imagined there would come the day when I would deliberately chop such plants to the ground. The thought almost shames me when I gaze on a *Daphne bholua* in full flower, pampered in cultivation. A jumble of rocks thrust their way through the canopy and for these we headed, guided by a curtain of Himalayan vine — *Parthenocissus himalayana* — whose long growths clad with brilliant crimson leaves gave the impression from a distance of newly spilt blood.

Climbing the rocks we were accompanied by a party of short-billed minivets, the males with scarlet and the females with canary-yellow underparts. On gaining the summit of the largest rock we found ourselves with a clear view into the valley below. The forest continued for perhaps a quarter of a mile giving way to what appeared to be grassland over which were scattered small huts and shelters. It suggested to us some kind of habitation so down we climbed from the rocks and once more continued our trail cutting. After an hour we thankfully broke out of the forest to find, to our dismay, that what had appeared as grassland was in fact a sea of head-high secondary vegetation covering land formerly cultivated. Undaunted we plunged onwards in the direction of the huts, our progress now even slower than before. The wretched mugwort was everywhere, its pollen making our eyes and noses smart. A particularly uncompromising trailing vine persistently tripped us and we lost count of the times we fell over. At regular intervals we ran into large specimens of a white-stemmed bramble — *Rubus biflorus* — which loomed out of the thicket like ghostly octopuses with viciously thorny tentacles. Also prevalent was a familiar plant in the bracken — *Pteridium aquilinum*.

Whilst falling to the ground on one occasion I came face to face with *Anemone vitifolia*, an herbaceous species with five-lobed leaves and fluffy cottonwool-like seed heads. Isolated trees of *Rhus succedanea* carried rich crimson leaves and these we carefully avoided, aware of the burning juice they contained. The sun blazed down and the aroma from the bruised mugwort made us feel sick, but still we staggered on until, two hours after leaving the forest, we gained the nearest hut. It was deserted and had been so for some years. From its dilapidated porch we saw several more huts lower down and we foolishly decided to head for them in the hope of finding at least a recently used track. Half-way to the first hut I stumbled and fell, my knee catching a rock hidden in the grass. I ended up on my back gazing at the sun which spun round like a ferris wheel. I managed to sit up and stare at the surrounding hills whose colour alternated between the natural and a curious monochrome. Then nausea took over and I lay back on the hillside. It looked as though we would be spending another night in the valley, but we were hungry and thirsty and had neither food nor water and this fact determined us to attempt the climb out of the valley before nightfall. It was a long haul, painfully slow and several times we sank down to rest and could have slept where we lay. Eventually we made the ridge and peering over the other side we could see the village of Chyamtang on the distant hillside. There was no chance, however, of us making the village before the following day and our attention was caught by a cluster of houses immediately at the foot of our ridge. There were obvious signs of activity — smoke from a fire, dogs barking, etc., and we made our way down through the forest of evergreen oak — *Quercus semecarpifolia* — and into the open space between the houses. Here we sank to the ground exhausted and thankful. The dogs, of course, had announced our arrival and two women emerged from the nearest house and approached us carrying a kind of giant cucumber which they split into three and offered to us. We stayed that night in the larger of the three houses and, after four or five glasses of chang, tucked into a meal of boiled chicken and rice. We were ravenous and picked the carcass clean, even sucking the bones. Afterwards, considerably satisfied, we laid out our bedrolls and settled down for a good night's rest, at least that was what we intended to do. But our presence in the hamlet was hot news and the single living room which we shared with the family soon filled with noisy neighbours, most of whom brought their food with them to cook on the fire, all the time watching us and chattering.

After a quick breakfast and profuse thanks to our hostess we were on the move again following a well defined track up the hillside. An attractive herbaceous spurge — *Euphorbia sikkimensis* — was plentiful amongst low scrub, its narrow leaves strikingly marked by the almost white midrib. This bold perennial is often seen in cultivation and is particularly ornamental in spring when the young growths are suffused coral pink or red.

From the ridge we could look down upon the River Arun and, almost directly across from where we stood, the village of Chyamtang. Our descent to the river was long and steep and we followed a track which, in places, fell almost vertically. It was an invigorating experience and there was plenty of interest on the way especially in the world of trees. First to catch our attention was a cherry tree 25 ft high in full bloom. It was *Prunus cerasoides*, the species we had last seen above Side Pokhara, where its hard-pruned existence had made little impression on us at the time. Its bark was close and grey and its new leaves, only just emerging, of a bronze-green fringed with bristle-tipped teeth. The blush-pink flowers 1 in. across were borne on drooping stalks, singly or in pairs. It was a lovely sight and yet strange that it should be flowering now in the middle of November. Later we saw many of these cherries scattered across the hillside above the river.

Two *Hydrangea* species were frequent by the track, both shrubs ranging in height from 10-15 ft. One was a narrow-leaved form of *H. aspera* with large drooping seed heads. In cultivation this has proved to be of a tender nature. The other, *H. robusta*, had very different broadly oval to orbicular leaves, occasionally as much as 12 in. long and wide. The flowerheads were equally large and flattened with creamy-white,

123

green-tinted ray florets. This species is rarely if ever seen in British gardens due no doubt to its tender nature and its lacking the flower quality of *H. aspera*. It would be worth its place in a collection however if only for its magnificent leaves.

Another plant we found which would grace gardens and arboretums in the milder areas of the British Isles was the Himalayan hornbeam — *Carpinus viminea*. This small- to medium-sized tree is not even mentioned in the recently revised edition of Bean's *Trees and Shrubs Hardy in the British Isles* and one must assume that amazingly it has never been introduced, or at any rate not successfully. The lance-shaped leaves, 2.5-3.5 in. long, are slender pointed and doubly toothed and of a delightful copper colour when emerging. Their finest character, however, are the veins which are boldly parallel.

The wealth of trees on the hillside amazed us after having seen endless *Rhododendron arboreum* and conifers and we were especially impressed by the representation of the bay family — *Lauraceae* — with *Cinnamomum glanduliferum*, *Litsea doshia* and *Lindera neesiana*, the three most common. The latter was a deciduous tree with oval leaves 2-3 in. long and small clusters of yellow flowers. *Lithocarpus elegans* appeared as a small evergreen tree with lance-shaped leathery leaves 6-10 in. long, not unlike those of the Chinese *L. henryi* which, in my opinion, is one of the finest hardy evergreen trees in cultivation. I was also pleased to see a 30 ft *Meliosma*, like *M. pungens*, with coarsely toothed, abruptly pointed leaves. It was later identified as *M. simplicifolia* ssp. *yunnanensis*. Crowding the sides of the track were many shrubs and perennials including *Aster trinervius*, its white daisy flowers 1 in. across borne in large loose heads on 2-3 ft stems. Far more spectacular, however, was *Senecio cappa* (*densiflora*) with stout erect woody stems 4-5 ft tall clothed with grey-backed coarsely toothed leaves 2.5-3.5 in. long. The yellow flowers were carried in dense bold terminal heads sometimes as much as a foot long. This would be a much sought after plant for the herbaceous border if only it were hardy. The hillside at this point would have been in the region of 8,000-9,000 ft, and, amazing though it may seem, to British gardeners this was a little too low to expect much in the way of hardy plants, although several might have succeeded out of doors in the mildest areas of the British Isles. It seemed to us at the time a pity that the transition zone should be placed on this richly clad hillside.

We reached the river which, at this point, was young and freshly emerged from Tibet, throwing itself at the rocks with terrific gusto, causing its waters to froth and foam. To cross it we were required to tread a bamboo bridge of the most slender proportions which bounced and swayed under the slightest pressure. Da Norbu would not cross whilst carrying his enormous pack, and I could hardly blame him, so Beer carried half of it, and the sight of him moving gingerly along what was little more than a gangplank is something I shall never forget. Once safely across we climbed the near vertical hillside and trod the stone-paved streets of Chyamtang to where our camp had been pitched in a field of stubble above the village. Having been expected the previous day we received a warm welcome from Morris and Dawa who, aware of our food situation, had been preparing a search party to come to meet us. Beer and I stopped just short of the camp insisting that Da Norbu should arrive first in recognition of his tremendous spirit and physical strength. Without him we would still have been groping about in the undergrowth and hopelessly lost. During the previous days never once had he grumbled or complained, nor had he disagreed with decisions once taken. He was a worthy son of a famous father.

10   A DEMON STRIKES

We spent three days in Chyamtang, and for most of this time our
activities attracted an audience of villagers. They presented a wild and
colourful appearance, sporting a variety of hats of which a trilby seemed
the most popular, usually decorated with peacock feathers, badges or
flowers, especially orange marigolds and white marguerites. Kukris were
carried by most males including quite small boys. They reminded me of
a gang of pirates looking for trouble, and the evil countenance of many
lent weight to my theory, which, however, dissolved whenever they
smiled. For then their faces split to reveal teeth tarnished and unevenly
worn through a lifetime's gnawing and smoking. Cheap Nepalese
cigarettes were available in many village stores in the lower valleys and
home-made varieties could be had wherever certain trees or shrubs such
as *Lyonia* grew.

The village lay spread over a large area of hillside, its houses separated
by small terraced fields in which many crops were grown. At night
villagers moved about with the aid of torches constructed of split
bamboo canes, one end lit from the fire. From our elevated position
their movements resembled fireflies — now converging, now separating,
creating a fascinating pattern of light. On reaching our camp the visitors
extinguished their torches, re-lighting them from our fire on leaving.
One night we heard music emanating from a house some distance away.
We decided to investigate, and on reaching the house entered through a
low doorway to find ourselves in a large room lit by a fire in the middle

126

of the earth floor. The place was seething, some people sitting, some standing, all drinking chang which was dispensed by several women who hovered over a large metal container. In one corner of the room two men sat cross-legged, each holding a long-handled drum which he struck regularly with a curved tong, chanting all the while. Opposite these sat a bearded man also chanting whilst shaking cymbals rigorously. We were told the bearded man was a lama performing some service for the owner of the house, and it seemed to us that everyone had joined the party including our Sherpas and many of the porters who sang and laughed and helped to keep the chang brewers busy at their cauldrons. Outside the house yet another fire burned around which danced a host of children.

Morris continued his morning 'surgeries' which were well attended, some patients travelling several miles for the privilege. Several brought gifts such as eggs, vegetables and even chickens. One man asked for medicine for his sister who had been kicked in the thigh by a bullock, whilst a woman asked for medicine for her husband whose head had been cut by a neighbour's kukri after an argument. Others had festering sores and stomach complaints to whom Morris administered as best he was able. As before in other villages we had passed through, it was depressing to see so many people with misshapen limbs as a result of unattended breakages and fractures.

We discussed village crops with the panchayat leader and learned that, in addition to millet and maize, which were everywhere apparent, wheat, barley, naked barley, potatoes, soya beans, buckwheat and radishes were grown. Several vegetables, including a variety of marrow, were also grown on a smaller scale.

One morning the Wabak Khola porters chopped down an old stump in a nearby field and brought it to burn on their fire. They were soon followed by an irate women who started shouting at us for taking the log from her field. Her tongue flapped like a flag in the wind and Berma, taking exception to some of the remarks, answered back in like fashion. Very soon the two were going at each other hammer and tongs until Dawa stepped in between and broke them apart, leaving Berma in tears with her tormentor laughing and making fun of her.

Most of the trees in the vicinity of the village had been cut down many years previously but occasional stands of Bhutan pine remained. The Himalayan ivy — *Hedera nepalensis* — was very common hereabouts, climbing over rocks and into shrubs and thickets. Its ovate pointed leaves were entire or occasionally with two basal lobes, quite unlike the boldly toothed version in British cultivation, which I suspect originated in Kashmir. The lovely pink flowered cherry was plentiful and, like the pine, had apparently been spared the axe due to its religious significance. *Viburnum erubescens* here made a large shrub of 15 ft or more with leaves polished green above and the occasional small cluster of white, pink-tinged flowers. With the last grew a splendid bramble — *Rubus niveus* — with vigorous purple-brown prickly stems up to 8 ft high coated with a white bloom. The leaves consisted of nine to eleven toothed, long-pointed leaflets, white felted beneath. Creeping over rocks and moist banks we found *Parochetus communis*, like a delicate clover with single blue pea flowers, and *Polygonum capitatum*, its red-flushed stems and pill-like pink flowerheads contrasting effectively with the blue of the other.

Spiraea micrantha reappeared, thrusting its strong erect stems 4-5 ft from the thicket and bearing terminal flattened heads of white flowers. In effect, this shrub resembles a white-flowered *S. japonica*, and seeds we collected have resulted in vigorous individuals with bold inflorescences, providing a striking contrast with the red and rose flowered kinds.

During this period in camp we checked through the specimens collected by Morris between Thudam and Ritak higher up the Arun. They included *Rhododendron ciliatum* and *Aconitum spicatum*, previously found by us on the Milke Danda. Two red-fruited brambles were collected as seed — *Rubus thomsonii* and *R. treutleri* — the latter with large palm-shaped downy leaves, its fruits partly enclosed by the large calyces. Another good find was the true *Sorbus cuspidata*. First he had seen a single 40 ft tree growing between two fields near the village of Ritak, but later found others in mixed woodland. The leaves of these trees were oval and pointed 5-6 in. long on 1-1.5 in. stalks. The leaf undersurface was densely white felted, whilst the fruits were like speckled crab-apples 0.75-1 in. across, green with a rose-flushed cheek. This species, both in leaf and fruit, differed from the closely related *S. hedlundii* we had seen on the Milke Danda. Young trees from this seed are now well established and growing strongly in several collections including the Hillier Arboretum and Wakehurst Place, Sussex.

The seed of several rhododendrons were in Morris's booty, but two seedlots which pleased us were the red berries of *Viburnum mullaha*, a shrub 8-10 ft high with toothed leaves 2-3 in. long, and the black fruits of a Himalayan dogwood — *Cornus macrophylla* — which he had gathered from a tree of some 30 ft. The former is of borderline hardiness in Britain where it is occasionally encountered in collections. The dogwood, however, is generally hardy and somewhat resembles *C. controversa* in its attractive tiered branches. *C. controversa* and the North American *C. alternifolia*, incidentally, are the only species with alternately arranged leaves and are thus easily recognised in cultivation.

The morning we left Chyamtang dawned bright and sunny. There was an air of excitement as tents were taken down and everything was packed into carryable bundles. Porters milled around and Sherpas shouted instructions, whilst, to judge by the size of the crowd, the entire village had turned up to watch the affair. Children played games with balloons we had distributed and several boys fired arrows from crudely made bows. Beer and I strolled through the village where the shrubs *Viburnum erubescens* and *Elaeagnus parvifolia* were commonly grown as rough hedges and where a tall shrub *Leucosceptrum canum* sported closely grey-felted leaves and shoots which terminated in conspicuous dense cylindrical flower spikes bristling with long creamy-white stamens. A group of porters were stripping the leaves from a large bush of *Lyonia ovalifolia* for use as cigarettes in the days to come. Returning to camp we found that all was ready and, to a rousing chorus from villagers and porters, we set off along a track down the valley towards Chepua.

On leaving the village we passed beneath a huge specimen of the pink cherry. It was at least 50 ft high with a girth of 8.5 ft at breast height. *Edgeworthia gardneri* occurred frequently as a shrub up to 6-7 ft with an 8 ft spread. The pale-brown shoots bore elliptic pointed leaves 2-2.5 in. long and terminated in tight nodding heads of greenish flower buds surrounded by narrow bracts. This is an attractive shrub, the yellow flowers imparting a delicious fragrance. It is, however, more tender than the Chinese *E. chrysantha*, from which it differs in its smaller evergreen leaves. Sharing the same gullies as this shrub was a small spreading tree to 15 ft whose large pinnate leaves, 12-18 in. long, had turned a brilliant orange and red. These trees, which we recognised as sumachs, fairly smouldered across the hillside and we could even see them on the opposite side of the valley. It was later identified by the British Museum (Natural History) as *Rhus semialata* which enjoys a tremendous distribution from the Himalaya eastwards to Japan and south to Sumatra. Not surprisingly it has received several names over the years and in the *Enumeration of the Flowering Plants of Nepal* the above name is placed as a synonym of *R. javanica* I.., whilst in Bean's *Trees and Shrubs Hardy in the British Isles* the name *R. chinensis* is preferred. The wide range of this tree obviously produces forms varying in hardiness, and hardy specimens in the Hillier Arboretum are admired for their handsome foliage and later flowering, without however producing the brilliant autumn colours described above.

In the thicket above the track occurred a large evergreen shrub or occasionally a small tree to 20 ft. It resembled at first glance *Camellia sasanqua*, but on examination proved to be *Eurya acuminata*. The young shoots were greyish-brown, pubescent and the leaves oblong-elliptic 2-2.5 in. long, toothed and abruptly pointed. They were of a dark glossy-green above, paler below. The flowers were quite small, 0.125 in. long, bell-shaped, creamy-white and crowded beneath the shoots of the second year. Our excitement increased however on finding another Rhododendron species — *R. virgatum* — by the track at a height of approximately 8,300 ft. It formed an erect shrub 3-4 ft high with slender straight brown scaly stems and oblong to narrowly lance-

A Woman
of Chepua

Paul
Chester.

shaped leaves 2 in. long, slightly longer on strong shoots. All leaves were of a distinct bronze-green in colour and densely glandular scaly below. The seed capsules 0.33 in. long were borne singly in the leaf axils, appearing racemose once the leaves had fallen. Several clumps of this shrub grew on a dry stony bank along with *R. triflorum*, *R. arboreum*, *Lyonia ovalifolia* and several of the shrubs just previously mentioned.

Dog and Pig
Sleeping in
Chepua

On arrival at Chepua we found ourselves in the compound of the police post and checkpoint where we were welcomed by the inspector, a likeable man aged about 60 who had served with the British Army in World War 2. We were invited to stay the night and, although we would have preferred to move on as it was early afternoon, we agreed to stay out of politeness. The inspector proved a great storyteller and in the comfort of his office he described to us many of his wartime exploits. Eventually a large bearskin on the floor caught our attention and elicited another story from the inspector who, when his English failed him, spoke urgently in Nepali with Dawa translating. The bear had been shot by the inspector close to the village and he then told us how, when the millet and maize are being harvested, the bears descend the hillside at night in search of food. Every year several villagers, mostly children, are mauled.

Having spent the night in the inspector's quarters, we headed down the track to Hatia. It was our intention to reach there before nightfall. The sun blazed down upon us and much of the vegetation around bore a withered appearance except for the ubiquitous bamboo and a handful of interesting shrubs, chief amongst which was a large *Buddleja* — *B. paniculata* — 6-8 ft tall, whose 5-7 in. long leaves were covered below, like the shoots, with a dense grey pelt of hairs. The flower spikes were still developing, but when open are perhaps amongst the least ornamental of the genus, being small and lilac or lavender. It is, however, too tender for general cultivation in the British Isles except in a cool greenhouse. Amongst the Rhododendrons we found several plants of *Deutzia staminea*, a shrub of 4-5 ft with roughly hairy shoots and leaves. The clusters of white flowers were long since spent but, like the *Buddleja*, are rarely seen in British cultivation owing to this species's tender nature. Indeed most, if not all the plants in this area were of borderline hardiness, and although 8,000 ft may seem a good altitude by European standards, it was low by Himalayan standards and we were constantly reminded of this during the following days.

Vaccinium dunalianum was another shrub of the borderline zone. It was an evergreen, 2-3 ft high with arching reddish-brown branches clothed with elliptic leathery leaves 2-3 in. long, each ending in a slender tail-like point and of a shining dark green above. We had missed the flowers but the resultant fruits were globular, 0.25 in. across and red in colour, turning to black. They were carried in slender spikes 1.5-2 in. long from the leaf axils. I planted this handsome shrub in the Hillier Arboretum but it perished and as far as I am aware it is now only grown from our seed at the Royal Botanic Garden, Edinburgh. *Anaphalis triplinervis* was scattered across the hillside, its grey herbaceous clumps up to 1.5 ft, the elliptic leaves with three to five main veins.

After lunch we hurried on until we reached an area of large rocks and cliffs where we decided to wait for the Sherpas and porters to catch us up. It was a fascinating place covered in dense vegetation, amongst which we found several interesting and unusual plants. First of all we spied a banana — *Musa balbisiana* perhaps — growing above the track, its conspicuous paddle-shaped leaves waving above the low herbage. *Hydrangea anomala* climbed its way up the trunks of many trees to heights of 50-60 ft. Unfortunately this too is rather tender in the British Isles where its place is taken by the hardier and more ornamental Japanese species *H. petiolaris*. Other climbers here included *Jasminum dispermum*, a twining jasmine with pinnate leaves and, in season, sweetly scented white flowers pink in bud, and *Embelia floribunda*, a member of a large, mainly tropical genus, with green glabrous stems and oblong, slender pointed leaves 3-3.5 in. long. The most conspicuous aspect of this powerful climber however was the small scarlet berry-like fruits which hung in large, dense, conical clusters often 2-3 ft long. Seeds of this magnificent plant have produced an abundant supply of plants, but one could only recommend it for a conservatory or, if outside, in a warm sheltered corner in the mildest areas of the British Isles.

Two *Clematis* species grew amongst the boulders, where their stems tumbled down the rockface. *C. buchananiana* bore pinnate leaves with three to five rounded, coarsely toothed leaflets, the whole plant covered with short soft hairs. The second species *C. grewiiflora*, unlike the other, was in full flower, the bell-shaped blooms 1-1.25 in. long, pale golden yellow in colour with tepals slightly recurved at the tips. These were carried in three to five flowered drooping clusters and looked most ornamental. The entire plant was clothed in a thick velvety pad of golden-brown hairs.

Clematis grewiiflora

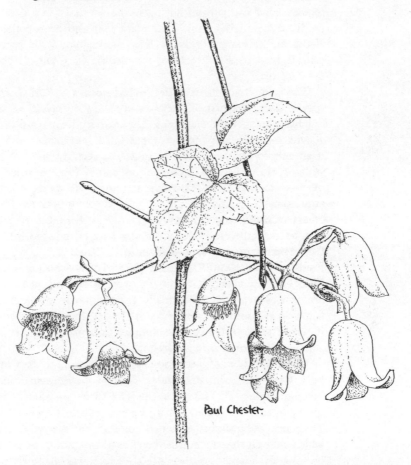

Paul Chester.

Debregeasia longifolia was a common shrub, a member of the mulberry family, but very different in general appearance from that well-known tree. It attained 10-15 ft in height with numerous long downy branches and lance-shaped, roughly hairy leaves 3.5-4.5 in. long, silvery-white beneath. Both male and female plants were present and the latter bore clusters of small bright orange fruits all along the second-year shoots. By far the most productive area, however, was a group of tall boulders covered in debris from the overhanging trees. Growing in the debris were three plants which caused a great deal of excitement. The first and most noticeable was *Vaccinium gaultheriifolium*, an evergreen shrub rather like a taller version of *V. glauco-album*. Its reddish-brown arching stems reached fully 9 ft and carried bold leathery leaves 4-5 in. long of a polished dark green above, vivid blue-white bloomy beneath. The shining black berries too were covered by a blue-white bloom and were gathered into dense bunches in the leaf axils and beneath the branches. It really was a striking species and I recognised it easily from having seen a specimen in a cool greenhouse in the Hillier Arboretum. That plant had also been collected in East Nepal in the early 1960s by Tom Spring-Smyth. It is worth trying outside in the milder parts of the British Isles, but is hopeless in the face of frost.

The other two plants were rhododendrons — *R. dalhousiae* and *R. vaccinioides*. The first of these we later saw on several occasions as an epiphyte on rocks and in trees. The leathery leaves, 4-5 in. long, were generally concentrated in the upper third of each stem, whilst the stem itself terminated in a large fat bud. The straggly habit of this species, which is also a feature in cultivation, can be forgiven when the clusters of two to six tubular flowers are borne in spring. Each flower is approximately 4 in. long and can vary in colour between forms, usually cream or white or occasionally lemon-yellow. Fragrance too varies and can be powerful and heady. It was first introduced into cultivation from Sikkim by Sir Joseph Hooker in 1849 and is named after Christine Ramsay, Countess of Dalhousie (1786-1839) who collected plants in India and elsewhere. It is usually seen in cultivation as a cool greenhouse subject, but is occasionally grown outside in the milder areas of the west and south-west of the British Isles. I have often wondered how it would fare, grown as an epiphyte, in some of the damp woodland gardens of Cornwall and SW Ireland.

When we found *R. vaccinioides*, both Beer and I first mistook it to be a *Vaccinium* with its slender, flexible, grey-brown stems and small box-like leaves. The stems reached 12-18 in. in length and were produced from a thickened tuber-like base which lay embedded in moss. The wiry young shoots were rust coloured and warty, whilst the leaves, which were clustered towards the ends of the shoots, measured 0.5-0.66 in. long, broadening towards the tip which was shallowly notched and possessed a small point. The leaf upper surface was dark green and shining, whilst the underside was paler and bore scattered glands. We found several clumps of this *Rhododendron* on these damp moss-covered rocks and later found it growing from the crotch of a tree. Although distinct and fascinating botanically, it is said to be of little ornamental merit, the flowers being rather small and insignificant.

Having exhausted the immediate area we decided to explore the hillside below the track, but before we could do so we were interrupted by the arrival of one of the porters to say that the rest of the party were still in Hongoan and preparing to stay the night. Annoyed by this we turned the porter round with instructions to go and tell Dawa that we intended moving on and that he must bring the porters down as quickly as possible. It was obvious to us that the Sherpas had been tempted to stay the night in Hongoan with promise of a party or some such celebration, but time was short – it was 20 November and although this area was interesting botanically, it was nevertheless warm temperate and no hardy plants would ensue. We were anxious to reach the Iswa Khola before winter set in and every delay meant lost time and less seed collected.

The next morning we set off down the track which here was well frequented by travellers and villagers. A small tree with stout shoots and large magnolia-like leathery leaves 12 in. long occurred in some quantity by the track. It was indeed a handsome tree for foliage effect and reminded me of a loquat – *Eriobotrya* sp. – but later proved to be *Saurauia napaulensis*.

We had not seen a maple for some time and so we were pleased to find *Acer oblongum*, several trees of 30-40 ft scattered along a gully below the track. The lance-shaped leaves 3-4 in. long were entirely without lobes or teeth and were dark glossy-green above, blue-white beneath. Emerging leaves were reddish-green or coppery, whilst those of strong sucker shoots were even more colourful and reached 6 in. in length. Although this maple was first introduced to cultivation from the Himalaya as long ago as 1824, it was not truly hardy and was eventually replaced in gardens by a hardier form collected by E. H. Wilson in W. China in 1901. Several trees of the latter may be found in collections in the south and west of the British Isles and it has proved a most handsome addition to the garden.

The only other tree to draw our attention that morning was *Alangium alpinum* which I mistook for a *Styrax*. It reached a height of 40 ft and had large rounded leaves 5-6 in. long, pointed, heart-shaped at base and covered with soft short hairs beneath.

Hatia lay basking in the sun when we arrived. It was surrounded by paddy fields which were now dry and only the stubble gave any hint of their recent use. Here we spent the rest of the day sorting out supplies, seed and notes whilst Morris and Dawa engaged new porters to replace those from the Wabak Khola and Thudam who now wished to return to their homes.

After a sleepless night during which Beer's yak tail had been snatched from his tent and carried off by a dog, we marched up a stony track out of the village. We were surprised to find two familiar British plants growing amongst the stones. These were *Plantago major*, the broad-leaved plantain, and *Polygonum hydropiper*, the water pepper. The pink cherry – *Prunus cerasoides* – was still everywhere apparent and looked decidedly out of place amongst the surrounding 'sub-tropical' vegetation.

Hatia

All day we toiled in the heat up the steep hillside until at approximately 7,000 ft we stopped to rest beneath a huge rock. Beer and I climbed up the obstacle to examine the vegetation growing in the moss on its summit and were delighted to discover several epiphytic shrubs. *Rhododendron dalhousiae*, *Agapetes serpens* and *Vaccinium dunalianum* were present but were dwarfed by five small trees of *Acer sikkimense*, a most unusual and attractive maple. Their stems reached 15-18 ft, strong, stout and green. The magnificent leaves 4-6 in. long — larger on sucker shoots — were ovate with a heart-shaped base and an abrupt point. In colour they were glossy dark-green above, paler and matt beneath, their margins shallowly and distantly toothed. Both surfaces were smooth except for minute tufts of chocolate-coloured hairs in the axils of the veins beneath. Young leaves were a delightful coppery-red when unfolding, whilst the leaves of two trees had already turned to orange and red prior to falling. I suspect that this species is closely related to *A. hookeri* and both have been and still are cultivated in cool greenhouses or outside in the milder areas of the British Isles, but always in the ground, and it might be worth experimenting with them epiphytically where conditions are suitable.

136

Late in the afternoon we entered virgin forest and forsook the sun-drenched world outside for one of darkness and gloom. Huge trees soared towards the sky including *Acer campbellii* and *Quercus lamellosa*, and beneath them several species of *Araliaceae* of which a *Schefflera* was the most common. Their stems were clothed with a variety of creepers, amongst which *Hedera nepalensis*, *Hydrangea anomala*, *Euonymus echinatus* and *Celastrus stylosus* were prominent. *Daphne bholua*, an evergreen form, was plentiful in the undergrowth, its white flowers already well open and scenting the air around. We also spotted another *Acer sikkimense* approximately 35 ft tall growing in the crotch of a tree some 30 ft above the ground, its leaves turning to yellow.

We slept around the fire that night, and I lay in my sleeping-bag watching the forest trees in the glow of the fire, their stems tall and stout like columns in a cathedral nave. Their dense canopies formed a roof above our heads except for one gaping hole through which I could see the stars in the night sky. Early in the morning we heard a loud shriek and on investigating, Dawa told us that a porter had been bitten by a demon. We had to wait until light to investigate the incident and when the porter was brought to us for treatment he dropped his shorts and showed us a large red mark on his behind. The demon, he explained, had struck him as he was about to relieve himself, upon which he had panicked and rushed back to camp fearful of his life. We asked him to take us to the scene of the crime and he led us out of camp through the vegetation to a point some 10-15 yds away and there was the demon — or rather demons — because there were lots of them — nettles! But these were no ordinary nettles; they were 10-15 ft high with stout stems and large lobed leaves clothed with stinging hairs. It was *Girardinia diversifolia* — or giant nettle — and I remembered an incident in my student days at the University Botanic Garden, Cambridge, when a colleague of mine was watering a batch of plants in pots, one of which was a young *Girardinia*. He accidentally brushed against this plant and let out a yell at the same time dropping his can. For at least a week the hand was swollen and painful and although he may have been especially allergic to stings the incident left me with a healthy respect for the *Girardinia*'s reputation. The porter suffered considerable discomfort for several days after and always stood at mealtimes.

Halfway through the morning and still in the dark forest, we heard a noise somewhere along the track ahead of us. Birds were fleeing the disturbance, and as the noise was getting louder and was heading in our direction we stopped, slightly apprehensive, wondering if some animal was the cause. The crashing and clattering of bamboo was unmistakable and we braced ourselves for a surprise, taking the precaution of stepping off the track into the undergrowth. Suddenly from out of the thicket ahead burst several men trotting in single file each hauling a bundle of green bamboo. The canes measured 10-12 ft in length and 0.75-1 in.

*Girardinia
diversifolia*

thick and were packed 80-100 per bundle. The weight of the smallest
bundle was as much as I could lift let alone carry and I could only stare
in amazement. The men had cut the canes from thickets on the ridge
and were taking them down to Hatia where they would be used to repair
roofs and fences. The bundles were tightly bound with rope, and all the
weight was laid on one end only. After a brief exchange of news the
bamboo men continued on their way singing as they ran, the bamboos
clattering against the trees and over roots and stones in their wake.
Later we heard another group somewhere in the forest, their calls

138

echoing through the trees.

We reached the bamboo thickets and I wandered alone for some way along the ridge and settled down between the canes closing my eyes so that I might hear the gentle clicking of the canes and the soft urgent whispering of their myriad leaves. A new porter had arrived from Hatia to guide us along a track which, to his knowledge, had not been used for several years. As one would expect, the track was, in parts at least, long overgrown and without our guide would have been invisible to our eyes.

The thicket produced several shrubs which kept up our interest. A beautiful bramble – *Rubus lineatus* – was particularly plentiful, its arching, silvery-silky shoots, 6-8 ft high, carrying leaves 4-6 in. long made up of several slender leaflets, green and parallel-veined above, silvery-silky below. This is a desirable shrub but unfortunately of borderline hardiness in the British Isles where it is generally represented in collections in the milder areas. A well-established plant suckers freely in a sheltered border in the Hillier Arboretum but is cut to the ground in a hard winter. In the same thicket we found a single tree of *Ilex sikkimensis*, a handsome holly 15 ft high with smooth pale greyish-brown stems and bold evergreen leaves 4-5 in. long, sharply toothed along the margin. Later on, the silver-backed *Rhododendron arboreum* appeared and beneath its canopy our track descended between clumps of *Viburnum grandiflorum* and *Berberis insignis* to the bottom of a narrow valley. Here in the shelter of the steep hills, oaks and maples flourished, and I was particularly impressed with an *Acer campbellii* which must have been all of 100 ft with a huge trunk straight as a gun-barrel supporting a beautiful autumn canopy of golden leaves. Both *Hydrangea anomala* and *Euonymus echinatus* climbed up many of these trees and nearby rocks. The latter, a charming evergreen spindle, resembled somewhat the Japanese *E. fortunei* var. *radicans* which is so common in cultivation, but the two are easily separated when in fruit, those of the Japanese plant having smooth capsules, whilst those of the present species had capsules covered with tiny points or prickles, hence the name *echinatus* (with prickles, like a hedgehog). *E. echinatus* is rarely seen in cultivation, possibly because of its somewhat tender nature, although it grows in a border in the Hillier Aboretum without, however, showing any inclination to flourish.

Our camp was surrounded by bamboo mainly, although a few trees came to the water's edge including *Lindera assamica*, a small tree of 15-18 ft bearing glaucous-backed deep-green leaves, 4-6 in. long and small axillary clusters of greenish-white flowers. It is a member of a large family, most members of which are unfortunately too tender for cultivation out of doors in the British Isles.

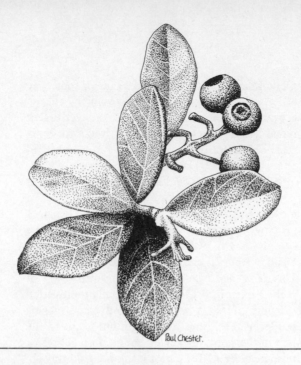

Vaccinium
sikkimense

Paul Chester.

11 THE MAKALU TRAIL

Next morning we crossed the torrent by way of a hastily constructed bundle of branches which moved about beneath our weight. Once across we began the long haul up the thickly wooded side of the ravine which in places was vertical, entailing ropes and persuasion and a fair amount of swearing. The most difficult stretches occurred in bamboo thickets where projecting spikes of broken canes made our passage doubly hazardous. So dense was the undergrowth and so totally consuming our progress that we had climbed 1,000 feet before we were able to examine the trees around, and then only because we found ourselves in a small clearing on a gentle slope. Here grew several trees 60 ft high of *Magnolia campbellii* whose fruiting spikes we collected from the leaves at our feet. Here too we found the sycamore-like *Acer sterculiaceum* which we had first encountered on the Milke Danda. It reached heights of 50-60 ft here, its branches carrying large drooping bunches of shortly hairy fruits with parallel wings 1.5 in. long. Large bushes of the evergreen *Mahonia napaulensis* now appeared, standing 6-8 ft tall with ruffs of bold pinnate leaves 12-18 in. long, each composed of 17-19 spine-toothed oblong leaves 1-2 in. long and glossy-green above. Authorities at the British Museum (Natural History) have since suggested that this plant is related more to *M. borealis* than to *M. napaulensis*.

Eventually we attained the ridge at a height of 9,500 ft, having climbed 2,000 ft above the torrent. A track now led along the ridge

140

climbing gently through the trees, several of which we had encountered before, including *Sorbus cuspidata*, *Populus jacquemontiana* var. *glauca*, *Acer pectinatum* and *Betula utilis*. The evergreen *Pieris formosa* appeared, some bushes up to 25 ft in height, creating what must be a wonderful spectacle in spring when the white flower clusters drape the branches. Both *Rhododendron barbatum* and the buff-backed *R. arboreum* now formed thickets, and in the leaf mould beneath these crept a dwarf evergreen spindleberry — *Euonymus vagans*. Here it reached 12 in. in height though we found it again later up to 4 ft. The slender green four-angled stems bore pairs of narrow, long-pointed leaves 2.5-3.5 in. long x 0.75 in. across, the margins shallowly toothed and wavy. They were a dark glossy-green above, paler beneath and quite smooth. They carried a few fruits singly on slender drooping stalks, the pink capsules opening to reveal orange-coated seeds. The conspicuous buds were purple and up to 0.5 in. long. This struck me as being a delightful creeping shrub, quite different in looks to others I have seen of a similar nature and yet, as far as I am aware, it is not in cultivation and unfortunately, of those seeds we managed to collect I have heard no more.

The track soon left the ridge and continued along the slope at just below the 10,000 ft contour. We passed a large rock-face down which water trickled and were delighted to see here the Himalayan maidenhair fern *Adiantum venustum* with its delicate fronds flowing in green waves over the wet rock surface. Here too were *Primula glomerata* and *P. bracteosa*, the latter with pale mauve yellow-eyed primrose flowers protruding from tufts of slightly powdered, toothed leaves. In the crotch of a tree 6 ft above the ground we found a plant which I am convinced was *Dianella ensifolia*, although, according to the Nepal Enumeration, this plant has not been recorded from Nepal, though, in his *Flora of British India*, Hooker gives its distribution as Nepal eastwards. Our plant had tufts of grass-like dark-green leaves 9-12 in. long from out of which arose an 18 in. arching stem bearing towards its summit a cluster of deep blue berries. The fruits and a specimen were collected but neither have been heard of since.

Following close on the heels of the last, we discovered another plant which I have since had cause to ponder upon. It was a tree of some 60 ft with slightly downswept branches, the slender branchlets bearing what appeared to be ranks of long slender drooping catkins of seed. Most of the leaves had already fallen and we were able to retrieve a good number for examination. These were ovate to elliptic, 4-5 in. long and rather leathery in texture. They were pointed and possessed an obliquely rounded or straight base with sharply toothed margins, the main veins emanating fan-like from the base. I have reason to believe this tree to have been the monotypic *Tetracentron sinense*, with which I am quite familiar from cultivated specimens in the Hillier Arboretum and especially in the wood at Caerhayes, Cornwall. All those in

141

cultivation, however, are of Chinese origin, having been introduced by E. H. Wilson when collecting for the nurseryman Veitch in 1901. In his book *A Naturalist in Western China* Wilson makes several references to this tree where he remarks on its often large size, trees of 60-70 ft being not uncommon, and to its thin and characteristic leafage. The first record of *Tetracentron* from East Nepal was made by the Japanese in the early 1960s and later by L. H. J. Williams in 1969. According to Professor Hara of the University of Tokyo, the Nepal tree belongs to a western race, differing in the generally larger leaves, abruptly pointed and with smaller more pointed teeth.

Our track continued along the slope for most of the day before veering rapidly downwards to the Barun Khola. Here we found the Sherpas had made camp in a bamboo thicket. Bamboos are ornamental and most acceptable in a garden, where they can be looked at and admired from a distance but after several days of toiling through vast thickets in the wild, I was beginning to change my mind about their attributes. Where a track has been cut through bamboo, the severed canes can gash legs and arms, and pointing, as they do, in all directions, they are a constant danger to one's face, especially the eyes. Pieces of bamboo lying on the ground, particularly when covered by dead leaves, caused us to slip or trip. Bamboo thickets are hot and dusty on sunny days, and a track, unless it is broad and straight, soon becomes obscured. On the other side of the coin the catalogue of useful attributes of the bamboo is endless. During our travels in Nepal we had seen it used for bridges, supports of many kinds, houses, shelters and other structures, baskets, trays, containers, head bands for carrying, ropes, fences, tree guards, whistles, flutes, mats, cow muzzles, flagpoles, utensil handles, water carriers, drainpipes, churns, stakes, packing material, wrappers, cigarette holders, swings, pea-shooters, bows and arrows and other things. Nevertheless, I found myself cursing the bamboo all night as I was bitten all over by crab lice, one in particular on the inside of my arm caused me a lot of pain. We were thankful, therefore, the next morning to be up and away from this cursed place, our trail following the river over boulders and rocks, occasionally climbing the steep bank where waterfalls made direct progress impossible. The day gave us sunshine all morning deteriorating to mist and drizzle in the afternoon, by which time we cleared the forest.

A last search amongst the trees revealed a wealth of interesting plants including large clumps of *Vaccinium nummularia* hanging from mossy trunks and boulders. Two trees in particular caught our eyes, one of which we recognised as a hazel. There were several specimens, similar to our native species – *Corylus avellana* – in habit with several grey-barked main stems 30-35 ft tall with parallel-veined, elliptic to obovate leaves 4-5 in. long which were smooth above, downy beneath. Several trees had their branches draped with bunches of pretty pink catkins 1.5-2.5 in. long adding a warm tinge to the now decidedly wintry scene above. It proved to be *Corylus ferox*. Rooting about in the fallen leaves we found a few old fruiting clusters covered in short branched spines, hence the name *ferox* (ferocious, spiny). This unusual species is rare, if at all, in British cultivation but has been re-introduced more recently by A. Schilling, amongst others.

Near the hazel we found a small multi-stemmed tree with stout pithy branches up to 15-20 ft. These carried large alternately arranged leaves over 12 in. across, borne on 10-15 in. stalks. The leaf blade varied from entire to three lobed, each lobe rounded, slender-pointed and finely downy all over, more so on the underside where it was more or less mealy. Some leaves had turned an attractive bronze-purple. The tree, which has since been named as *Toricellia tiliifolia*, was in fruit with large drooping terminal clusters of black berries, rather like elderberries, the juice of which left dark stains on our hands. It was a handsome if unusual tree related to *Cornus* and as far as I am aware is not in cultivation in the British Isles.

At one point during the morning we walked through a grove of a Himalayan whitebeam which, in its broad, almost rounded leaves 6-10 in. long, put me in mind of the tree in cultivation known by the name *Sorbus* 'Mitchellii'. This handsome tree originated at Westonbirt and is now considered to be a clone of *S. thibetica*. Strangely enough, a specimen collected by Beer above Sedua on a later trip in 1975 has since been assigned to this species by the *Sorbus* authority Eleonora Gabrielian, and I am tempted to believe that the trees in the Barun Valley also belonged here. It was certainly an invigorating experience walking beneath these trees which reached 40-50 ft in height and had littered the ground with their bold leaves; brown or occasionally still green above, greyish-white beneath, creating a bi-coloured carpet of exceptional beauty.

On returning to the river, we found our way blocked by a sheer-sided gorge through which there was no possible access. We turned about-face to climb the hillside again but before doing so stopped to examine two more trees which spread their branches above the water. The first of these, *Litsea confertiflora*, had all but dropped its leathery leaves and our attempts to climb it only succeeded in dislodging the remainder which fell to the river and were carried away like sampans. A few however settled on the bank and we were able to retrieve them for examination. They were quite handsome, measuring 4-5 in. with three to five main veins arising from the base. The upper surface was a dark-green and glossy, the lower surface pale or blue-green and softly hairy. The tree itself had an attractive grey-born flaking bark and stout hairy twigs with conspicuous chestnut-brown buds. More intriguing was a neighbouring tree some 15-20 ft in height with a spreading head of branches. The young shoots were a deep red, whilst the leaves, mostly fallen, were elliptic to oblong-elliptic, 5-6 in. long, slender-pointed with a rounded base. They were green and smooth above, greyish-green below and had a bold curving venation. Small dark-blue fruits were carried in flattened heads. From this seed, we germinated in the Hillier Arboretum plants of a seemingly different character, with ornamental deep-red shoots with dark-coloured buds and large attractive leaves. These seedlings, which have yet to flower, look more like a typical dogwood and appear very similar to the Chinese *C. hemsleyi*. They have also proved somewhat tender, which has been our experience with the last-named species. It seems extraordinary therefore that the specimens we collected are considered by the authorities to be *Cornus macrophylla*, and I await with interest the further development of these plants.

Ilex intricata

Paul Chester.

At approximately 10,500 ft there was hoar frost in a gully and the air became colder as the sun was swallowed up by cloud. *Rhododendron hodgsonii* appeared, the intervening spaces being occupied by large bold clumps of the bamboo *Arundinaria spathiflora*. The dwarf, box-leaved holly — *Ilex intricata* — formed an understorey, sharing the debris beneath the rhododendrons with *Euonymus vagans*. We were surprised to renew our acquaintance with *Rhododendron camelliiflorum*, a small bush of which we found growing 10 ft up in the crotch of a hemlock — *Tsuga dumosa*.

On rounding a corner of the hillside we saw groups of a large yellow daisy-flowered perennial growing by a stream. It was *Inula hookeri*, its erect downy stems 3-4 ft tall clothed with narrow leaves 5-6 in. long. The flowerheads measured 2-3 in. across and bore conspicuous narrow strap-shaped marginal florets which in turn were surrounded by dense, crowded and recurved downy bracts. With the *Inula* grew a shrubby honeysuckle — *Lonicera hispida* — a bush 5-6 ft high with ovate, hairy leaves 1-2 in. long and ovoid berries 0.25 in. long, black with a blue-white bloom. Growing on the slope above the track Beer came upon a small plant of *Daphne bholua* whose leaves were splashed with yellow and pale-green, rather like those of the popular cultivated holly *Ilex* x *altaclarensis* 'Lawsoniana'. We could only imagine what a winner this might have been in cultivation.

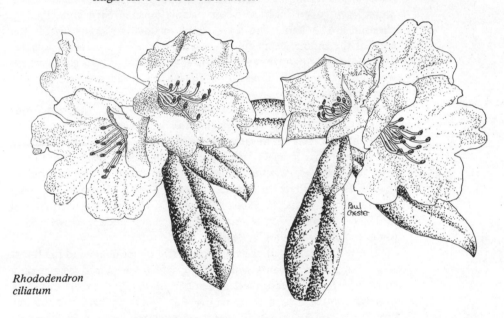

Rhododendron ciliatum

The porters had all this time followed in our wake and were still behind us when we descended to the river to take a closer look at a low evergreen shrub which covered a wide area, crowding its way between boulders on both sides of the river. It was *Gaultheria semi-infera*, and as most plants were fruiting we called up the porters to help us gather in the harvest. Morris, Beer and I produced cotton bags in which to collect the fruits which were of a striking China-blue colour. In no time at all we had filled our bags and eager for a large haul we stopped to check how the porters were progressing. To our consternation we found that they were picking the fruits faster than we and popping them straight into their mouths. We called Dawa over asking him to explain what it was we wanted, and on being told they looked mystified,

145

retorting that they thought we were collecting the fruits to eat later. Continuing our harvest we filled four more bags before calling it a day and moving on. We headed for a gully down which a stream flowed and found the whole area covered with a mixture of two dwarf rhododendrons — *R. ciliatum* and *R. glaucophyllum*. Both species we had already seen on the Milke Danda but these had been isolated individuals, whilst before us in the gully stretched a continuous low cover of the two intermixed. *R. ciliatum* formed dense spreading bushes up to 2 ft high, the stems and branches with peeling bark. The elliptic leaves 2-3.5 in. long were glossy-green and hairy above, the margins fringed with long hairs, hence the name. Some bushes had occasional early flowers which were bell-shaped 1.5-2 in. long and white with a faint pink flush. *R. glaucophyllum* on the other hand, although of similar height, was a more leggy, open bush with wiry stems covered in a thin, flaking, chestnut-brown bark. The leaves were mainly clustered towards the ends of the shoots, being elliptic to narrowly so, 1-2 in. long, pointed, dark glossy-green above, white beneath and speckled with glands which were aromatic when rubbed. Even the young shoots and fruit clusters were glandular scaly.

During the rest of that day we encountered both rhododendrons often growing in large colonies together with *Gaultheria semi-infera*, either by the river or in lateral gullies. Nearly always they inhabited wet places either in shade or on north-facing slopes. Seed of both was introduced and *R. ciliatum* is represented in several collections including the Hillier Arboretum, where, however, its early flowering is usually frustrated by frosts. *R. glaucophyllum* was also well distributed and in 1977 a plant in flower was exhibited at the Chelsea Flower Show under the clonal name 'Len Beer'.

The whole stretch of riverside for a mile or more beyond the forest was a paradise for plants which, being late in the year, were mainly shrubs in fruit. I recognised a number of familiar 'faces' including *Deutzia compacta* with its attractive flaking brown bark and the low growing *Coriaria terminalis* var. *xanthocarpa* bearing its terminal cylindrical spikes of amber-yellow fruits containing black seeds. Eventually the mist, which had been gathering strength for several hours, made plant hunting impossible and we were pleased therefore to find that camp had been established on a flat piece of ground above the river.

Although Makalu (27,807 ft) was some way up the valley, out of sight of our camp, it was not our intention to continue in its direction. Snow had already fallen on the higher slopes above the valley and if we were to attempt to gain access to the Iswa Khola then we would need to leave the Barun as quickly as possible.

The way out of the Barun lay via the so-called Makalu Trail, a track by which climbers reached the mountain from the Arun Valley by way of Sedua and the Kasuwa Khola. This track ran along the opposite flank of the river and for the best part of the afternoon Dawa and the others had been looking for a way across by a bridge which our Hatia guide had assured us we would find. It was to locate the bridge that we sent Da Norbu and Namgyal next morning and in their absence we searched the hillside above our camp. The sun was out early and conditions were pleasant if a little cold. There were many *Rhododendron* species present forming thickets and bold groups. *R. campanulatum*, *R. campylocarpum* and *R. hodgsonii* often growing together, with *R. lepidotum* and *R. anthopogon* forming dense low ground cover. By far the most dominant species however was *R. barbatum*, including an unusual form with leaves a distinct sea-green above. Specimens of this plant were later considered by one authority to be nearer the species *R. imberbe* which, however, appears to be no more than a hairless form of *R. barbatum*. *R. ciliatum* continued to inhabit the damp hollows which, in some instances, were little more than bogs, and it suggested to me that moisture must be an important factor in the successful cultivation of this species. In another area *R. cinnabarinum* and *R. thomsonii* occurred, the latter forming mixed stands with *R. barbatum*. We even found a lone bush of *R. lepidotum* bearing umbels of purple flowers 0.75 in. across.

We returned to camp along the river, a route which proved lucky because on one area of stony bank we found three species of *Gaultheria* and a *Vaccinium*. *G. trichophylla* we had seen previously at Topke Gola and elsewhere, whilst *G. semi-infera* was everywhere around. *G. pyroloides* we had also seen below Topke Gola, but *Vaccinium sikkimense* was quite new to us. This shrub here formed a low mound 6-9 in. in height with roughly hairy shoots bearing several extra large, conspicuous, red-pointed buds in the upper leaf axils. The leaves themselves were obovate to elliptic-obovate 1.5-2 in. long, rounded and with a short sharp point, narrowing gradually to the base. The margins were sharply toothed especially towards the apex and there were hairs on the midrib beneath, otherwise quite smooth and green.

We followed the Makalu Trail as it wound its way up the hillside away from the threshing and noisome waters of the Barun. Soon we were walking through a dense forest of hemlock and silver fir where birch and maple made tentative intrusions. Rhododendrons again formed thickets between the trees, whilst creeping gaultherias and primulas coated the banks by the track. Walking through the giant trees was a dreamlike experience after the bamboo nightmare of Hatia and the cold damp valley of the Barun Khola. The sun occupied the sky sending great arms of light and warmth down through the canopy, illuminating the numerous clearings like stages in a darkened theatre.

Two Himalayan tree creepers appeared on several occasions, playing hide-and-seek amongst the trees, moving jerkily over the bark like slender brown and white mice. The higher we climbed the colder it became and the first stray patches of snow gradually united until the slopes above were completely white. Where the track passed through *Rhododendron* thicket it was easy to follow. At 13,000 ft the dominant rhododendrons were *R. wightii* and *R. fulgens*, and through many fine stands of these a broad passageway had been cleared. Once the track left these areas, however, conditions became more difficult and, although we knew roughly where the pass lay, the snow on the track and in our eyes made progress slow and separated the party several times, each occasion necessitating a halt and roll-call.

We tramped upwards, our feet catching in the dense tangled growth of *Rhododendron anthopogon*, hidden beneath the snow. The slope steepened appreciably and soon, every few steps were followed by a slide, and to cap it all the mist descended, making further progress virtually impossible. The track appeared barely discernible but we followed its erratic course all the way to the pass where a chorten marked the summit at 14,600 ft. On crossing the pass we were relieved to see the track continuing down the other side clear of snow, and a few hundred feet below we made our camp by a frozen lake. The porters trailed in for some time, carrying loads of dry wood on their packs and set to making their fires. That night was the coldest we had experienced and for the first and only time I wore my sweater in my sleeping-bag.

After supper we sat round the fire discussing what to do. It was obvious that we would not now be able to enter the Iswa Valley. The delaying tactics of the porters in the Arun Valley were borne of a natural reluctance on their part to enter a high valley which, at the best of times, was difficult to get to and would now be fraught with problems. Those Sherpas who had accompanied Beer on his reconnaissance were even more aware of the risks and their response to the plan was, not surprisingly, lukewarm. We were all three bitterly disappointed, especially Beer, who had been to the Iswa, but all agreed that, time and weather being against us, the most sensible plan was for Beer to push on to Sedua and there begin the final seed cleaning and drying, whilst Morris and I followed at a more leisurely pace collecting whatever seed we could. Next morning, after Beer and Namgyal had left, Morris and I climbed back to the pass and continued up the hillside to the ridge, where we were presented with a magnificent view of the Iswa Valley. Most of its length was bathed in sunshine, but this did little to detract from the menace of the place. In parts it was a steep-sided gorge and innumerable hanging glaciers stood seemingly poised to fall. Beer had described to us the awful desolation he had found in the upper reaches where ice, snow and rock combined to form the most bizarre effects. Progress had been painfully slow, and having reached the terminal glacier, he had then to make a hurried exit when one of his porters fell seriously ill. Yet, despite the undoubted difficulties he had encountered, Beer had discovered many rare plants, several of which are as yet unnamed and probably new to science including two yellow-flowered species of *Saxifraga*. Amongst the more exciting plants collected as specimens by Beer in the Iswa, the following give an idea of the floral riches to be found there.

Gentiana elwesii with trumpet-shaped blue flowers, white at the base; *Meconopsis bella*, a delicate plant with large blue flowers, growing in crevices, sometimes from the roofs of over-hanging rocks; *Aconitum orochryseum*, with creamy-yellow helmeted flowers; *Androsace lehmanii* and *A. globifera*, both forming large hummocks of tightly packed rosettes.

Our party left the campsite around mid-morning and, having skirted the frozen lake, began the long haul up the opposite slope. We took a different route from the one used by Beer and Namgyal, whose footprints we could trace very clearly in the snow. We reached the summit of the col at 14,400 ft where our lama added a piece of white cloth to the prayer flags fluttering from canes on the chorten. We dropped down the south slope to a ridge track and with mist gathering the conditions were fast deteriorating. We moved along the ridge at a brisk rate, stopping only once to examine a tiny plant growing in tufts by the side of the track. It reminded me of a narrow-leaved stonecrop — *Sedum* sp. — with wiry woody stems 1-3 in. high. In the event it proved to be *Diplarche multiflora*, a member of the heather family — *Ericaceae*. Another member of this family grew with it and it was only when we crouched to look at the *Diplarche* that we noticed the miniature *Rhododendron pumilum*, a gem of a species with slender branches prostrate or ascending to 3 in. carrying elliptic, pointed leaves 0.5-1 in. long. These were a shining bronze-green above, pale green and speckled with brown scales below. Indeed the whole plant was speckled with scales including the slender seed capsules borne singly or up to three in a cluster from the shoot tips. This is a charming shrublet with pink or rose bell-shaped flowers, but it is rarely met with in cultivation where it demands a high degree of skill and not a little bit of luck. Its growths are repeatedly damaged by frosts which, of course, would not normally happen in the wild where they are protected by the snow.

Whilst we were examining these plants, our porters had gone on ahead and on resuming our walk we discovered two sets of tracks in the snow. We followed what appeared to be the most popular route, to find after half-an-hour that it veered steeply downhill and on the wrong side of the ridge. Then we found tracks going straight up the hill back towards the ridge and we guessed rightly that some of our porters had missed their way. For two miles we plodded through snow, occasionally floundering, climbing to our feet and plodding on until at last we broke through to the crest of the ridge again and refound the Makalu Trail.

Shortly afterwards, the track left the ridge and plunged steeply down the slope, this time on the correct side, cutting its way through dense thickets of rhododendron in similar mixture to those we had seen in the Barun Valley. Gradually we left the mist and snow behind and progress became easier and more leisurely. The dwarf box-leaved holly — *Ilex intricata* — was very common here as a ground cover but gave way lower down the slope to another evergreen shrub 3-5 ft high with spreading or shortly ascending branches crowded with obovate to oblanceolate, sharply toothed and abruptly pointed leaves 3.5-4.5 in. long, polished dark-green above, paler beneath. Small flower buds were present, borne singly or in pairs in the leaf axils. Specimens of this shrub have been identified at the British Museum as *Eurya cavinervis*, which constitutes a new record for Nepal although it has long been known in nearby Sikkim.

The site of our evening camp was still some way off and as the light was beginning to fade we broke into a jog. It is amazing that one of us did not at least sprain an ankle as we descended the steep track through thicket and boulders. We entered the forest at a run, catching up with the tail-end of our porters as they entered camp, which was situated within a large natural cave at the base of a gigantic rock wall.

Our arrival was the signal for Pema to start cooking, and whilst waiting for supper we entered our notes by the light of the fire, darkness having already descended. Later, fully satisfied, we lay back in our sleeping bags listening to the Sherpas singing and watching the fires glow. At one point we saw a sizeable creature gliding across the mouth of the cave to land with a crash in the hanging branches of a nearby tree. It then scrambled up into the dense heart of the tree. We saw no more of it and concluded that it must have been a flying squirrel.

Next morning, the mouth of the cave was alive with people moving about in all directions, calling and chattering, to which was added the gurgle of water boiling in pots and the spiralling smoke of several rekindled fires. Outside in the forest, shafts of sunlight pierced the branches of a giant magnolia tree and somewhere close to hand a bird made wolf-whistles until it changed to an equally monotonous single note version. The rock was higher than I had imagined, its damp face masked by green and brown moss and partially concealed by the long roots of trees and creepers which hung like a veil of dark string.

I wandered down through the forest on my own, enjoying the changing vegetation and what Farrer once called 'the sweet rotting smell of autumn', except that autumn here was later — it was the end of November. We were still in the cool temperate zone, just about, and with my eyes I drank in the plants which would, all too soon, be replaced by others from the warmer valleys. Many of the trees and shrubs we had seen before including *Helwingia himalaica*, *Taxus wallichiana*, *Ilex dipyrena* and *Hydrangea robusta* with its rounded leaves big as frying pans. *Lyonia ovalifolia* was common, its leaves apparently varying in size depending on altitude. The lower the altitude the larger the leaf. Indeed I had several times mistaken these latter trees for magnolias.

Campbell's maple — *Acer campbellii* — reached a great size, resembling an English elm in its branching and autumn colour. It is a pity that this tree is too tender for the majority of the British Isles. Into several of these trees two by now familiar plants climbed — *Hydrangea anomala* and *Euonymus echinatus*, both of which ascended to heights of 50-60 ft. *Rhododendron vaccinioides* appeared 7 ft up on the moss covered branch of a maple. Any doubts we may have had as to its identity were now cleared by the evidence of small curved seed capsules 1-1.25 in. long borne singly on a slender stalk from the tip of each shoot.

Several large whitebeams came into the picture, one specimen at least 70 ft high with a correspondingly large girth. As far as I could tell by the fallen leaves, it was similar to those we had seen in the Barun Valley and in retrospect this may well have been the *Sorbus thibetica* collected 'above Sedua' by Beer when he again visited this region in 1975.

Gradually the vegetation began to change and the *Viburnum grandiflorum* which had accompanied me downhill most of the morning now handed over to *V. erubescens*. Clearings appeared where large trees had been drastically pollarded for firewood. These included *Actinodaphne reticulata*, a member of the bay family.

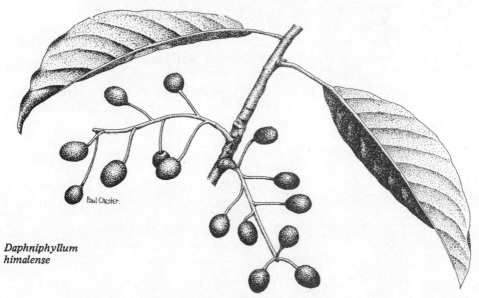

*Daphniphyllum
himalense*

Walking through open grassy areas between groves of trees I encountered a magnificent evergreen with tall straight stems occasionally up to

70 ft in height. It was *Daphniphyllum himalense*, a member of the spurge family — *Euphorbiaceae* — and its stout green shoots carried large elliptic leaves 10-12 in. long, even longer on vigorous shoots. These were a dark glossy-green above, blue-green beneath with reddish veins and stalk. The flowers of this tree are dioecious, i.e. male and female on separate trees, and I saw a good number of female trees carrying their drooping clusters of purplish-black, plum-like fruits 0.66 in. long each containing a single stone-like seed 0.5 in. long. Seedlings raised and planted out of doors in the Hillier Arboretum sadly perished in the first cold winter.

I saw *Rhododendron dalhousiae* again several times, either on boulders or sprouting from the tops of dead tree stumps, whilst in the undergrowth an unusual shrub — *Dichroa febrifuga* — became dominant. Its erect stems to 5-6 ft carried pairs of elliptic, sharply toothed leaves 5-6 in. long and terminal as well as axillary heads of blue fruits. It is related to *Hydrangea* and is a very important medicinal plant particularly useful in reducing fevers especially in malaria. It enjoys a tremendous distribution in the wild, ranging from Nepal to Taiwan and Malaysia.

At approximately 7,000 ft the track skirted a gully crowded with trees supporting an abundance of epiphytes, mainly ferns and orchids. Amongst the latter I was delighted to find *Pleione praecox*, a single clump in full flower, its fig-shaped green mottled-purple pseudobulbs embedded in deep moss on a branch. The flowers, each 2 in. long, were pale-purple except for the base of the tube which was white. The inner surface of the lacerated tip was yellow, with five raised toothed ribs. The 1 in. long ovary curved like a swan's neck and each flower was borne on a 2 in.-long stalk which was green mottled-purple. A green capsule with six prominent ribs was also present.

I emerged from the gully feeling elated and as I rejoined the track met Da Norbu and together we strode down the hill into the village of Sedua.

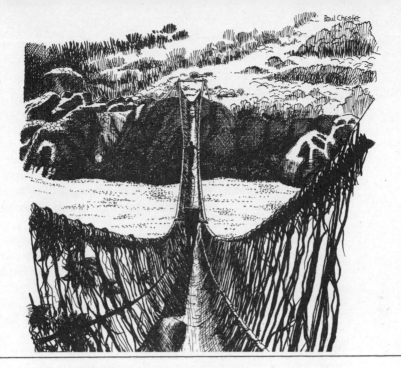

12

THE BRIDGE AT NUM

For two of the Sherpas — Dorje and Tende — Sedua was home and both their families turned out to greet us, leading us excitedly through the village to Tende's house where, sitting outside in the sun surrounded by an ocean of seed, we found Deei. That night we had a party in the open space between several houses, to which the families and friends of Tende and Dorje were invited, but which, in the event, proved a free-for-all with most of the village turning up.

The activities increased as the night wore on and I lost count of the dances I took part in and the glasses of chang I drank. I cannot even remember at what time I staggered to my tent, but I do know that the village throng continued to make merry, singing and dancing into the early hours of the morning, and when they finally drifted home they were replaced by dogs whose incessant howling and barking prevented sleep.

In a gully above the village, I made some last minute collections, including a climbing rose with powerful prickle-clad stems and leaves composed of five to seven elliptic, abruptly pointed leaflets of a characteristic polished green. On the fruiting branches leaves were trifoliolate. The hips were ellipsoid, just over 0.5 in. long, and russet red in colour, carried in loose clusters along the arching older stems. Plants germinated from this seed have proved vigorous in cultivation, but in Hampshire at least, unfortunately subject to frost damage. However, such is its habit and leaf characters that I strongly suspect it to be *Rosa longicuspis* with which I am familiar in cultivation; only time will tell. Should it prove to be the above species it will constitute a new record for Nepal. I found a plant of *Agapetes serpens* with green-washed white flowers, a pleasant contrast to the normally red veined ones growing as an epiphyte in a moss-covered tree. I did not collect this plant but two years later a similar form was collected by Harry van de Laar of Boskoop during a spring trek I led to the Milke Banjgang. This plant has been distributed in cultivation, rooting easily from cuttings, and is to be found in the temperate houses of Kew and Wisley and other places under the cultivar name 'Nepal Cream'.

A common tree in the gullies is *Alnus nepalensis*, the Nepalese alder. It follows rivers and streams for several thousand feet into the hills, in places forming a tall tree 60-70 ft high with grey bark and greyish-green, downy, angled shoots with stalked buds. The leaves are elliptic to ovate-elliptic, 5-7 in. long with a short slender point and a rounded base. They are obscurely toothed and in colour are glossy-green and smooth above, pale greyish-green and downy beneath, borne on downy stalks 0.5-0.75 in. long. The young leaves are a pretty bronze or coppery green. Although this is an autumn-flowering species, the long drooping male catkins had long since fallen. This is a tender tree in cultivation in the British Isles.

Dorje's Father
at Sedua

154

Back in Chepua, one of our Thudam porters had sold Morris, Beer and me each a pair of home-made boots, or rather the colourful woven uppers. On reaching Sedua, Da Norbu arranged to have the bottoms made and sewn on and, on completion, filled the boots with earth and proceeded to bury them in the ground outside our tents, an operation designed to keep the hide bottoms soft and pliable as they dried. At night Da Norbu placed rocks over the buried boots to prevent their being dug up and chewed by dogs.

That night we visited Dorje's home where his parents squatted either side of a fire. Others present included a young harelipped brother, an older brother wearing a cap and boots from a French Makalu Expedition, for which he had been a porter, and a deaf mute brother-in-law, husband of Dorje's bossy sister Berma. We sat on goatskins on the earth floor and were given tompas of chang and bowls of roasted maize, both of which were refilled as soon as they were emptied. After a couple of hours Dorje's father undressed and retired beneath a large blanket in the corner of the room, and although this gesture was by no means meant as a hint that we should leave, we welcomed the opportunity to thank our hostess and claim an early night's sleep. Outside, the air was cold and crisp and the sky was clear and sprinkled with stars. In the distance we could see the whole length of the Jaljale Himal along which we had trekked on our way to Topke Gola.

The next morning was the first of December and we awoke again to a brilliantly sunny day. There was much to be done and we quickly set to, sorting and packing, throwing in a heap those items we would not be requiring any more and distributing our unwanted gear and clothing to Dorje's and Tende's parents and to some of our favourite porters. All those who have employed porters in Nepal know that there are good and bad porters and until one is well into the march it is difficult to know how lucky or otherwise one has been in his choice. Some porters did all and often more than one expected of them without expecting any extra remuneration. These porters put up with the worst conditions and accepted the characteristics and surprises of a route without complaint and could always be relied upon. Others, however, could be idle, disobedient or even dishonest. They might complain incessantly about food, pay, conditions and everything else and rarely showed appreciation when luck or compassion brought them a reward or a change of fortune. Some porters drank themselves silly whilst others changed their minds somewhere along the way and would drop out to return home. The unreliable porter could be a danger to his colleagues and, at the very least, cause despondency or dissension. Happily, such porters were a minority.

At last we were on the move and struck off through cultivated fields on our descent to the Kasuwa Khola where we intended spending the night. On the outskirts of the village we passed several clumps of a giant bamboo — *Dendrocalamus hamiltonii* — with canes 40-60 ft tall — canes of 80 ft are recorded — and 4-7 in. in diameter. This commonly planted bamboo is a native of NE Himalaya and in these regions is universally employed for building and basket and mat work. Most villages in the warm valleys are marked by their bamboo clumps and it is referred to as Tama in Nepalese. The young shoots are sometimes eaten as a vegetable whilst, according to Gamble in his 'Bambusae of British India', the inner layer of the culm sheaths was once used for covering Burmese cigarettes.

Gradually the vegetation assumed a more tropical appearance and I was surprised to see one of the so-called screw pines — *Pandanus nepalensis*. This peculiar tree is not unlike a *Cordyline* or a *Yucca* in appearance, its main stem branching in the upper half, each branch supporting a great cluster of bold, sharply toothed, sword-shaped leaves. The Nepalese tree is one of a group of 600 species native of the Old World tropics and sub-tropics. Despite the common name, these trees have no relation to the pine, being more closely, though distantly, related to the palms. The male and female flowers are borne on separate trees, the females, when fertilised, producing pineapple-like fruits. The stems often twist spirally like a screw. In India the fragrant flowers of the most common species — *P. odoratissimus* — are used in making Kewda Attar, whilst its leaves are used for thatching.

Epiphytic orchids abounded, none in flower. Beer made a limited collection for the University Botanic Garden, Bangor, including four which grew on the same rock above the track.

We arrived at the river and there made camp at a height of approximately 4,200 ft. Here we found a colourful spider — *Argiope amoena* — its large abdomen strikingly banded yellow and brown. It resembled a humbug with legs and we took several photographs before it tired of basking and moved into the shade of a deep crevice. The Sherpas sang round the fire that night and I lay in my sleeping-bag watching fireflies amongst the trees. In the light of the moon I could see the vast blanket-like webs of the giant wood spider (*Nephila maculata*) stretching between branches and occasionally connecting the canopies of separate trees. This species is just as striking as the 'humbug' spider, differing in its long narrow grey and black abdomen marked with two longitudinal yellow stripes.

The next day we climbed out of the gorge of the Kasuwa Khola. The whole area was a maze of fields, each the size of a pocket-handkerchief, in many of which wheat was being harvested, whilst others previously supporting rice now lay fallow. Bananas were grown in every village and we were delighted to be approached at one point by an old woman offering bananas for sale. They were the fattest bananas I had ever seen, huge by western standards, though lacking the characteristic shape.

Our track led us through villages where the flowers of tall poinsettias glowed scarlet against whitewashed walls, and babies swung gently in cradles suspended from the eaves. We reached a point where the track ran downhill towards the River Arun, and there connecting the high banks at its narrowest point we saw that remarkable structure, the Bridge at Num. It was constructed entirely of bamboo, U-shaped in section and approximately 235 ft long. The bridge sank towards the middle and the whole structure bounced and swayed as we crossed one at a time. The river, though powerful enough, was almost at its lowest and we could imagine the perils involved in crossing at the height of the monsoon or after the spring thaw in the mountains. We had been told of the porters who had been lost whilst crossing the bridge and it required no imagination to believe such stories. On this occasion however there were no problems and after an hour the whole party was safely assembled on the other side where we made camp.

*Nephila
maculata*

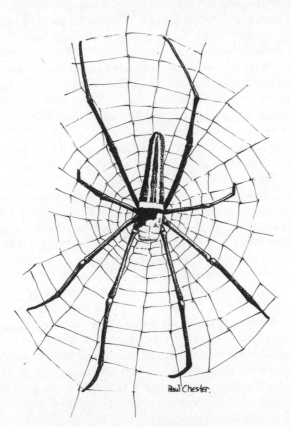

At the bridge we met a government official, an engineer charged with constructing a new bridge with steel instead of bamboo. It was his first field assignment and he was excited at the thought of the task ahead. The bridge he told us was being assembled in Khambari and brought to the site by porters. Each steel cable needed 100 porters to carry it, which, in this terrain, was quite some feat. He seemed confident that the bridge would be constructed within six months.

The climb from the bridge up to the village of Num was long and steep and it took us the whole of the next morning. In the village the autumn-flowering cherry was again common, but our interest was mainly centred around a large evergreen shrub of 8-10 ft with erect branches, brown hairy when young, and elliptic to obovate-elliptic leaves 2.5-3 in. long. These were polished dark-green above, with a slender point and small teeth. The flowers, borne singly in the leaf axils, measured 1 in. across with creamy-white, obovate petals and a central bundle of yellow-anthered stamens. They possessed a slight musky fragrance and were quite obviously those of a *Camellia*, an opinion which was later confirmed by the Botany Department of the British Museum (Natural History) who named our specimen *C. kissi*, a species rarely seen in cultivation because of its tender nature and small flowers.

After taking lunch at Num we continued along the track which climbed the ridge, rising in one place to 7,000 ft. Here many interesting plants appeared including *Gleichenia volubilis*, a large fern which scrambled into small trees displaying its magnificent paired fronds in impressive feathery green walls. The yellow-flowered *Clematis grewiiflora* occurred again and *Viburnum grandiflorum*, one specimen with leaves to 8 in. long. It was another *Viburnum*, however, which next occupied our attention. *V. cylindricum* is a large shrub, occasionally a small tree up to 20 ft, producing large flattened clusters of tubular white flowers with conspicuous protruding lilac anthers. Its main interest, however, certainly to the botanically inclined, lies in its large leaves, the upper surfaces of which are coated with a thin wax which cracks and turns white when handled. It is sometimes seen in cultivation especially in southern and western areas of the British Isles. We had previously seen it on Phulchoki in the Kathmandu Valley.

The track continued through a narrow defile with thickly mossy banks where *Rhododendron ciliatum* occurred as a few scattered mounds. It then ran downhill into a dark dank area of the silver-backed form of *Rhododendron arboreum*, their branches and stems heavily encrusted with epiphytes including several specimens of the maple — *Acer sikkimense* — 30-35 ft tall, their leaves turning orange and yellow. Several plants first seen in similar woods on the Milke Danda now re-appeared and we were pleased to renew our acquaintance with the red-fruited *Paris polyphylla* and the delicate scrambling *Dicentra scandens* with its purple, bullet-shaped fruits.

All next day our track led along a sun-drenched ridge with tremendous views on either side. The little spindle bush — *Euonymus vagans* — which we had seen above the Barun Valley we found again bearing pale greenish-white, hanging capsules containing two to four orange-coated seeds. A huge climbing shrub also attracted our attention. It looked to me like an *Elaeagnus* species and indeed so it proved to be. *E. infundibularis* is a powerful species with long scandent, brown scaly stems and elliptic evergreen leaves 2.5-3.5 in. long, glossy-green above covered with silvery scales beneath. The flowers too, are silvery scaly on the outside and are carried in dense axillary clusters. Close by another climber, this time a honeysuckle — *Lonicera glabrata* — twined its slender brown shoots 15 ft into surrounding trees and shrubs. Its shining black berries 0.25 in. across were borne in clusters in the axils of the long pointed elliptic leaves 1.5-2.5 in. long. These were smooth and glossy above but minutely downy beneath. Plants grown from a seedling of this species collected by Harry van de Laar in 1973 have proved hardy in the Hillier Arboretum, but it is not the most ornamental of the group and I doubt if it will be widely grown in cultivation.

Growing on a grassy bank by the track, in full sun, we found a large group of low perennial plants sporting large yellow salver-shaped flowers. This really was a spectacular flowering display and we were pleased to have specimens later identified as *Reinwardtia cicanoba*, a tender relative of *Linium*, the flax, and not unlike a large-flowered flax in general appearance. These were amongst the last plants of which we collected specimens as from here our route lay through warm temperate and sub-tropical regions where the only areas not under cultivation contained plant species unsuited to cultivation out of doors in Britain.

Our lunch break that day was taken on a hillside scattered with large plants of the angel's trumpet — *Datura suaveolens* — its huge pendent white trumpets creating a scene more reminiscent of its native Peruvian Andes. Several travellers shared our hillside and one of these produced from his pocket a bamboo flute on which he proceeded to play. It was a plaintive tune yet at home in this place of giant hills and deep valleys and we all listened attentively, each in his own private world shaped by the experience of the last three months.

Our camp for the night was in a dried-up paddy field in the village of Chiplagong. Bananas and tangerines were now available in every village and we purchased enough of each to fill our packs and spare pockets. We walked along the ridge all morning, stopping for lunch in Khambari, a one-street town with paving and shops. A porter picked a rose for me to wear in my buttonhole and then kept pace with me pointing out all those plants which were known for their medicinal value. Early in the afternoon we again sighted the River Arun and could see the air strip at Tumlingtar.

Next morning we beheld the Arun Valley filled with mist like some ghostly river. Shortly afterwards we entered this strange wonderland where spiders hung their intricate webs from grasses and herbs. We left the mist behind in Tumlingtar emerging to brilliant sunshine, and saw the flash of a flock of green pigeons alighting in a nearby field. Soon

159

after, we encountered a flock of rose-ringed parakeets, screeching their way through the trees. Before mid-day we had reached our previous crossing point of the Sabhaya Khola, thus completing a circle which had lasted almost three months and had taken us through some of the most fantastic terrain on earth. This time we waded across the river, and so hot was the sun, that within ten minutes we were completely dry again.

Our route lay along the valley bottom and all day we sweated in the sun thankful for the occasional stops to replenish our water bottles. The track was now broad and well travelled. The porters who used it regularly were the long distance 'lorry drivers' of Nepal. They knew every inch of the route: the best stops, the best tea houses, the best river crossings and the best places to spend the night. Essentially, things could hardly have changed along these routes for hundreds of years and one wondered for how much longer this state of affairs would remain.

For the best part of two days we followed the river before climbing a steep wooded hill to the village of Hile where we sampled our last chang, unfortunately of inferior quality to what we had drunk in the mountains. Moving on from Hile we walked along an open ridge before descending the hill to the village of Dhankuta where we spent the night in a woodland consisting almost entirely of Chir pine — *Pinus roxburghii* — its fallen needles forming a soft thick carpet over the ground.

On our way through the village we called in at the British Medical Trust to have breakfast with Dr Don Patterson and his wife. They had been in Dhankuta for twelve months and seemed settled and happy. Like the Trust in Chainpur, this was financed mainly by OXFAM and dealt primarily with the treatment of tuberculosis. Treatment consisted of a two months' course of daily injections followed by an eight to ten months' daily course of pills. Whilst receiving injections the patients stayed in the vicinity, many of them living in temples. We crossed the Tamur River at Mogart by way of a narrow suspension bridge constructed of steel and wood by the Gurkhas. Shortly afterwards we began the long haul up to the Sanguri Ridge — 3,500 ft above the river. At the summit of the trail is a small tea house dispensing hot tea, and after several glasses we were ready for the descent.

The walk down to Dharan Bazaar was excruciating, but we were intent on reaching Gopa Camp before we collapsed. Here we were reunited with Witcombe who together with Mortimer had journeyed to Sedua and then moved westwards eventually to arrive in Namche Bazaar. They had made large collections of seed of cereal crops as well as samples of other food crops and a smattering of seed of ornamental plants including silver fir and several junipers. Finally they had returned to Kathmandu where both of them had become ill; Mortimer was still unwell and Witcombe had had to leave him in order to come to meet us.

It was at this time that we heard about the India-Pakistan confrontation and we wondered whether we would be able to leave Kathmandu. No one seemed to know which Indian airports were open to civilian traffic and someone told us that Calcutta airport had been closed for some time. As always in such situations, rumours were rife and varied in content so we decided to ignore them and concentrate on repacking our gear and our precious seed which arrived with the porters the next day.

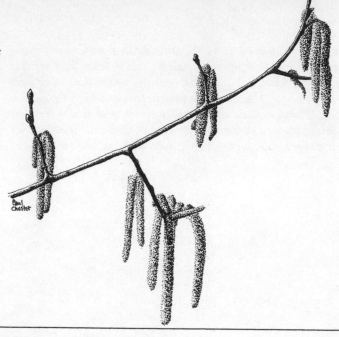

Corylus ferox

13 HOME AGAIN

We arrived in England on Christmas Eve. The freight did not arrive until January when Beer drove in a newly acquired car to Heathrow to extract the herbarium specimens for the Natural History Museum, and the seed. The successful outcome of our expedition seemed about to take place. Beer decided to stay the night in London in order to visit the Botany Department at the Museum when it opened the next morning. Having booked into an hotel he drove into the West End, parked his car in a side street and went to see a show. When he returned to where he had parked the car, he found to his horror that it was gone. He called at the local police station to report the loss and was informed that so many cars were stolen in London each night that they held out very little promise for its return. Beer told them of the car's contents, to which the officer shrugged his shoulders, saying that more than likely the car was in some back-street workshop being resprayed and that the seed and dried plants would probably be burned as rubbish. Beer then told them of the British and American Ambassadors' efforts in having the cargo flown out of Kathmandu and the suggestion of a diplomatic involvement seemed to lend a sudden urgency to the enquiries. Beer was told to return to his hotel whilst the police pursued their investigations. Of course he could not sleep at all and almost panicked at breakfast next morning when told he had a telephone call. It was the police and to Beer's joy he was told that his car had been returned to the place where he had parked it the previous night. It was with some trepidation

162

that Beer approached the car, trepidation which turned into ecstasy when he discovered that both seed and specimens were intact and even his camera, which he had left unthinkingly under the driver's seat, was still there. Beer asked no further questions and having first delivered the specimens to the Museum headed for home.

The packeting of seed and distribution of shares lasted several weeks and involved the help of several others in addition to expedition members. A total of 396 seed collections had been made by the Horticultural Project, to which the Agricultural Project had added a further 21, making 417 collections in all. The Agricultural Project made seed collections of cereal crops from 110 different sites. The seed shares were distributed to over 100 individuals and organisations who had together finally contributed approximately £3,000 to the expedition's total budget of £7,200.

Holders of general shares (£25 each) received 80 packets of seed, whilst special shareholders (£50) received the 80 packets plus a special collection of 60 packets, making 140 packets in all. Seed lots in excess of 8,000 were eventually distributed to shareholders in Britain and Europe, North America and Australia. Despite our written request for details of germination and cultivation results, few of our shareholders bothered to contact us and such information that we collected was based mainly on the results of shareholders known to us. But many shareholders shared their seed amongst friends. This was a commendable action and served to spread the results over an even greater area. Even today I come across our plants in gardens, often in the most isolated places.

A set of field notes accompanied each batch of seeds. In a comparatively short time the experts at the British Museum had furnished us with a number of identifications to add to those which we had made in the field.

Many of the plants which resulted from the seed we collected, have now had time to prove themselves in cultivation. From personal experience I have seen many undoubted successes. Amongst the trees the Himalayan birch — *Betula utilis* — has been one of our winners. Young plants showing vigour and early bark colour bring a welcome warm orange-brown to the many creams already long established. *Prunus rufa*, the Himalayan cherry, is still rather young but already its characteristic peeling bark is showing on comparatively slender stems. *Cotoneaster gamblei* has developed into a spectacular small tree of great vigour, displaying its white flowerheads and red fruits with gay abandon.

The Himalayan silver fir — *Abies spectabilis* collected in the Solo Khumbu area — though still comparatively small, has not succumbed to the frost, at least not in the south of England, and I have high hopes of its continued development. Two whitebeams — *Sorbus cuspidata* and *S. hedlundii* — have rapidly developed into handsome young specimens

8 ft and above and will undoubtedly hold their own amongst rivals.

Of the many shrubs to have thrived I regard the Rhododendrons to be amongst our greatest successes, and many of the species we collected are now represented in the foremost British collections notably at Wakehurst, Borde Hill and Sheffield Park in Sussex; Sandling Park in Kent; the Valley Gardens, Windsor; Glendoick, Perth, and the Hillier Arboretum in Hampshire.

Spiraea micrantha and *S. arcuata* have proved easy and floriferous, whilst at least one of our *Berberis* − *B. erythroclada* − is regarded by nurserymen as being a good commercial proposition. *Rubus nepalensis* quickly established itself and has already been used as a parent to produce at least one hybrid.

Another success has been the Hypericums, especially our superior forms of *H. hookeranum* and *H. uralum*, whilst *H. choisianum* and *H. tenuicaule* were new to cultivation. Amongst our perennials, *Cautleya cathcartii* was new to cultivation whilst the superb red-flowered seedling of *Meconopsis napaulensis*, selected by Jim Sanders at Longstock Water Gardens, is at least as good as any previously seen.

The form of *Polygonum capitatum* collected at Chyamtang has been widely grown and is highly thought of at Kew by Assistant Curator, Brian Halliwell. The same could be said of our *Polygonum amplexicaule* 'Arun Gem'.

Many of our *Primula* collections were widely distributed and from personal experience *P. capitata* ssp. *crispata* did well, although I expect others also flourished. Amongst our more spectacular collections *Rheum nobile* failed at Hillier's but grew with Jack Drake in Aviemore. Our *Saussurea gossypiphora* seedlings germinated then gradually withered away, whilst *S. obvallata* fared little better. Most of these high-altitude scree plants are impossible or notoriously difficult in cultivation and require exceptional patience and skill.

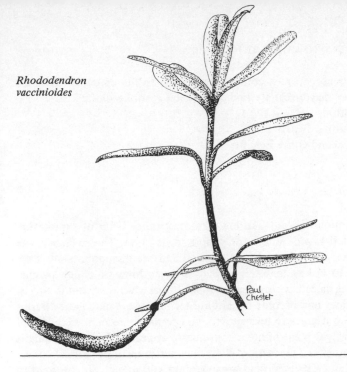

Rhododendron vaccinioides

14

SOME THOUGHTS ON PLANT HUNTING

In horticultural circles it is occasionally said that there is no future in plant hunting. Those who subscribe to this opinion offer several explanations. First of all they believe that all serious plant hunting ended with the death of Kingdon-Ward in 1958 and that, as far as hardy ornamental plants are concerned, all the interesting areas of the temperate world together with their desirable plants have been exhausted. They further point out that the early plant hunters, being first in the field, creamed off the best plants, leaving only the chaff for later collectors. On the basis of these premises, several pundits believe that nurseries have long ago absorbed the rich bounty of wild plant introductions and that today the only new plants of garden merit come not from the wild but from the nimble fingers and computer mind of the professional hybridist.

A major nail in the coffin of the plant hunter, so some people believe, is the growing importance placed on plant conservation in the wild. The 'leave-it-alone' fringe of the world conservation movement believes that nothing must disturb the delicate balance which exists in native plant communities. This means, amongst other things, that plants should not be dug up nor seeds removed.

But what *is* the present situation? Who are today's plant hunters, where do they go and why do they do it? How can they justify their continued activities?

There are several reasons why plant hunting survives and will continue

165

to do so, reasons which collectively give lie to the opinions expressed above. They may be categorised under three main headings:

Fascination

Horticultural Benefits

Botanical and Other Benefits

Fascination

The fascination of plant hunting, like most other fields of exploration has attracted a wide variety of people to its ranks. The challenge, the exhilaration, the magic, the satisfaction and the disappointments have combined to make a tempting and adventurous brew which few people, once having tasted it, can leave alone. It was always so and it still is. But how does one become a plant hunter? There are no college courses available, no degrees to be acquired, no commonly recognised ladder of progression, yet plant hunters continue to appear and plant hunting is still recognised as a profession albeit on a part-time or occasional basis.

An old and respected field botanist once said to me, 'So you want to be a plant hunter, then the world should be your textbook and your doorstep your first chapter. In other words,' he added kindly, 'study plants wherever you find them, starting in your own garden.' I was a schoolboy at the time and I believe this to have been one of the most important and influential pieces of advice I have ever received.

A plant hunter usually starts off with a love for plants. He may already be professionally involved as a gardener, a forester or a botanist. Alternatively his interest may stem from a hobby. Certainly he begins by studying plants, learning their names and histories. However, if most plants have already been seen or collected what is it that persuades people into treading well-trodden paths?

Man is curious and generally likes to find things out for himself. Just as a growing toddler moves further and further afield becoming bolder in his exploration of his home so adult man continues the process. As a schoolboy and afterwards I spent ten years exploring my local country-side, visiting places and finding plants which had been visited and found by perhaps thousands of others before me. For each individual, each new act of discovery is a personal and precious first experience which can be shared but never duplicated. The knowledge that countless botanising groups and individuals have combed the mountains of Greece did not, in 1977, rob me of the pleasure of finding hundreds of, to me, new and interesting plants. The discovery of two plants new to Greece was a splendid and unexpected bonus which, however, remained a small part of the whole experience. It is this thirst for personal experience which took me to Nepal in 1971 and again in 1973 and to other countries since. It is this same thirst which now fills me with excitement and curiosity when I contemplate my visits to China. Of course most of the plants I shall find there will already have been found many times by others but that will not spoil my own pleasure.

The knowledge gained by personal experience is surely the most valuable of all and though much of our everyday knowledge is based on what we have been told or read, the difference in conviction is that between the writer and the reader. That plant hunting is spiced with danger and adventure is proven by the many graves of those who have departed their lives in the world's wild places. The history of plant hunting is well endowed with drama and puzzling events. The dreadful death of the Scot David Douglas in a wild bull pit in Hawaii and the drowning of the American Frank Meyer in the River Yangtze are just two of many unexplained incidents. Reginald Farrer and George Forrest both died in the field, Farrer in Upper Burma and Forrest in Yunnan, China.

Anyone who has read accounts of the plant hunters and their travels will be aware of the frightening experiences and narrow escapes which attended their trips. George Forrest's account of his 25-day ordeal during which he was hunted by murderous lamas is a classic example of the kind of situation in which a plant hunter can find himself whilst in pursuance of a seemingly harmless and peaceful occupation. The hazards of wild terrain claim many lives and even the experienced E. H. Wilson in China suffered a broken leg in a sudden landslip.

Today the wild terrain, despite certain local improvements in communications, has not been tamed and dangers are ever present for the inexperienced or the unwary. Anyone who has followed the activities of climbers in the mountains of Asia and elsewhere will be aware that not all hazards occur above the snow line and that, in addition to permanent hazards, the presence of rain or mist can add a new and worrying dimension to a familiar situation whilst compounding existing dangers.

The fascination of plant hunting is as strong as ever and as long as there are plants left in the wild, plant hunters will want to travel to see them.

Horticultural Benefits

'And so finishes an era in horticulture' — with these words the late E. H. M. Cox concluded his scholarly account of plant hunting in China. His book covers one of the richest chapters in the history of plant hunting and one detects a personal sadness in Cox's finale which is not surprising since he was bound up in that era. He made his own contribution to a golden age that filled our gardens with countless new and ornamental plants and made household names of a host of plant explorers.

There is no doubt that the old-style plant hunter, who spent from two to three years at a time in the field noting plants in flower and returning several months later to harvest their seed is a thing of the past. The thought of George Forrest, for instance, at work in Yunnan with a team of 20 or more trained native collectors is mind-boggling by today's standards. Even more amazing are the quantities of seed collected. From his final expedition alone Forrest sent home two mule loads (300 lb approximately) of good clean seed, representing some 400-500 species. Other collectors of his generation were similarly industrious. But one of the tragedies of Forrest's efforts is that much of his seed came to nought. As Cox observed, 'Few private gardeners had the opportunity of doing justice to well over a hundred seed packets arriving at the same time, even if they were sufficiently enthusiastic to wish to cultivate in bulk this source of potential plants'. Those with special interests and ample propagation facilities such as the Rhododendron enthusiasts probably did better by Forrest's seed than others of more general interests. But the truth is that Forrest's seed collections drowned a gardening world which was ill prepared to cope. Many of his best collections arrived in a Britain preoccupied with a debilitating war and with most young gardeners and propagators away in the fields of France there were few people left to deal with them. I have heard stories from several 'old hands' of piles of seed packets mouldering in potting sheds or being burned on boilerhouse fires. Even the seeds that were sown and managed to germinate often survived through chance rather than as a result of skilled attention.

Forrest was not the only collector whose efforts in the field were not entirely matched by those to whom seed was sent. Cox again has expressed sympathy with E. H. Wilson who introduced over 1,000 plants new to cultivation. Unlike a good many other plant hunters, Wilson had a gardener's eye for a good plant and his collections contained few duds. There are few gardens today of any merit that do not contain at least one Wilson plant and yet more of Wilson's introductions have been lost than remain. Browsing through the descriptions of his introductions in the three volumes of *Plantae Wilsonianae* (1911-17) one is struck by the great number and calibre of plants which have been lost somewhere along the way. As Cox points out, Wilson's first two expeditions to China were financed by the nurserymen James Veitch and Sons at a time when that great firm was enjoying the last few years of its active existence and many of his best plants were later auctioned just as they were reaching flowering stage and before they had been propagated.

It is abundantly clear from past experiences that the greatest obstacles to the successful establishment of a newly collected plant in cultivation are apathy, ignorance, lack of facilities and insufficient time. Again and again one or more of these factors have resulted in a rare or desirable plant being written off before it has had a chance to prove itself. These obstacles unhappily are still present. A valuable batch of Rhododendron seedlings from our Nepal Expedition were lost by one propagator because he used unsuitable seed compost.

Knowing the amount of effort needed to collect a single packet of seed it is annoying and disappointing to learn that the seed or seedlings have been lost. I cannot begin to imagine how Forrest must have felt about his often wasted efforts. Today, if he is wise, the plant hunter will ensure that adequate facilities are available to receive his seed before he finalises his itinerary, and, just as important, that the propagator selected has the necessary desire, time and skill to do the seed justice.

At a time of great change in the nursery trade brought about by economic measures it is imperative that serious plant hunters, at least those collecting seed for horticultural purposes, consider carefully the fate of their seed collections. Few if any large nurseries are now in a position to deal with collections of seeds of unknown quantity. Even if the nursery staff have the necessary skills, facilities and enthusiasm, the time and space required in order to grow and prove the seed is usually more than commercial considerations will allow. To a plant hunter with no particular knowledge of propagation or nursery practice a quantity of seed in packets may seem to present few if any problems to the nurseryman but wild collected seed, when it is arriving from several sources and often at the wrong time of the year, can have an alarming effect on the otherwise smooth running of a commercial concern and I have seen situations where hundreds of boxes and pans containing many thousands of seedlings have threatened to clog the works. The amount of time, effort, materials and space required to deal adequately with a large quantity of seed consisting of small amounts of many different species is more than anyone now can afford.

In the wake of the change caused by large nurseries reducing their variety of stocks a whole vanguard of small specialist nurseries has blossomed. Often run by one or two persons and with small overheads these concerns have the abilities to deal with the more unusual garden-worthy plants and are careful to accept only as much as they can comfortably handle. Add to this situation the ever-present enthusiasm and determination of the amateur gardeners of Britain and the current interest in the conservation of garden plants, and there is no possible doubt that whatever plant hunters collect will be gratefully received and competently handled. The plant hunter on his part must be selective in his seed collecting. If he wants to collect seed of plants which are worth growing in gardens, then the onus is on him to know what he is looking for and to recognise it when he sees it. It is no shame to return from a trip with only a few collections, so long as they are of merit. Better five good garden plants than 500 weeds. There are many great gardens and notable specialist societies whose collective expertise should be sought by all intending plant hunters.

Some of the most notable successes with our Nepal seed were achieved by specialists — amateur and professional. Rhododendrons, gentians, Primulas, conifers, all have their followers and if the plant hunter is anxious to get the best results from his efforts it is up to him to ascertain who is most suitable to deal with seed of a given genus or group. As for the claim that nothing of garden merit remains to be collected, possibly the greatest understatement in the history of plant hunting was that made by Sir Harry Veitch to the young E. H. Wilson just before the latter went to China for the first time: 'My boy, stick to the one thing you are after and do not spend time and money wandering about. Probably almost every worthwhile plant in China has now been introduced to Europe.' As events have since proved, Veitch was not the last to be wrong.

Anyone who has travelled afar to look for plants will know that the chances of treading new ground and finding new plants are ever present and the wilder and more inaccessible the terrain, the greater the chances of making new discoveries. To suggest, even now, that China has been exhausted is foolish. One has only to study a map of China marked with the collecting routes of the major plant hunters to realise how dangerous such a premise is. I remember my own travels in East Nepal when we sometimes marched along a ridge track in the knowledge that, for several ridges east and west no similar tracks existed. There were times when, following such a track, we caught sight of a puzzling plant or a promising cliff or gully which, because of the intervening terrain or simply through lack of time, we were reluctantly forced to ignore.

Those who have read anything of the old plant hunters will recall similar admissions. Then there are those plants which, for one reason or another are missed by one plant hunter and found by another. A famous example of this is the Chinese *Rehderodendron macrocarpum*, a rare small tree of the *Styrax* family discovered on Mount Omei, in W. Szechwan by Dr H. H. Hu in 1932. According to its finder it is most probable that E. H. Wilson (that most diligent and observant plant collector, as W. J. Bean observed) passed by the type tree of *Rehderodendron* during his visit to Mt Omei in 1903. To be fair, having recently visited Mt Omei I am not in the least surprised that Wilson should have missed a plant, after all, there are 3,000 species recorded from the mountain and plants crowd the tracks in such numbers and variety that the blink of an eye would suffice to miss an individual. The genus *Rehderodendron* was established by Dr Hu in 1932 and by 1935 eight species had been described and later two more were added. These discoveries led Bean to conclude that it was further proof of the vast wealth of the temperate flora of China and one need only mention the discovery of *Metasequoia glyptostroboides*, the so-called living fossil tree in 1941 and of *Cathaya argyrophylla*, a relative of *Picea* and *Keteleeria* in 1955 to confirm this.

Good garden plants are not however the prerogative of China and by way of proof consider the number of species introduced from Nepal and south-western Asia — especially from Turkey and Iran — since World War 2. Even the southern hemisphere — New Zealand and the Andes of South America — has still much to offer British gardens.

A final consideration and perhaps the greatest justification for plant hunting today is the re-introduction of plants lost to cultivation and, just as important the selection and introduction of more desirable forms of plants already in cultivation. I have already indicated the great numbers of plants collected as seed by Wilson, Forrest and others which have been lost to cultivation. Examples which come to mind are *Clematis florida*, *C. lanuginosa*, and *Rosa chinensis*. There are hundreds of others, especially alpines and herbaceous perennials. This will be a rich source of activity for future plant hunters and equally so, the field of improved forms, whether they are hardier, easier to grow, larger flowered, freer fruiting, dwarfer, narrower or whatever qualities are currently desirable. As examples I might instance *Polygonum amplexicaule* 'Arun Gem' and the peeling-barked form of *Prunus rufa* introduced by us from Nepal in 1971. Both are considered decided improvements on the plants previously in cultivation.

Botanical and Other Benefits

Ornamental considerations apart, the value of cultivating plants from the wild is as great if not greater now than at any time previously. The Chinese for instance place great importance on the medicinal attributes of plants and their botanic gardens contain large collections of such plants representing medicines currently in use. Plant hunters in China are given every encouragement to seek out and collect samples of those plants which are known or suspected to have medicinal possibilities. No other country appears to place quite the same level of importance on their native flora. International research is currently taking place on a range of lesser known or previously obscure plants in an attempt to discover new uses, especially in third world countries. Until each species has been thoroughly checked out it is foolish to dismiss them as worthless. Who for instance 50 years ago would have believed that a low growing xerophytic shrub from the deserts of Mexico, Arizona and southern California would offer hope for the sperm whale. The seeds of the jojoba — *Simmondsia chinensis* — produce a liquid wax almost identical to the oil of the sperm whale. The sperm whale has been hunted mercilessly almost to the point of extinction and scientists studying the potential of the jojoba believe that farming methods would help increase the plant's oil production. Such plantations are already established in Arizona and Israel and it has been estimated that a minimum of 15 acres of jojoba is needed to save one sperm whale per year.

The food potential of plants is another area in which the plant hunter has an important role to play. The search for new and improved strains of established crop plants depends in part on the work of the plant hunter. New strains of old species, new species even, are still being discovered in the world's wild places and this aspect offers a particularly attractive specialisation to the plant hunter. It is worth noting that many of the best cultivars of soya bean grown in the United States have evolved from strains introduced 60-75 years ago by Frank N. Meyer from China. Meyer specialised in the introduction of economic plants − his tally was enormous but his name is rarely remembered today except through his introduction of the ornamental conifer *Juniperus squamata* 'Meyeri'.

From the botanical point of view, the plant hunter is a permanent fixture. As long as plants and their relationships need to be studied plant hunters will continue to collect them. To the botanist, especially the taxonomist, it is herbarium material rather than living material that interests him but he is not always averse to the idea of collecting seed and occasionally such material, especially if it is of known provenance, is of benefit to his research.

Another important contribution the plant hunter makes is to the study of plant geography. Despite man's great knowledge of this subject there remain many gaps, many inexplicable occurrences in the distribution of plants which the plant hunter can help solve. Before its being opened to outsiders in 1951, Nepal represented a huge gap in our knowledge of the Himalayan flora. To some extent a similar gap exists even today in the north-east territories of India (North East Frontier Agency). Our own expedition to East Nepal in 1971 resulted in a number of records which were extensions of previously know distributions and such work need not be restricted to countries far from home. In 1969, for instance, I found the sea plantain − *Plantago maritima* − on St Mary's in the Isles of Scilly. This is a common plant around the coasts of Britain and Europe but, according to the late J. E. Lousley, it had not been found in Scilly since the dubious reference in Gerards Herbal of 1633.

A piece of botanical detection such as this is one of the first and most practical contributions an aspiring plant hunter can make to the serious study of plants. To make such a contribution brings satisfaction and encouragement which the plant hunter, especially the novice, needs in order to flourish.

This brings me to the vexed question of conservation. The plant hunter needs to be guided in his work by consideration for a plant and the community to which it belongs. In these days of rapid communication facts concerning the destruction of natural habitats, entire eco-systems even, are brought to the world's attention almost overnight and such facts are frightening in their immensity. Man and his machines can and do change a landscape in the space of a few weeks or days even and equally horrific are the disasters inflicted upon native populations as a result of pests and diseases introduced by man from one country or continent to another. The Chestnut blight which has almost destroyed the American chestnut in the USA and the Dutch elm disease which has decimated the elms of America and Europe are two infamous examples of man's deadly ignorance. But how does the plant hunter fit into all this? Fortunately, gone are the days when gardeners ran amok in their native hills and forests digging up quantities of desirable plants. Such activities for instance reduced our native lady's slipper orchid — *Cypripedium calceolus* — to the present representative plant now under strict protection. The story can be duplicated over and over again with many different plants in many countries of the world. The Victorian and Edwardian amateur collectors between them almost stripped the Alps of their rare alpines and it makes one weep to think of the thousands of hampers stuffed with plants by enthusiastic amateurs to fill the rock gardens of England. That many of these failed to survive the first savage wrench goes without saying. By and large though, I believe it is fair to say that with few exceptions the serious and certainly the professional plant hunter was never a party to the pickaxe and hamper brigade. A famous professional was Robert Fortune who has been called the most successful introducer of living plants in history and most of his plants were purchased in Chinese nurseries. With the advent however of mass plant introductions by seed the threat of mass pillage by digging up lost favour although sadly, it still occurs where financial inducement is present. Happily the governments of several countries now take a serious view of such desecration for commercial gain and legislation now helps those who strive to protect their natural heritage.

It is difficult to monitor let alone control plant collecting by amateurs just as it is difficult if not impossible to prevent collectors taking the eggs of rare birds. One day a few years ago a man and his wife asked to see me at the Hillier Arboretum. They had recently collected some plants whilst on holiday in Greece and as the plants were not responding to cultivation they asked me if I would like them for the arboretum. I asked to see their plunder and when they opened the car boot I was sickened to behold a dozen pots and pans filled with *Ramonda nathaliae* and *Jankaea heldreichii*, in an advanced state of decay. Both these rare and delightful species are found wedged in narrow rock fissures and consequently are extremely difficult to extract. I prefer not to repeat the details of my reaction and I can only hope that the people in question never again contemplated such bestial operations.

I am not opposed to the amateur but as in all societies, those of ill repute are in a minority and the majority are not only aware of but actively support the ideals of plant conservation. To all those, therefore, who claim or even suspect the worst I offer the good news that plant hunting is alive and well and given the vagaries of horticultural fashion and scientific progress will continue to play an active and important role for many years to come.

APPENDIX: A LIST OF THE NUMBERS AND NAMES OF SEED COLLECTED BY BEER, LANCASTER AND MORRIS (B. L. & M.) IN NEPAL IN 1971.

1 Rubus paniculatus
2 Sambucus adnata
3 Zanthoxylum acanthopodium
4 Zanthoxylum oxyphyllum
5 Dicentra scandens
6 Tripterospermum volubile
7 Cautleya cathcartii
8 Arisaema sp.
9 Holboellia latifolia
10 Cautleya spicata
11 Lilium nepalense
12 Lilium nepalense
13 Paris polyphylla
14 Clematis tongluensis
15 Clematis tongluensis
16 Rubus calycinus
17 Helwingia himalaica
18 Acer pectinatum
19 Magnolia campbellii
20 Sorbus hedlundii
21 Vaccinium retusum
22 Symplocos theaefolia
23 Sorbus kurzii
24 Sorbus microphylla
25 Sorbus insignis
26 Rhododendron ciliatum
27 Sorbus microphylla
28 Aconitum spicatum
29 Geranium polyanthes
30 Sorbus microphylla
31 Rosa sericea
32 Codonopsis dicentrifolia
33 Betula utilis
34 Senecio alata
35 Acer pectinatum
36 Polygonum emodi
37 Meconopsis napaulensis
38 Gentiana prolata
39 Gentiana sikkimensis
40 Piptanthus nepalensis
41 Berberis erythroclada
42 Codonopsis dicentrifolia
43 Polygonum milletii
44 Euphorbia himalayensis
45 Jurinea macrocephala
46 Saxifraga sp.
47 Gaultheria pyroloides
48 Saussurea taraxicifolia
49 Prunus cornuta
50 Sorbus kurzii
51 Ribes laciniatum
52 Cyananthus inflatus

53 Rheum acuminatum
54 Juniperus squamata
55 Primula dickieana
56 Primula obliqua
57 Vaccinium nummularia
58 Cicerbita macrantha
59 Aster himalaicus
60 Saussurea gossypiphora
61 Cremanthodium ellisii
62 Salix sp.
63 Saussurea uniflora
64 Cremanthodium reniforme
65 Aconitum spicatum
66 Bergenia purpurascens
67 Iris kumaonensis
68 Morina nepalensis
69 Megacodon stylophorus
70 Rheum nobile
71 Salix sp.
72 Juniperus squamata
73 Juniperus indica
74 Geum elatum
75 Anemone polyanthes
76 Ligularia sp.
77 Swertia multicaulis
78 Salix sp.
79 Primula capitata ssp. crispata
80 Cremanthodium pinnatifidum
81 Cremanthodium oblongatum
82 Juniperus recurva
83 Gaultheria trichophylla
84 Cotoneaster microphyllus
    var. cochleatus
85 Abies densa
86 Aconitum spicatum
87 Spiraea arcuata
88 Berberis sp.
89 Cyananthus sp.
90 Sorbus ursina
91 Sorbus microphylla
92 Rhododendron wightii
93 Pleurospermopsis sikkimensis
94 Megacodon stylophorus
95 Potentilla cuneata
96 Myricaria rosea

97 Primula hopeana
98 Primula macrophylla var.
    macrocarpa
99 Meconopsis grandis
100 Betula utilis
101 Clematis montana
102 Lonicera myrtillus
103 Stellaria sp.
104 Parnassia nubicola
105 Cremanthodium reniforme
106 Rubus nepalensis
107 Prunus rufa
108 Ribes luridum
109 Acer papilio
110 Meconopsis paniculata
111 Saussurea obvallata
112 Meconopsis sinuata
113 Saussurea taraxicifolia
114 Mandragora caulescens
115 Soroseris pumila
116 Silene setisperma
117 Draba sp.
118 Silene sp.
119 Polygonum sp.
120 Fritillaria cirrhosa
121 Aster himalaicus
122 Rheum sp.
123 Morina nepalensis
124 Potentilla peduncularis
125 Anemone polyanthes
126 Thalictrum elegans
127 Paris polyphylla
128 Delphinium viscosum
129 Salix disperma
130 Salix sp.
131 Salix sp.
132 Aster stracheyi
133 Leontopodium himalayanum
134 Primula buryana
135 Silene sp.
136 Saxifraga moorcroftiana
137 Juniperus recurva
138 Rosa sericea
139 Gueldenstaedtia himalaica
140 Stachyurus himalaicus

141 Gaultheria semi-infera
142 Neillia thyrsiflora
143 Rubus spendidissimus
144 Gaultheria griffithiana
145 Berberis insignis
146 Sarcococca hookerana
147 Hypericum choisianum
148 Clematis connata
149 Ribes himalense
150 Ilex intricata
151 Viburnum nervosum
152 Rubus nepalensis
153 Rhododendron camelliiflorum
154 Vaccinium glauco-album
155 Rubus thomsonii
156 Berberis sp.
157 Berberis sp.
158 Cimicifuga foetida
159 Primula geraniifolia
160 Cardiocrinum giganteum
161 Tsuga dumosa
162 Euphorbia pseudosikkimensis
163 Cotoneaster acuminatus
164 Ligularia amplexicaule
165 Compositae
166 Umbelliferae
167 Cotoneaster microphyllus
168 Meconopsis discigera
169 Hemiphragma heterophyllum
170 Juniperus indica
171 Meconopsis horridula
172 Cortiella hookeri
173 Potentilla argyrophylla var.
        leucochroa
174 Leontopodium
        monocephalum
175 Potentilla microphylla var.
        depressa
176 Potentilla eriocarpa
177 Potentilla sp.
178 Saxifraga pseudopallida
179 Potentilla arbuscula
180 Anaphalis cavei
181 Waldheimia glabra
182 Aconitum hookeri

183 Cremanthodium ellisii
184 Anemone polyanthes
185 Aster albescens
186 Juniperus recurva
187 Spiraea bella
188 Senecio alata
189 Allium sp.
190 Potentilla fruticosa
191 Pedicularis sp.
192 Scopolia stramonifolia
193 Aconitum spicatum
194 Saxifraga brunonis
195 Unnamed
196 Sorbus microphylla
197 Thalictrum virgatum
198 Aruncus dioicus ssp.
        triternatus
199 Androsace hookerana
200 Polygonum amplexicaule var.
        pendulum
201 Acer pectinatum
202 Polygonum polystachyum
203 Oryzopsis munroi
204 Sorbus microphylla
205 Lyonia villosa
206 Fritillaria cirrhosa
207 Saussurea hieracioides
208 Lomatogonium sikkimense
209 Juniperus indica
210 Polygonum affine
211 Saxifraga sp.
212 Clematis sp.
213 Primula macrophylla
214 Deyeuxia pulchella
215 Rosa sericea
216 Eriophytum wallichii
217 Rhododendron setosum
218 Delphinium sp.
219 Betula utilis
220 Rhododendron cinnabarinum
221 Betula utilis
222 Hydrangea heteromalla
223 Berberis sp.
224 Rubus nepalensis
225 Pieris formosa

226 Senecio wallichii
227 Allium sp.
228 Rhododendron thomsonii
229 Lobelia erectiuscula
230 Lyonia sp.
231 Rhododendron anthopogon
232 Ilex intricata
233 Rhododendron hodgsonii
234 Rhododendron cinnabarinum
235 Polygonum vacciniifolium
236 Polygonum amplexicaule
    var. pendulum
237 Hypericum uralum
238 Hypericum tenuicaule
239 Rhododendron triflorum
240 Hypericum hookeranum
241 Jasminum humile f.
    wallichianum
242 Miscanthus nepalensis
243 Erianthus rufipilus
244 Iris decora
245 Boehninghausenia albiflora
246 Anemone vitifolia
247 Hydrangea aspera
248 Calamagrostis emodensis
249 Gaultheria semi-infera
250 Cotoneaster gamblei
251 Vaccinium glauco-album
252 Vaccinium nummularia
253 Hypericum hookeranum
254 Gaultheria nummularioides
255 Senecio tetranthus
256 Rubus treutleri
257 Rubus thomsonii
258 Polygonum sp.
259 Aconitum spicatum
260 Rhododendron thomsonii
261 (Number omitted in the field)
262 Sorbus microphylla
263 Cotoneaster sp.
264 Umbelliferae
265 Circium involucratum
266 Cotoneaster microphyllus var.
    cochleatus
267 Potentilla cuneata

268 Gaultheria trichophylla
269 Sorbus cuspidata
270 Ilex dipyrena
271 Viburnum mullaha
272 Ficus sp.
273 Sambucus adnata
274 Rubia manjith
275 Cornus macrophylla
276 Leycesteria formosa
277 Strobilanthes sp.
278 Fritillaria cirrhosa
279 Rhododendron lepidotum
280 Rhododendron cinnabarinum
281 Rhododendron anthopogon
282 Rosa sericea
283 Rhododendron
    campanulatum
284 Meconopsis napaulensis
285 Arisaema sp.
286 Rhododendron setosum
287 Rhododendron wightii
288 Senecio cappa
289 Inula cappa
290 Polygonum capitatum
291 Berberis sp.
292 Spiraea micrantha
293 Arisaema sp.
294 Rhododendron
    campanulatum
295 Piptanthus nepalensis
296 Boehmeria polystachya
297 Pinus wallichiana
298 Rhododendron virgatum
299 Vaccinium dunalianum
300 Rhododendron dalhousiae
301 Debregeasia salicifolia
302 Vaccinium gaultheriifolium
303 Embelia floribunda
304 Clematis buchananiana
305 Rhododendron dalhousiae
306 Euonymus echinatus
307 Acer sterculiaceum
308 Magnolia campbellii
309 Dianella ensifolia
310 Inula hookeri

311 Lonicera hispida
312 Rubus nepalensis
313 Rubus sp.
314 Rhododendron ciliatum
315 Rhododendron
    glaucophyllum
316 Rubus treutleri
317 Arisaema sp.
318 Cornus sp.
319 Vaccinium glauco-album
320 Gaultheria semi-infera
321 Coriaria terminalis var.
    xanthocarpa
322 Viburnum grandiflorum
323 Rhododendron hodgsonii
324 Rhododendron ciliatum
325 Rhododendron barbatum
326 Arisaema sp.
327 Rhododendron
    campanulatum
328 Gaultheria nummularioides
329 Rhododendron
    glaucophyllum
330 Rhododendron fulgens
331 Lonicera hispida
332 Rhododendron anthopogon
333 Juniperus squamata
334 Pedicularis sp.
335 Toricellia tiliifolia
336 Rhododendron vaccinioides
337 Pleione praecox
338 Rosa longicuspis
339 Corylus ferox
340 Gynura cusimbua
341 Daphniphyllum himalense
342 Rubus sp.
343 Polygonum sp.
344 Rhododendron
    campanulatum
345 Symplocos sp.
346 Paris polyphylla
347 Dichroa febrifuga
348 Hypericum uralum
349 Euonymus vagans
350 Lonicera glabrata

351 Quercus sp.
352 Gesneriaceae
353 Agapetes serpens
354 Mahonia napaulensis
355 Unnamed
356 Primula sp.
357 Primula sp.
358 Primula sp.
359 Corydalis sp.
360 Clematis montana
361 Corydalis sp.
362 Meconopsis discigera
363 Primula sp.
364 Gentiana recurvata
365 Gentiana sp.
366 Dicentra scandens
367 Corydalis sp.
368 Androsace globifera
369 Tetrastigma rumicisperma
370 Corydalis sp.
371 Lyonia villosa
372 Myricaria rosea
373 Leontopodium jacotianum
374 Salix fruticulosa
375 Potentilla microphylla
376 Rubus sp.
377 Cruciferae
378 Primula vernicosa
379 Primula calderana
380 Meconopsis villosa
381 Primula strumosa
382 Unnamed
383 Polygonum molle
384 Leguminosae
385 Fragaria daltoniana
386 Fragaria nubicola
387 Cardiocrinum giganteum
388 Potentilla microphylla var.
    achilleifolia
389 Fragaria nubicola
390 Unnamed
391 Hypericum monanthemum
392 Columnea sp.
393 Leguminosae
394 Mimosa pudica

Appendix

395 Saxifraga brunonis
396 Pyrus pashia
397 Iris sp.
398 Abies spectabilis
399 Iris sp.
400 Leguminosae
401 Juniperus recurva
402 Juniperus squamata
403 Juniperus squamata
404 Juniperus squamata
405 Juniperus squamata
406 Juniperus recurva

407 Juniperus recurva
408 Juniperus squamata
409 Juniperus indica
410 Juniperus indica
411 Juniperus sp.
412 Juniperus sp.
413 Pinus wallichiana
414 Juniperus sp.
415 Abies spectabilis
416 Abies spectabilis
417 Abies spectabilis

SELECT BIBLIOGRAPHY

Bean, W. J. *Trees and Shrubs Hardy in the British Isles*, 8th edn, revised vols. 1-4 (1970-80)

Cowan, A. M. and J. M. *The Trees of North Bengal* (1929)

Cox, E. H. M. *Plant Hunting in China* (1945)

Desmond, Ray *Dictionary of British and Irish Botanists and Horticulturists* (1977)

Farrer, Reginald *The English Rock Garden*, vols. 1 & 2 (1919)

Gabrielian, E. *The Genus Sorbus in Eastern Asia and the Himalayas* (1978)

Gamble, J.S. 'The Bambuseae of British India', *Ann. Roy. Bot. Gard. Calcutta*, 7:1-133, t. 1-119 (1896)

Green, Roy 'Asiatic Primulas', *Alpine Garden Society Guide* (1976)

Hagen, Toni *Nepal* (1972)

Hara, H., Stearn, W. T. and Williams, L. H. J. *An Enumeration of the Flowering Plants of Nepal*, vol. 1 (1978)

Hara, H. and Williams, L. H. J. *An Enumeration of the Flowering Plants of Nepal*, vol. 2 (1979)

—— *An Enumeration of the Flowering Plants of Nepal*, vol. 3 (1981)

Heywood, V. H. (ed.) *Flowering Plants of the World* (1979)

Hooker, J. D. *Himalayan Journals* (1854)

—— *Flora of British India*, 7 vols. (1872-9)

Lancaster, Roy 'An Account of the Species of *Rhododendron* collected by the University College Bangor Nepal Expedition 1971' Rhododendrons 24-32 (Royal Horticultural Society, 1972)

—— 'Maples of the Himalaya', *The Garden*, vol. 101, pt 12, 589-93 (1976)

Stainton, J. D. A. *Forests of Nepal* (1972)

Select Bibliography

Stearn, W. T. and Smith, A. W. *A Gardeners Dictionary of Plant Names* (1972)

Stewart, R. R. *An Annotated Catalogue of the Vascular Plants of West Pakistan and Kashmir* (1972)

Willis, J. C. *A Dictionary of the Flowering Plants and Ferns*, 8th edn, revised (1973)

Wilson, E. H. *A Naturalist in Western China*, vol. 1 (1913)

GLOSSARY

Technical and botanical terms have been used in this book only when necessary for precision and brevity. The following are the most frequently used examples.

Acicular	Needle shaped
Acuminate	Tapering at the end, long pointed
Acute	Sharply pointed
Anther	The pollen-bearing part of the stamen
Adpressed	Lying close and flat against
Awl-shaped	Tapering from the base to a slender and stiff point
Bloom(y)	A white or pale-blue powdery-like wax covering as on a fruit
Bract	A modified, usually reduced leaf at the base of a flower stalk, flower cluster or shoot
Bullate	Blistered or puckered
Calyx	The outer part of the flower, the sepals
Campanulate	Bell-shaped
Capitate	Head-like, collected into a dense cluster
Capsule	A dry, several-celled pod
Ciliate	Fringed with hairs
Cordate	Shaped like a heart, as base of leaf
Coriaceous	Leathery
Corolla	The inner, normally conspicuous part of a flower, the petals
Corymb	A flat-topped or dome-shaped flowerhead with the outer flowers opening first
Corymbose	Having flowers in corymbs
Crenate	Toothed with shallow, rounded teeth
Cuneate	Wedge-shaped
Cuspidate	Abruptly sharp pointed

Cyme	A flat-topped or dome-shaped flowerhead with the inner flowers opening first
Cymose	Having flowers in cymes
Decurrent	Extending down the stem
Dentate	Toothed with teeth directed outward
Denticulate	Minutely dentate
Downy	Softly hairy
Elliptic	Widest at or about the middle, narrowing equally at both ends
Emarginate	With a shallow notch at the apex
Entire	Undivided and without teeth
Exfoliating	Peeling off in thin strips
Exserted	Projecting beyond (stamens from corolla)
Ferruginous	Rust-coloured
Florets	Small, individual flowers of a dense inflorescence
Glabrous	Hairless
Glandular	With secreting organs
Glaucous	Covered with a 'bloom', bluish-white or bluish-grey
Hispid	Beset with rigid hairs or bristles
Indumentum	Dense hairy covering
Inflorescence	The flowering part of the plant
Lanceolate	Lance-shaped, widening above the base and long tapering to the apex
Linear	Long and narrow with nearly parallel margins
Lobe	Any protruding part of an organ (as in leaf, corolla or calyx)
Midrib	The central vein or rib on a leaf
Monocarpic	Dying after flowering and seeding
Mucro	A short fine point
Mucronate	Terminated abruptly by a spiny tip
Oblanceolate	Inversely lanceolate
Oblique	Unequal-sided
Oblong	Longer than broad, with nearly parallel sides
Obovate	Inversely ovate
Obtuse	Blunt (as in apex of leaf or petal)
Orbicular	Almost circular in outline
Ovary	The basal 'box' part of the pistil, containing the ovules
Ovate	Broadest below the middle (like a hen's egg)
Palmate	Lobed or divided in hand-like fashion, usually five or seven-lobed
Panicle	A branching raceme
Paniculate	Having flowers in panicles
Pectinate	Comb-like (as teeth on leaf margin)
Pedicel	The stalk of an individual flower in an inflorescence
Peduncle	The stalk of a flower cluster or of a solitary flower

Petal	One of the separate segments of a corolla
Petiole	The leaf-stalk
Pilose	With long, soft, straight hairs
Pinnate	With leaflets arranged on either side of a central stalk
Pinnatifid	Cleft or parted in a pinnate way
Plumose	Feathery, as the down of a thistle
Prostrate	Lying flat on the ground
Pruinose	Bloomy
Pubescent	Covered with short, soft hairs, downy
Raceme	A simple elongated inflorescence with stalked flowers
Racemose	Having flowers in racemes
Rachis	An axis bearing flowers or leaflets
Recurved	Curved downward or backward
Reflexed	Abruptly turned downward
Reticulate	Like a network (as in veins)
Revolute	Rolled backwards, margin rolled under (as in leaf)
Rib	A prominent vein in a leaf
Rufous	Reddish-brown
Scabrid	Rough to the touch
Scale	A minute leaf or bract, or a flat gland-like appendage on the surface of a leaf, flower or shoot
Scandent	With climbing stems
Scape	A leafless flowering stem rising from the ground
Sepal	One of the segments of a calyx
Serrate	Saw-toothed (teeth pointing forward)
Serrulate	Minutely serrate
Sessile	Not stalked
Setose	Clothed with bristles
Spathulate	Spoon-shaped
Spike	A simple, elongated inflorescence with sessile flowers
Stamen	The male organ of a flower comprising filament and anther
Stellate	Star-shaped
Stigma	The summit of the pistil which receives the pollen, often sticky or feathery
Stipule	Appendage (normally two) at base of some petioles
Stolon	A shoot at or below the surface of the ground which produces a new plant at its tip
Stomata	Breathing pores in leaf surface
Strigose	Clothed with flattened fine, bristle-like hairs
Style	The middle part of the pistil, often elongated between the ovary and stigma
Tepals	Petals and sepals of similar appearance
Tomentose	With dense, woolly pubescence
Tomentum	Dense covering of matted hairs

Glossary

Trifoliolate	A leaf with three separate leaflets
Type	Strictly the original (type) specimen, but used in a general sense to indicate the typical form in cultivation
Umbel	A normally flat-topped inflorescence in which the pedicels or peduncles all arise from a common point
Umbellate	Flowers in umbels
Umbellifer	Plant of the family Umbelliferae
Undulate	With wavy margins
Venation	The arrangement of the veins
Verrucose	Having a wart-like or nodular surface
Villous	Bearing long and soft hairs
Whorl	Three or more flowers or leaves arranged in a ring

PLANT INDEX

Only those plants seen by the Expedition in Nepal are included here. All names are accompanied by their authorities (person/s responsible for the name/s). Plant names in italics are synonyms. Within the text, synonyms are shown in parentheses.

187

Plant Index

Camellia Kissi *Wall.* 158
Cardiocrinum giganteum (*Wall.*) *Makino* 89
Carpinus viminea *Wall. ex Lindle.* 93, 124
Cassiope fastigiata (*Wall.*) *D. Don* 56, 62
Castanopsis tribuloides (*Sm.*) *A. DC.* 39
Cautleya cathcartii *Baker* 42, 164
  spicata (*Smith*) *Baker* 49
Celastrus stylosus *Wall.* 137
Cheilanthes farinosa (*Forsk.*) *Klf.* 44
Chrysanthemum atkinsonii C.B. Clarke 64
  gossypinum (*Hook. f. & Thoms.*) *Kitamura* 68, 84
Cicerbita macrantha (*C.B. Clarke*) *Beauv.* 59
Cinnamomum glanduliferum (*Wall.*) *Meisn.* 124
Clematis buchananiana *DC.* 41, 132
  connata *DC.* 92
  grewiiflora *DC.* 133, 158
  montana *Buch.-Ham.* 79
  tongluensis (*Brühl*) *Tamura* 45
Codonopsis dicentrifolia (*C.B. Clarke*) *W.W. Sm.* 54
Coriaria napalensis *Wall.* 26
  terminalis var. xanthocarpa *Rehder & Wilson* 146
Cornus macrophylla *Wall.* 128, 144
Cortiella *glacialis Bonner* 102
  hookeri (*C.B. Clarke*) *C. Norman* 102
Corydalis cashmeriana *Royle* 60
  juncea *Wall.* 52
  meifolia *Wall.* 64
Corylopsis himalayan *Hook. f.* 44
Corylus ferox *Wall.* 143
Cotoneaster acuminatus *Lindl.* 77
  cavei *Klotz* 56
  frigidus *Wall.* 120
  gamblei *Flinck* 120, 163
  integrifolius (*Roxb.*) *Klotz* 51
  meuselii *Klotz* 89
  microphyllus *Wall. ex Lindl.* 89, 110
  microphyllus var. cochleatus (*Franch.*) *Rehder* 75, 89
  microphyllus var. thymifolius (*Baker*) *Koehne* 51
  milkedandai *Hylmo* 56
  sanguineus *Yü* 105
Crémanthodium ellisii (*Hook. f.*) *Kitam.* 63, 68
  pinnatifidum *Benth.* 65, 68
  plantagineum Maxim. 63
  reniforme *Benth.* 56, 77
Cryptogramma crispa (*L.*) *Hook.* 68
Cyananthus inflatus *Hook. f. & Thoms.* 52
  lobatus *Wall. ex Benth.* 59, 64
  pedunculatus *C.B. Clarke* 67

Daphne bholua *Buch.-Ham. ex D. Don* 28, 42, 117, 121, 137
  bholua (variegated forms) 57, 145
Daphniphyllum himalense (*Benth.*) *Muell.-Arg.* 152

Datura suaveolens *Humb. & Bonpland* 37, 159
Debregeasia longifolia (*Burm. f.*) *Wedd.* 133
Delphinium glaciale *Hook. f. & Thoms.* 84
  nepalense *Kitam. & Tamura* 69
  trilobatum *Huth* 59
  viscosum *Hook. f. & Thoms.* 59, 64, 67
Dendrocalamus hamiltonii *Nees & Arn. ex Munro* 156
Deutzia compacta *Craib* 146
  staminea *R. Br. ex Wall.* 132
Dianella ensifolia (*L.*) *DC.* 141
Dicentra scandens (*D. Don*) *Walp.* 41, 158, 175
Dichroa febrifuga *Lour.* 152
Diospyros kaki *Thumb.* 29
Diplarche multiflora *Hook. f. & Thoms.* 149

Edgeworthia gardneri (*Wall.*) *Meisn.* 42, 129
Elaeagnus infundibularis *Momiyama* 159
  parvifolia *Wall. ex Royle* 121, 129
Eleusine coracana (*L.*) *Gaertn.* 41
Elsholtzia fruticosa (*D. Don*) *Rehder* 42, 121
  polystachya Benth. 42
  strobilifera *Benth.* 49
Embelia floribunda *Wall.* 132
Enkianthus deflexus (*Griff.*) *Schneid.* 44, 50
Ephedra gerardiana var. sikkimensis *Stapf* 69, 110
Erianthus rufipilus (*Steudel*) *Griseb.* 121
Eriobotrya japonica (*Thunb.*) *Lindl.* 29
Eriophytum wallichii *Benth.* 101
Eucalyptus globulus *Labill.* 29
Euonymus echinatus *Wall.* 137, 139, 151
  tingens *Wall.* 120
  vagans *Wall.* 141, 144, 158
Eupatorium adenophorum *Spreng* 40
Euphorbia himalayensis *Klotzsch* 56
  pseudosikkimensis (*Hurusawa & Ya. Tanaka*) *Radcliffe-Smith* 93
  sikkimensis *Boiss.* 123
Eurya acuminata *DC.* 129
  cavinervis *Vesque* 150

Fagopyrum esculentum *Moench* 37
Ficus benghalensis *L.* 35
  religiosa *L.* 35
Fritillaria cirrhosa *D. Don.* 88, 110

Gaultheria griffithiana *Wight* 96
  nummularioides *D. Don* 96
  pyroloides *Hook f. & Thoms. ex Miq.* 56, 59, 147
  semi-infera (*C.B. Clarke*) *Airy-*

188